3/6.

D1387394

SELECTED ENGLISH CLASSICS
General Editor: A. H. R. Ball, M.A.

THREE COMEDIES

THE KNIGHT OF THE BURNING PESTLE
THE CRITIC
THE IMPORTANCE OF BEING EARNEST

RICHARD TARLTON, THE FAMOUS JESTER (Harleian MS.)

THREE COMEDIES

THE KNIGHT OF THE BURNING PESTLE
THE CRITIC
THE IMPORTANCE OF BEING EARNEST

Edited by

G. P. W. EARLE, B.A.

Formerly Chief English Master, Dulwich College

GINN AND COMPANY LTD.
QUEEN SQUARE, LONDON, W.C.1

GINN AND COMPANY LTD.

All Rights Reserved

054005

PRINTED IN GREAT BRITAIN
BY R. & R. CLARK, LIMITED, EDINBURGH

ACKNOWLEDGMENTS

THE thanks of the editor are due to Mr Philip Nutt
for permission to draw occasionally on the text of
The Critic in Fraser Rae's edition of *Sheridan's Plays
now printed as he wrote them* (David Nutt, 1902) ;
to Professor Nettleton and Ginn and Company for
allowing him to draw upon the Notes to *The Critic*
in *The Major Dramas of Richard Brinsley Sheridan*
(Athenæum Press Series) ; to the executors of Oscar
Wilde for permission to include the text of *The Importance of Being Earnest* (Methuen & Co. Ltd.). The
editor is also indebted to the Director and Secretary
of the Victoria and Albert Museum for permission to
reproduce drawings of *Drury Lane* based on engravings
from the *Enthoven Collection* ; to the Keeper of MSS.,
the British Museum, for the picture of *Tarlton* from a
Harleian MS. ; to the Librarian of the Bodleian Library
for *Mediaeval Pageants* from a *Bodleian MS.* ; and to
the London Electrotype Agency for the illustration to
The Importance of Being Earnest, from a photograph in
The Sketch, March 20th, 1895.

PREFACE

In a collection of plays such as this it is perhaps desirable to justify, or at least to give the reasons for one's choice. Obviously the possible permutations and combinations are endless when one is selecting three comedies from the wide field of English drama. It would of course have been easy to select three landmarks in the drama, but it does not follow that these would have been as suitable for reading and acting in schools as the three plays in this volume are. This therefore was my first criterion of judgment. My second aim was to separate the three plays as far as possible in time so that each should reflect something of its age. Thus there is one play, not by Shakespeare, but of his period, one of the eighteenth century, avoiding the more usual *Rivals* and *The School for Scandal*, and one which is on the threshold of the drama of to-day. It would have been very difficult to select one full-length play which could have been regarded as typical of modern comedy.

Finally, each play has intrinsic merit, quite apart from its place in the history of the development of the drama. The first two are burlesques : *The Knight of the Burning Pestle*, the first complete example of this type in the story of the drama, contains in addition the characters of the Citizen and his Wife, which alone would make it worthy of inclusion ; *The Critic*, a masterpiece of its class, forms a fitting companion, is an interesting reflection on the type of tragedy it burlesques, and gives us Sir Fretful Plagiary and Puff. *The Importance of Being Earnest* is a perfect example, not of burlesque, but of "society" comedy, and apart from its verbal brilliance contains superb satire on a good many facets of this society.

For my purpose it was essential to give some idea of the beginnings of the drama and its development between the periods represented by these plays. I have tried to do this in the general introduction and inter-chapters. The serious student of the drama will find omissions which have been necessary to keep this introductory matter within reasonable compass. In short, I have not attem   1 to give a complete history of the drama in little, but t   ik up the plays to preserve continuity.

THE ILLUSTRATIONS

Richard Tarlton was a famous jester of the Elizabethan stage. He and Skelton played many of the comic parts in contemporary plays. I thought him both sufficiently decorative and expressive of the comic spirit to serve here as a frontispiece.

Though Professor Allardyce Nicoll notes that the " Mediaeval Pageants " from a Bodleian MS. may be puppet shows, these shows had much in common with the pageants in their early stages.

The well-known De Witt drawing of the interior of the Swan Theatre illustrates the main features of the Elizabethan theatre — the apron stage, the balcony and tiring house, with the flag flying as it always did during a performance.

The pictures of Drury Lane show the theatre as it was in the days of Sheridan's management.

The illustration to *The Importance of Being Earnest* is taken from a photograph of the original production. The gentleman behind the handkerchief is George Alexander as Ernest, with Miss Evelyn Millard as Cecily.

G. P. W. E.

CONTENTS

I
THE DRAMA TO SHAKESPEARE

MEDIAEVAL PAGEANTS (Bodleian MS.)

THE DRAMA TO SHAKESPEARE

In any attempt to trace the development of our drama, the main point to be borne in mind is that we are dealing with something continuous. It is like a stream that we can trace back to its source; at one time we almost lose sight of it in an overgrowth of Puritan denunciation, sometimes it flows very sluggishly, and then again it is wild and turbulent, and there are, of course, many tributaries which have to be reckoned with; but it is always there, flowing onwards from its original spring.

At first sight there seems little connection between the theatre and the Church, yet it is there that we must look for the beginnings of our drama, although Christianity had set its face sternly against the " spectacula ", the surviving element of the old classical drama.

The Classical drama has its influence on our English drama — that is one of the tributaries — but scholars are agreed that it is in the Church that we find the seeds of our native drama, and it is really easy enough to show their germination.

It was doubtless some enterprising priest who, in the Middle Ages, first conceived the idea of driving home more powerfully to a simple-hearted people a particular lesson of the Church by a simple dramatic ceremony. But it was some time before this ceremony was elaborated to contain dialogue and action. Eastertide was chosen, not only because the story of the Resurrection was one of the most important in the teaching of the Church, but also because the events in themselves have essential dramatic value. At first all would be done very simply; the crucifix, draped in mourning, would be hidden behind the altar, and three priests would advance up the church towards

3

it ; it would finally be brought out from its place of concealment and borne round the church in triumph. Here is the
first hint of dramatic action. Dramatic dialogue developed
from the antiphonal singing of the choir. As far back as the
sixth century the practice of interpolating " Ah " 's and " Oh " 's
in pauses in this alternate choral chanting had arisen, and this
custom was gradually elaborated and special texts were composed. This embellishment of the Easter service has progressed
a long way when we come to the " Quem Quaeritis " trope of
the tenth century.

Now it is a priest that is concealed in a sepulchre of painted
canvas and wood (or occasionally stone) richly adorned, and
the three priests, representing the three women, enter the
church, and, as if looking for the tomb of the Saviour, proceed
towards the sepulchre. From within the sepulchre comes the
chant of the hidden priest " in a dulcet voice, of medium
pitch " : " Quem quaeritis in sepulchro, Christicolae ? "
To which they answer : " Iesum Nazarenum crucifixum, o
caelicolae ". And again the hidden priest speaks : " Non est
hic ; surrexit sicut praedixerat. Ite, nuniate quia surrexit
de sepulchro ". Then the three chant " Alleluia ! surrexit
Dominus " and an anthem " Venite et Videte locum " [1] is sung,
the priest in the sepulchre then showing the tomb empty save
for the cloths in which the cross was wrapped. The little
drama ends with the joyous pealing of bells, and the singing of
the " Te Deum " by the congregation.[2]

Here was obviously the birth of the drama — both on the
Continent and later in England — and such drama was comparatively quick in widening its scope. Another service of

[1] " Whom do you seek in the sepulchre, O Christians ". " The crucified
Jesus of Nazareth, O heavenly ones ". " He is not here ; he has risen as he
foretold. Go and announce that he has risen from the dead ". " Alleluia,
the Lord has risen ". " Come and see the place ".

[2] Based on the full " stage directions ", as we may almost call them, of
the *Concordia Regularis*, by Ethelwold, Bishop of Winchester, translated
by E. K. Chambers in his *The Mediaeval Stage*.

the Church which obviously lends itself to a similar embellish-ment is that at Christmas. Here the three priests represented the three shepherds, and the " Quem quaeritis " would be adapted to " Quem quaeritis in praesepe pastores ? " [1] A variation was that of the Magi or Three Kings, and the " Star " was represented by a fixed or movable light. Other incidents were included : the Massacre of the Innocents ; the introduc-tion of Herod as a " stock " character and his interview with the Magi. These form the nucleus of a group of Epiphany plays.

We may see at once that there were certain limitations on these little " tropes ", as these interpolations are called, which precluded much further internal development until they could become secularised. For material they were limited fairly strictly to the appropriate lesson the Church was trying to teach ; the dialogue was definitely laid down, and was in Latin ; and the production was entirely in the hands of the clergy, and always took place in the church. Therefore the move outside the church was an important one, and occurred mainly owing to the immense popularity of these little " plays ", as we may almost call them, and the resulting difficulty of housing the " audiences " who came to see them. This necessitated an overflow into the churchyard, where the graves were desecrated by the throng, so that they were finally banished even from there. Another feature which may have helped in establishing this move away from the church may be traced in an early Norman play *Adam,* the structure of which necessitated that parts of it should be played outside the church. It is full of most interesting stage-directions and, most important of all, written partly in the vernacular. Pollard dates this play contemporaneously with those of Hilarius which, though written in Latin, introduce refrains and speeches in the old French vernacular. At least two, then, of the limitations noted above were thus on the way to being removed entirely. To trace in detail the development of the drama from the elaboration of the ritual of the Mass to the flourishing Miracle plays performed by the Guilds of

[1] "Whom do ye seek in the manger, shepherds ? "

For example :

> 2 cotes and payre of hosen for Eve steyned.
> A cote and hosen for Adam steyned.
> A cote wt hosen and tayle for ye serpent, steyned.

> .   .   .   .

> 2 hearys for Adam and Eve.
>   (Grocers' Company, Norwich, 1565).[1]

Although the actors were all members of the Guilds, and this was merely an interlude in their daily work, payment ranging from fourteenpence to four shillings was apparently made for their performances, and they, in turn, contributed towards the cost of production, which was carefully prepared and rehearsed.

The subjects are all Biblical, and there is no doubt that actors and audience alike had a great sense of the reverence due to such plays.   Yet again it is inevitable that humour and fun should creep in as, of course, it did in passages which are not concerned with God or Christ.

There are two passages often quoted to illustrate this out-crop of native humour, and they afford excellent examples. The first is in the play of *The Three Shepherds*, the second shepherds' play of the Townley cycle.   The shepherds are seated on the ground watching their flocks, when one Mak enters to them.   After some conversation they sleep, and Mak steals a ram from the fold.   When the shepherds awake they soon discover their loss, and, rather naturally, connect it with Mak's disappearance.   They go to his house and rouse him, but he begs them to be quiet, as they may wake his wife and her new-born baby.   They insist, however, on searching his house, but can find no evidence of his guilt.   Soon after they have left they remember that they gave no present to the new-born baby, and, much to Mak's displeasure we may imagine, return to remedy this omission.   One of the shepherds says :

[1] Allardyce Nicholl, *British Drama*, p. 26.

Give me lefe him to kys and lyft up the clowte (clothes).
What the devill is this ?   He has a long snowte (snout).

There is the sheep in the cradle — dressed in swaddling clothes !
Mak's efforts, in which he is ably backed up by his wife, to
brazen it out are of no avail, and the incident ends with a bit
of horseplay, in which Mak is tossed in a blanket.   There is a
definite humour of comic situation here.   You can picture the
rough shepherds trying to tiptoe round the house, and the
discovery of the cradled sheep.

Another play in which a similar type of rough, knock-about
humour occurs is in the Chester play of *Noah and the Flood*.
Here is an early portrayal of a shrew in Noah's wife.   She
declines to enter the ark unless she can have her " gossips " to
drink and to chat with.   Noah refuses, and she peevishly does
her best to hamper the building of the ark, and even when it
is completed, still refuses to come in without her friends.   Noah
in desperation sends Shem to carry her in, and, as she is bundled
in willy-nilly, Noah rather tactlessly says : " Welcome, wife,
into this boate ", to which her only reply is : " And have thou
that for thy note ", and gives him a hearty slap.   " Aha !
Mary ! this is hotte (hot), it is good for to be still ", says the
wounded Noah !   It is noteworthy that it is those characters
which are not strictly sacred which lend themselves to this
" comic " treatment.   The sacred characters were treated and
played with real religious feeling and simple beauty.

It is not only humour that we find here presaging native
English comedy.   More than a hint of pathos, even tragedy,
is present too, in such a play as *Abraham and Isaac*, where
Isaac, bearing on his back the faggots for the sacrificial fire,
follows his father in blind obedience to the will of God, while
Abraham's heart is breaking at the naïve chatter of his son and
the duty that confronts him.

In all these plays we have progressed a long way from the
early embellishments of the ritual of the Mass, but even now
some of the drawbacks to further development previously noted

are still there, notably perhaps the lack of scope for much originality in the scenes portrayed, or in the choice of characters, though there is considerable variety in their portrayal. At any rate, here is a drama of a sort popularised to a certain extent, and certainly popular right up to the sixteenth century. They spanned a wide area, these Miracle plays. Chaucer's Absalom had " played Herod on scaffolds high ", and Shakespeare certainly had witnessed performances in his youth, and is thinking of one of them in Hamlet's advice to the Players : " it out-herods Herod ". Herod is the forerunner of the stock villain of melodrama, and was always played as a ranting, roaring figure. " Here Herod rages in the pageant and in the street also ", runs one of the stage-directions in the Coventry play.

The exact steps that led to the next obvious development, the Morality plays, cannot be traced here — for that matter they are by no means clear — but again it is certain that in the early sixteenth century this type of play was taking the place of the Miracle plays. The main difference lies in the fact that the Miracle plays take as their basis the history and legends of the Church, whereas the Moralities deal with its sacramental and moral teaching. The Morality is a dramatised allegory in which the common theme is the struggle between Good and Evil in the soul of man. Moralities are not very interesting in themselves to-day, but in marking another milestone in the development of drama they are indeed noteworthy. An interesting point is that the most notable feature of these plays, the characterisation, is at the same time hampering and furthering development. The characters are all allegorical, as their names, " Good Deeds ", " Evil Counsel ", " Mercy ", and " Worldly Affection ", show, and therefore in a sense lack life, moving always to the inevitable conclusion of the triumph of Good over Evil. On the other hand, in many plays the characters do have more definite contemporary characteristics in much the same way as, later, Shakespeare introduced local colour and typical Elizabethan figures even if the setting were Athens or Naples. Again, though some are stilted, here is a new group of characters having no connection with the Biblical figures which have occupied the " stage " for the preceding 150 years or more, and therefore tending to allow the author more originality of treatment than had been the case. In the same way, although the plot is stereotyped, the struggle between Good and Evil in the soul of man is the forerunner of a similar struggle in some of the great tragedies.·

That " Moralities " grew up side by side with the Miracle plays, and eventually ousted them from popular favour, is obvious, and an important part of the change is the fact that the Moralities and Interludes were played by professional actors. The best-known Morality is the fifteenth-century play of *Everyman*, adapted, as many think, from the Dutch play, *Elckerlijk*. Everyman — and the same character appears in other Moralities as Humanum Genus, Mankynd, etc. — is summoned by Death. In vain he seeks companions for this long journey, but Fellowship, Kindred, Goods, even Knowledge, Beauty and Discretion forsake him, and only Good Deeds accompanies him to speak for him before God.

The majority of Moralities are variants on this theme, though in any estimate of this type of play we must remember that a huge proportion of the plays is lost to us. So far we have been concerned with the more serious moral side which gives the plays their name, but just as humour appears in the Miracle plays, so here such a vital part of a people's make-up finds its place, and we can trace broadly the transition to the Interludes. It is from the characters presenting evil and worldly traits that this humour springs, just as in the Miracle plays the Devils disporting themselves with their smoke and noise in Hell-mouth provided some crude humour and coarse by-play, and such characters provide some of the rude farce and rough humour which was to furnish the writers of the Interludes with their comic material. Chief of all, it is the Vice (of whom his successor and descendant, Feste, speaks in *Twelfth Night*), with his dagger of lath, who with his pranks and quips provides much of the humorous material of these Moralities.

When we come to talk of Interludes we are in a rather difficult position, for the Moralities had often a sub-title of an " Interlude ", and sometimes were actually called Interludes. Again, some of the Interludes preserve many characteristics of the Moralities, so that it is, as has been said, a transitional period with no strict boundary line between the two until we come to such a realistic play as the *Four P's* (usually attributed to John Heywood), where we have a purely secular play with no religious or moral characteristics, paving the way for early Comedy.

A 'Pothecary, a Palmer, a Pardoner, and a Pedlar hold a competition in lying, with a prize for the best — or worst — lie. The Pardoner narrates his marvellous cures, the 'Pothecary tells of his magic medicines. The 'Pothecary and the Pedlar are coarse and not always funny, but the Pardoner tells a marvellous story of how he went to Hell to look for a lady friend of his, and the Devil promised to release her if the Pardoner would guarantee that no more women should come there, as they were such a nuisance ! The Palmer retaliates that this seems strange, as throughout his life he has never seen a woman out of patience. This supposedly colossal lie wins the in-voluntary admiration of the other contestants, and he bears off the prize. The descriptions of the Devils in gala dress — there is some festivity in progress — with their horns gilded and their nails all clean, playing a game with firebrands for rackets, are delightful, and the dialogue is excellently brisk. There is also considerable dramatic interest in the characterisation, and in this play Heywood has broken right away from the traditions of the Morality.

And now we have reached what we may call the first regular comedies in the English drama, *Ralph Roister Doister* and *Gammer Gurton's Needle.* The former play, written by Nicholas Udall, Headmaster of Westminster, about 1550, is the more " academic " of the two, *Gammer Gurton* being more broadly

farcical in theme and treatment. They are near enough together to be typical of a period, and excellent examples of
early comedy. *Ralph Roister Doister* owes something to the
classical tradition, and the figure of Ralph is a true-to-type
example of the " Miles gloriosus " stock, a vainglorious braggart.
On the other hand, the native stock is equally obvious in
Mathew Merygreke, who is in the line of descent from the Vice
of earlier plays. The plot structure is good, and the situations
amusing. Ralph Roister Doister falls in love with Dame
Custance, who is betrothed to a merchant at the moment abroad
on a voyage. In his foolish pride Ralph imagines Dame
Custance has only to see him to reciprocate his passion, whereas
she will in reality have none of him. His friend Merygreke,
who uses Ralph at will to feather his own nest, urges him on
to besiege her house and take the lady by force, but Ralph is
shamefully defeated by Custance's serving maids, who use their
domestic utensils as weapons of offence. There is a delightful
and typical touch when, during the battle, Merygreke soundly
belabours the luckless Ralph, apologising at every blow and
pretending it was aimed elsewhere. Gawyn Goodluck,
Custance's betrothed, returns, Ralph apologises, and all parties
sit down to supper at peace. The medium employed is rhymed
doggerel verse.

The other play mentioned above, *Gammer Gurton's Needle*,
is ascribed to John Still, and was produced at Christ's College,
Cambridge. A good deal of the long, rhymed doggerel verse is
in dialect, and the whole play gives a lively and excellent picture
of English rustic life at the period. The theme is farcical, and
concerns the loss and subsequent recovery of the Gammer's
needle, which she has mislaid while patching the breeches of
her husband Hodge. Diccon, the village mischief-maker —
another example of the Vice tradition — has not only a finger
but both hands in the pie, and confounds confusion by his
plotting. He tells Dame Chat, the Gurtons' neighbour (after
Gib the cat has been blamed and suspected), that Gammer
accuses her of having stolen a chicken. To Madam Gurton

he suggests that Dame Chat has found the needle and appropriated it to her own use. The two ladies (Dame Chat having expressed the pious hope that her nails may be long enough for the imminent fray !) meet and talk — at cross purposes, certainly, but they talk with a remarkable flow of scurrilous abuse until, words failing, they join battle with tooth and nail. The help of Dr Rat, the village curate, is enlisted, and again Diccon seizes a glorious chance of meddling. He tells Dame Chat that Hodge intends to creep through a hole in the dividing fence that night and to rob her hen-roost in vengeance for the violence his wife suffered. To Dr Rat he hints that if he will creep through the hole at nightfall he will surprise Dame Chat with the stolen needle, and her guilt will be made manifest. The sequel is obvious ; the unhappy little Doctor gets what was intended for the marauding Hodge, and is soundly belaboured. The Bailiff is finally called to unravel the tangle, and Diccon confesses his duplicity. He is ordered to kneel and apologise to all concerned ; he does so, but cannot resist a sly blow at Hodge. Hodge leaps up with a roar of pain, and the lost needle is found where Gammer Gurton left it — in the seat of his breeches ! Farcical as it is, this search for a needle in the rural domestic haystack is spirited and well-contrived.

So much for the earliest English comedy. Almost contemporaneously we have the first example of Tragedy in *Gorboduc, or Ferrex and Porrex,* the work of Sackville and Norton (1562). The classical influence noted in *Ralph Roister Doister* is more obvious here, and the play is modelled on the Senecan type of tragedy. The themes of this Roman philosopher were lust, bloodshed, murder, and revenge. In *Gorboduc* dumb shows, a chorus, and messengers all have their place, and practically no action takes place on the stage, the story dealing with murders, rebellions, and the struggle for supremacy between Ferrex and Porrex, King Gorboduc's two sons. The play has far more historical than intrinsic interest in that it is the first tragedy we have, and that it is written in blank verse, of a sort. It is actually an extremely correct ten-syllable line, but severely end-stopped and monotonous, and has no hint of the flexibility and sweetness it was to have at the hands of a master. In addition the " blood and thunder " tragedy had a marked influence on English drama for some time.

And now we must discuss the contribution of the " University Wits ", as this group of Oxford and Cambridge men have been called — Marlowe and Kyd to tragedy ; Lyly, Greene, and Peele to comedy. The names of Lodge and Nashe should be mentioned too, but their work is mainly other than dramatic, and it is with the larger group that we are more concerned. All were born between 1554 and 1567, and although two lived on into the seventeenth century, for practical purposes their work falls into the last half of the sixteenth century.

Christopher Marlowe (1564-93) handed on two great gifts. He did almost more than any one man of this group, though they all had a hand in it, to remove blank verse from the shackles which bound it in *Gorboduc*, and set it on the way to becoming the unfettered, flexible, varying medium it was to be. His fame rests not only on the " mighty clanging lines " of *Tamburlaine the Great*, his first play, but on the sweeter quality which his passionate love of beauty of thought and word gives his verse in such passages as Tamburlaine's farewell to the dying Zenocrate, which is, as it were, a variation on a theme, returning always to the dominant : " To entertain divine Zenocrate ".

> Black is the beauty of the brightest day,
> The Golden Ball of Heaven's eternal fire,
> That danced with glory on the silver waves,
> Now wants the fuel that enflamed his beams,
> And all with faintness, and for foul disgrace,
> He binds his temples with a frowning cloud.

And again in the well-known lines from *Dr Faustus* we see something of this quality :

> Was this the face that launched a thousand ships
> And burnt the topless towers of Ilium ?

> Sweet Helen make me immortal with a kiss ;
> Her lips suck forth my soul, see where it flies !
>
> .   .   .   .
>
> O thou art fairer than the evening air,
> Clad in the beauty of a thousand stars ".

And in one more gem, torn from its setting, the last words of
Faustus :

> O soul be changed into little water drops,

there is combined poetic imagination and a perfection of
phrasing.   One more example from the abdication scene in
Edward II will serve to show how much freer he has made his
verse ; the break and the run-on lines may be noticed particularly.

> O would that I might ! but heavens and earth conspire
> To make me miserable.   Here, receive my crown.
> Receive it ? no, these innocent hands of mine
> Shall not be guilty of so foul a crime.

Apart from this important contribution to the development
of blank verse as a vehicle of expression for the drama, particularly tragedy, Marlowe leaves a notable legacy in the
central figures of his tragedies.   He does not give us a Macbeth
or an Othello, but he prepares the canvas for Shakespeare to
paint such portraits, by showing us the struggle in the mind
of an individual or the attempt to reach an unattainable ideal,
and he shows us, too, his heroic or tragic figure beaten by
circumstances.

If Marlowe deserves credit for paving the way for Shakespeare's *Macbeth* or *Othello*, Thomas Kyd must be given his meed
of praise for developing another type of tragedy (exemplified
and perfected in *Hamlet*) in his *Spanish Tragedy*.   Modelled on
the Senecan type again, it popularises it to satisfy what was a
public demand.   It may be of the horror type — Shakespeare
himself wrote what one may describe as a " Shocker " in *Titus*

Andronicus — but it is full of hearty, exciting action. The theme is of the revenge type, and the hero, vacillating, accomplishes his end, like Hamlet, only after much indecision. The introduction of the ghost and the play within the play engineered by Jeronimo provide other points of contact with *Hamlet*. In his verse he rarely reaches the heights attained by Marlowe and makes a good deal of use of rhyme, but there are passages (particularly in *Jeronimo*, if it be his) where he achieves greater freedom.

John Lyly (1554-1606), the eldest of the group and the first to be considered in the development of Comedy, stands, in a way, apart from the others. He wrote more for the Court than the public theatre, and is in every way more " courtly " than the others of his group — had not his " Euphues ", with its balanced, antithetical style, set the fashion at Court ? And though it is parodied by Shakespeare in *Henry IV*, Part I, yet he was himself influenced by it in *Love's Labour's Lost* and *Richard III*. So popular did Euphuism prove that Lyly's contribution was inevitably in the development of prose rather than verse as a means of expression in comedy. On the other hand, he is as well a poet with a lyrical gift which he employs to advantage in the lyrics scattered through his plays. Here again we may trace another debt Shakespeare owes — this infusion of lyrics in comedy, not extraneously but with some bearing on the plot, or reflecting the mood of some character or theme of the play. In addition, Lyly develops the mingling of verse and prose and realises that the blank verse of tragedy as developed by Marlowe and Kyd is not so suitable for comedy, but requires a lighter, more fanciful touch. His plays are often allegorical, mythical, and masque-like, possibly because of the Court influence, but he begins the work — carried on by Greene and Peele and completed by Shakespeare — of weaving a romantic comedy, a web of romance, reality, and humour. Finally, the device of dressing a girl in boy's clothes, used so effectively in the case of Rosalind and Viola, may be credited to Lyly, as the first to make use of it in English comedy. It may be mentioned that not only did this device obviously lend itself to amusing situations of mistaken identity, but as women's parts were played by boys their task must thus have been rendered easier.

George Peele (1557–96) has given us five known plays diverse in type, and in most of these plays, different as they are, the verse reaches at times a very high level. There is a great deal of variety in rhythm and cadence which makes his an important contribution in this respect, though it is not poetry alone that will make a play, and Peele is usually weak on the side of dramatic structure. However, in addition to his verse he does hand on, in the case of the *Old Wive's Tale*, the harmonious mingling of reality and romance which, we know, is such an important feature of romantic comedy.

He uses not only blank verse, but rhymed verse and prose, though two plays, *The Battle of Alcazar* and *David and Bethsabe*, are entirely in blank verse. Two quotations must serve to illustrate his technique:

> To joy her love I'll build a kingly bower,
> Seated in hearing of a hundred streams,
> That, for their homage to her sovereign joys,
> Shall, as the serpents fold into their nests
> In oblique turnings, wind their nimble waves
> About the circles of her curious walks ;
> And with their murmur summon easeful sleep
> To lay his golden sceptre on her brows.
>
> *(David and Bethsabe)*

> Cast, as was Eva, from that glorious soil,
> Where all delights sat bating, winged with thoughts
> Ready to nestle in her naked breasts,
> To bare and barren vales with floods made waste —
> To desert woods and hills with lightning scorched
> Where death, where shame, where hell, where horror sit.

Robert Greene (1558–92) has also left five plays, of which two only are really important, *Friar Bacon and Friar Bungay* and *James IV*, in both of which are again examples of this essential juxtaposition of reality and romance. In the *Midsummer Night's Dream* we have fairies, Bottom and his friends, the human lovers, and the Duke ; in *Friar Bacon* we have the magic art of the Friars, the clowning of Miles, the servant, and a devil, and the love story of Margaret, the keeper's daughter, and Lacy, Earl of Lincoln. This is the very stuff of Romantic Comedy ; in any of Shakespeare's great comedies you find it. Feste, Malvolio, Sir Toby, and Sir Andrew can and must exist beside the loves of Orsino, Olivia, and Viola. It is in Greene's work more than in that of any of his contemporaries of this group, and his gift, then, is the realisation that these divergent types can grace the same picture, and that in this welding of the real and the ideal lies the material for this type of Romantic Comedy. He makes, too, a notable contribution in his portraits of women. They have sweetness, modesty, nobility and a real " living " quality. Shakespeare created Rosalind, Viola, and Imogen, but he had as patterns Margaret and Dorothea.

Such is the contribution of these immediate predecessors of Shakespeare (whose work is not under detailed consideration here), and we are nearing the jumping-off ground of our first play, in that glorious outburst of drama which almost above all things characterises the first twenty years of the seventeenth century. The fact that Shakespeare towers head and shoulders above his contemporaries is apt to dwarf their achievements. There is, however, an imposing list of other dramatists — headed by Ben Jonson — writing at this period, whose work presents a notable contribution to the development and practice of the drama. Ben Jonson was regarded by Dryden as only by a very little a lesser man than Shakespeare.

Jonson's first play, *Every Man in his Humour* (1598), gives by its title the clue to his aim. He returns in a sense to the comedies of Terence for his models, and shows his revolt against the romantic comedy and tragedy, the farcical comedy and revenge tragedy of his predecessors and contemporaries by his introduction of a realistic satirical comedy of humours. This word " humours " in its medical sense meant those subtle exhalations of a man's body which influenced his character. Thus a " humour " was responsible for a particular characteristic of a man, and so came to have the sense of peculiarity or idiosyncrasy. This, then, is Jonson's aim — to lampoon and ridicule upon the stage the eccentricities of human nature ; in other words, he is initiating the comedy of manners which supplied so often the themes of Restoration Drama, gave Sheridan the rod to castigate society in the *School for Scandal*, and has proved one of the most fruitful sources of inspiration to modern dramatists.

In *Every Man in his Humour* he presents us with a boastful coward (akin to the Miles gloriosus of Terence, of whom we have already had a hint in *Ralph Roister Doister*), a tyrannous father, and a foolish " gull ". All are exaggerated for the purpose of satire, but all escape the stigma of mere classical imitation by their liveliness. Jonson is an excellent satirist, and pricks with vigour the foibles of his age. He has, too, wit in his dialogue, though not the jewelled, sparkling wit of Congreve, so typical of that age. He showed as well considerable skill in the plots and construction of his plays, particularly *The Silent Woman* and *The Alchemist*, which contains in addition the superb creation of Sir Epicure Mammon.

This, then, is the contribution of Jonson (1573-1637) — a realistic, satirical comedy of manners. We must be content here with bare mention of the names of the remainder — Dekker, Marston, Middleton, Webster, Tourneur ; and of course in this same group come Beaumont and Fletcher.

II

INTRODUCTION TO
THE KNIGHT OF THE BURNING PESTLE

common with several of his relatives and connections. In
addition to his intimate friendship with Fletcher, he knew Ben
Jonson well, and, according to Dryden, acted as valued critic
of Jonson's plays. He died in 1616.

Such is a brief sketch of some of the known facts of the lives
of these two men who together made such a large contribution
to part of the drama in the early seventeenth century. They
handled almost entirely the romantic tragedy, and romantic
comedy, of which Shakespeare is the supreme exponent, but
in many respects they come indeed close to him, and their
plays had, and for a long time held, a tremendous popularity.
Dryden, in fact, said, " Their plays are now the most pleasant
and frequent entertainments of the stage, two of them being
acted through the year for one of Shakespeare's and Jonson's ".
This in itself is a striking testimony to their merits, although,
if the inference is that their work is of greater value than that
of Shakespeare, obviously later posterity does not endorse that
judgment. However, in the three great plays which are
undoubtedly their joint work, *Philaster*, *The Maid's Tragedy*,
and *A King and no King*, there are some of the best features
of the finest drama of the period. Their verse is loose and
flexible with a strong tendency to the extra syllable in the
line, usually ascribed particularly to Fletcher. There are some
truly lovely lyrics — a common feature of the drama which
was noted in Lyly and of which Shakespeare made such telling
use. Their stage-craft and plot structure are usually sound.
In *Philaster* the elements of romantic comedy are well and
charmingly handled, and in the incident of Euphrasia, who
follows her lover in the disguise of a page, Bellario, we
find another favourite device of romantic comedy again used
so successfully by Shakespeare in the cases of Viola, Rosalind,
Imogen, and Portia.

The Maid's Tragedy is the best example of their work in the
field of Romantic tragedy. Apart from a certain morbidity
in the theme, there is tremendous power in the handling of the
conflicting emotions of friendship, love, and loyalty, allied to

some very lovely verse. There is no humour in either of these plays, but in *A King and no King* there is a comic sub-plot, while the rich vein of humour in *The Knight of the Burning Pestle* is one of the main reasons for its inclusion in this volume.

The Knight of the Burning Pestle has several points in common with the tradition of Elizabethan comedy, although mainly it is admittedly a burlesque. There is first the " romantic love-story " of Luce and Jasper, although it is doubtful whether we can take them entirely seriously. It is a mere shadow of Shakespeare's probable treatment of a like theme, but it is, as we know, an indispensable feature of romantic comedy. The " clowning " is to a large extent supplied by Merrythought, with his rather infuriating snatches of song, but the main feature which supplies a great deal of the humour is the intro-duction on to the stage of the citizen and his wife. Their delightful interference with the plot, their demand for con-ventional situations, and insistence on the frequent appearance of Ralph, their apprentice, in the most inconsequential inter-ludes, are a great deal funnier than the actual burlesquing of Cervantes' *Don Quixote*, though this is interesting enough, particularly as it is the earliest example of the use of burlesque on the English stage, if we except the interlude of Bottom and his friends and their parody of romantic tragedy in *The Mid-summer Night's Dream*. It is a feature of farce and comedy which has always been popular, and though Sheridan, in *The Critic*, owes no direct debt to the Elizabethans, here at least is the first example of what he accomplishes so successfully. The wife, with her chatter and childlike belief in the reality of it all, and her almost invariable misdirection of her sympathies, and the efforts of the citizen, who was " the frowningest little thing when he was angry", to check her garrulity, are deliciously humorous and serve to give us in addition an excellent picture of part of a typical audience of the period.

Shakespeare gives us some excellent " low " portraits in Dogberry and Bottom, in the gravediggers and Macbeth's porter, but these pictures here certainly stand comparison.

It is very largely of course owing to the presence of this jolly pair that the main plot is interrupted and held up by the scenes in which Ralph figures, and therefore we cannot judge the plot structure very strictly because of the very form the play takes. However, the main action is straightforward enough, though it is always subordinate to the delightful interruptions of the "audience" and the interpolations of Ralph's burlesque of knight-errantry. In the first scene we learn of the love of Jasper and Luce, and the reward it meets at the hands of Jasper's master, her father, Venturewell. The presence of a rival and a plot to outwit him are hinted at, and in the second scene the rival materialises in the person of the foolish Humphrey, with his inane rhyming couplets, and the plot is partially disclosed by the preparation for the pretended elopement. Jasper's return home to his father, Merrythought, and departure with his "fortune", and Mistress Merrythought's quarrel with her light-hearted husband and her departure with the unpleasantly priggish little Michael conclude the act.

In Act II details of the supposed elopement are divulged to Venturewell, who gives his approval, and the various parties meet in Waltham Forest during the first three scenes. Here Ralph, with his pseudo-knight-errantry, becomes for a moment an actor in the main plot. In Scene iv the development of Jasper's plot takes place, the luckless Humphrey has been brought into the trap by Luce, Jasper meets them, seizes his love and sends Humphrey, beaten, away home to Venturewell, who starts off in pursuit — after an unsatisfactory interview with Jasper's father, whose conversation is plentifully interlarded, as usual, with snatches of song.

So far things seem to be going smoothly for the lovers, but in Act III Jasper is surprised while putting Luce's love to the test, a favourite device of lovers, and has her snatched from his arms by Venturewell and his men — the climax of the plot. Here Ralph again intrudes with the overthrow of the giant Barbaroso, but in Act IV, Scene iv, after another wild interlude of Ralph and the King of Moldavia's daughter, a boy brings to

Venturewell a supposed last request from Jasper, that Jasper's coffin, containing his presumably dead body may be brought to Luce. To this Venturewell conveniently gives consent, and the live Jasper rises from the coffin to confront his mourning love. She takes his place in the shroud and is borne out to freedom, while he hides in her room. More carefree singing from Merrythought and another quick change by Ralph to a May-Lord bring us to Act V, and towards the dénouement of the plot. Jasper appears as a convincing ghost to Venturewell and by threats of lifelong haunting persuades him to "beat fond Humphrey out-of-doors". Humphrey, who times his entries most unfortunately for himself, receives his second beating of the play and retires to mourn in seclusion under St Paul's. After Ralph has given another display of his versatility as Captain of his troops in a sort of Field Day at Mile End, we reach the dénouement in Scene iii, where Jasper, with his Luce, reaches his father's house. Mistress Merrythought has returned with Michael and is reconciled to her husband after paying forfeit with a song. Here Venturewell comes to crave Merrythought's forgiveness for so wronging the still supposedly dead Jasper, and father, daughter, and son-in-law are reconciled. We have not quite exhausted all Ralph's possibilities, and he appears as a ghost and recapitulates his recent activities, upon which the show concludes with a song.

VERSIFICATION

There is nothing very outstanding about the quality of the verse. It is, on the whole, of the usual iambic structure with the accent falling normally on the second syllable of each foot. Most of the usual variations are present, the weak or feminine ending, where the line has eleven syllables with the final syllable unstressed, being particularly common.

> No my best friend ; I cannot either fear,
> Or entertain a weary thought, whilst you
> (The end of all my full desires) stand by me :

Let them that lose their hopes, and live to languish
Amongst the number of forsaken lovers,
Tell the long weary steps, and number time,
Start at a shadow, and shrink up their blood,
Whilst I (possessed with all content and quiet)
Thus take my pretty love, and thus embrace him.

Act III, Sc. i.

In lines six and seven above may be noted also the inverted stress on the first foot.

Humphrey's speeches are nearly always in rhymed couplets, deliberately banal, with some occasional amusing rhymes. There is, of course, as is usual in comedy, a good deal of prose, and its use follows quite closely the custom of putting prose into the mouths of " low " or humorous characters, and leaving verse for the higher characters or as a vehicle of expression for deeper emotions.

III

THE KNIGHT OF THE BURNING PESTLE

BY

FRANCIS BEAUMONT
(1584–1616)

AND

JOHN FLETCHER
(1579–1625)

DRAMATIS PERSONÆ

SPEAKER OF THE PROLOGUE
A CITIZEN
HIS WIFE
RALPH, *his Apprentice*
TIM,
GEORGE, } *Apprentices*
Boys

VENTUREWELL, *a Merchant*
HUMPHREY
MERRYTHOUGHT
JASPER,
MICHAEL, } *His Sons*
Host

Tapster
Barber
Three Men, *supposed captives*
Sergeant
WILLIAM HAMMERTON
GEORGE GREENGOOSE
Soldiers, and Attendants

LUCE, *Daughter of Venturewell*
Mistress MERRYTHOUGHT
Woman, *supposed a captive*
POMPIONA, *Daughter of the King
of Moldavia*

SCENE.—London and the neighbouring Country, excepting
Act IV, Sc. ii, where it is in Moldavia.

*The play was probably written between 1609 and 1611, and was
first printed in 1613. It was at first apparently a failure but was
revived successfully in 1635 when another edition was published,
quickly followed by a third. Since that date it has been presented
intermittently with some success. In the 1635 edition the names of
the authors — Beaumont and Fletcher — are given, though the play is
attributed by some solely to Beaumont.*

*Improvements and slight alterations in the text have been made in
subsequent editions by Weber (1812), Dyce (1843-46), and J. St L.
Strachey (1887). This text is based mainly on that of Dyce. The
last part of the Barber scene, which is inordinately long and has little
dramatic value, has been cut, and four lines have been deleted from the
final scene.*

THE KNIGHT OF THE BURNING PESTLE

INDUCTION

Several Gentlemen sitting on Stools upon the Stage. The
CITIZEN, *his* WIFE, *and* RALPH *sitting below among the*
Audience.

Enter SPEAKER OF THE PROLOGUE.

SPEAKER OF THE PROLOGUE. " From all that 's near the
    court, from all that 's great,
Within the compass of the city-walls,
We now have brought our scene——"

CITIZEN *leaps on the Stage.*

CITIZEN. Hold your peace, goodman boy !

SPEAKER OF THE PROLOGUE. What do you mean, sir ?   5

CITIZEN. That you have no good meaning : this seven
years there hath been plays at this house, I have observed
it, you have still girds at citizens ; and now you call your
play " The London Merchant ". Down with your title,
boy ! down with your title !   10

SPEAKER OF THE PROLOGUE. Are you a member of the
noble city ?

CITIZEN. I am.

SPEAKER OF THE PROLOGUE. And a freeman ?

CITIZEN. Yea, and a grocer.   15

SPEAKER OF THE PROLOGUE. So, grocer, then, by your
sweet favour, we intend no abuse to the city.

CITIZEN. No, sir ? yes, sir : if you were not resolved to
play the Jacks, what need you study for new subjects,
purposely to abuse your betters ? why could not you be   20

31

contented, as well as others, with " The Legend of Whit-
tington ", or " The Life and Death of Sir Thomas Gresham,
with the building of the Royal Exchange ", or " The Story
of Queen Eleanor, with the rearing of London Bridge upon
5 Woolsacks " ?

SPEAKER OF THE PROLOGUE. You seem to be an under-
standing man : what would you have us do, sir ?

CITIZEN. Why, present something notably in honour of
the commons of the city.

10   SPEAKER OF THE PROLOGUE. Why, what do you say to
" The Life and Death of Fat Drake, or the Repairing of
Fleet-privies " ?

CITIZEN. I do not like that ; but I will have a citizen,
and he shall be of my own trade.

15   SPEAKER OF THE PROLOGUE. Oh, you should have told us
your mind a month since ; our play is ready to begin now.

CITIZEN. 'Tis all one for that ; I will have a grocer, and
he shall do admirable things.

SPEAKER OF THE PROLOGUE. What will you have him
20 do ?

CITIZEN. Marry, I will have him——

WIFE [*below*]. Husband, husband !

RALPH [*below*]. Peace, mistress.

WIFE [*below*]. Hold thy peace, Ralph ; I know what I
25 do, I warrant ye.—Husband, husband !

CITIZEN. What sayst thou, cony ?

WIFE [*below*]. Let him kill a lion with a pestle, husband !
let him kill a lion with a pestle !

CITIZEN. So he shall.—I'll have him kill a lion with a
30 pestle.

WIFE [*below*]. Husband ! shall I come up, husband ?

CITIZEN. Aye, cony,—Ralph, help your mistress this
way.—Pray, gentlemen, make her a little room.—I pray
you, sir, lend me your hand to help up my wife : I thank
35 you, sir.—So.   [WIFE *comes on the Stage.*

WIFE. By your leave, gentlemen all ; I'm something

troublesome : I'm a stranger here ; I was ne'er at one of these plays, as they say, before ; but I should have seen " Jane Shore " once ; and my husband hath promised me, any time this twelvemonth, to carry me to " The Bold Beauchamps ", but in truth he did not.   I pray you, bear 5 with me.

CITIZEN. Boy, let my wife and I have a couple of stools, and then begin ; and let the grocer do rare things.

[*Stools are brought.*

SPEAKER OF THE PROLOGUE. But, sir, we have never a boy to play him : every one hath a part already. 10

WIFE. Husband, husband, for God's sake, let Ralph play him ! beshrew me, if I do not think he will go beyond them all.

CITIZEN. Well remembered, wife.—Come up, Ralph.— I'll tell you, gentlemen ; let them but lend him a suit of 15 reparel and necessaries, and, by gad, if any of them all blow wind in the tail on him, I'll be hanged.

[RALPH *comes on the Stage.*

WIFE. I pray you, youth, let him have a suit of reparel. —I'll be sworn, gentlemen, my husband tells you true : he will act you sometimes at our house, that all the neighbours 20 cry out on him ; he will fetch you up a couraging part so in the garret, that we are all as feared, I warrant you, that we quake again : we'll fear our children with him ; if they be never so unruly, do but cry, " Ralph comes, Ralph comes ! " to them, and they'll be as quiet as lambs.—Hold 25 up thy head, Ralph ; show the gentlemen what thou canst do ; speak a huffing part ; I warrant you, the gentlemen will accept of it.

CITIZEN. Do, Ralph, do.

RALPH. " By Heavens, methinks, it were an easy leap 30
To pluck bright honour from the pale-faced moon ;
Or dive into the bottom of the sea,
Where never fathom-line touched any ground,
And pluck up drowned honour from the lake of hell ".

CITIZEN. How say you, gentlemen, is it not as I told you ?

WIFE. Nay, gentlemen, he hath played before, my husband says, Mucedorus, before the wardens of our 5 company.

CITIZEN. Aye, and he should have played Jeronimo with a shoemaker for a wager.

SPEAKER OF THE PROLOGUE. He shall have a suit of apparel, if he will go in.

10 CITIZEN. In, Ralph, in, Ralph ; and set out the grocery in their kind, if thou lovest me. [*Exit* RALPH.

WIFE. I warrant, our Ralph will look finely when he 's dressed.

SPEAKER OF THE PROLOGUE. But what will you have it 15 called ?

CITIZEN. " The Grocer's Honour ".

SPEAKER OF THE PROLOGUE. Methinks " The Knight of the Burning Pestle " were better.

WIFE. I'll be sworn, husband, that 's as good a name 20 as can be.

CITIZEN. Let it be so.—Begin, begin ; my wife and I will sit down.

SPEAKER OF THE PROLOGUE. I pray you, do.

CITIZEN. What stately music have you ? you have 25 shawms ?

SPEAKER OF THE PROLOGUE. Shawms ! no.

CITIZEN. No ? I'm a thief, if my mind did not give me so. Ralph plays a stately part, and he must needs have shawms : I'll be at the charge of them myself, rather than 30 we'll be without them.

SPEAKER OF THE PROLOGUE. So you are like to be.

CITIZEN. Why, and so I will be : there 's two shillings ;— [*gives money*]—let 's have the waits of Southwark ; they are as rare fellows as any are in England ; and that will 35 fetch them all o'er the water with a vengeance, as if they were mad.

SPEAKER OF THE PROLOGUE. You shall have them.   Will you sit down, then ?

CITIZEN. Aye.—Come, wife.

WIFE. Sit you merry all, gentlemen ; I'm bold to sit amongst you for my ease.   [CITIZEN *and* WIFE *sit down.* 5

SPEAKER OF THE PROLOGUE. " From all that 's near the court, for all that 's great.
Within the compass of the city-walls,
We now have brought our scene.   Fly far from hence
All private taxes, immodest phrases,   10
Whatever may but show like vicious !
For wicked mirth never true pleasure brings,
But honest minds are pleased with honest things ".—
Thus much for that we do ; but for Ralph's part you must answer for yourself.   15

CITIZEN. Take you no care for Ralph ; he'll discharge himself, I warrant you.   [*Exit* SPEAKER OF PROLOGUE.

WIFE. I' faith, gentlemen, I'll give my word for Ralph.

ACT THE FIRST

SCENE I.—*A Room in the House of* VENTUREWELL.

Enter VENTUREWELL *and* JASPER.

VENTUREWELL. Sirrah, I'll make you know you are my prentice,
And whom my charitable love redeemed   20
Even from the fall of fortune ; gave thee heat
And growth, to be what now thou art ; new-cast thee ;
Adding the trust of all I have, at home,
In foreign staples, or upon the sea,
To thy direction ; tied the good opinions   25
Both of myself and friends to thy endeavours ;
So fair were thy beginnings.   But with these,

As I remember, you had never charge
To love your master's daughter, and even then
When I had found a wealthy husband for her,
I take it, sir, you had not : but, however,
5　I'll break the neck of that commission,
And make you know you are but a merchant's factor.
　　　JASPER.　Sir, I do liberally confess I am yours,
Bound both by love and duty to your service,
In which my labour hath been all my profit :
10　I have not lost in bargain, nor delighted
To wear your honest gains upon my back ;
Nor have I given a pension to my blood,
Or lavishly in play consumed your stock ;
These, and the miseries that do attend them,
15　I dare with innocence proclaim are strangers
To all my temperate actions.　For your daughter,
If there be any love to my deservings
Borne by her virtuous self, I cannot stop it ;
Nor am I able to refrain her wishes.
20　She's private to herself, and best of knowledge
Whom she will make so happy as to sigh for :
Besides, I cannot think you mean to match her
Unto a fellow of so lame a presence,
One that hath little left of nature in him.
25　　　VENTUREWELL.　'Tis very well, sir :　I can tell your wisdom
How all this shall be cured.
　　　JASPER.　　　　　　　　Your care becomes you.
　　　VENTUREWELL.　And thus it shall be, sir :　I here dis-
charge you
My house and service ;　take your liberty ;
And when I want a son, I'll send for you.　　　[*Exit.*
30　　　JASPER.　These be the fair rewards of them that love !
Oh, you that live in freedom, never prove
The travail of a mind led by desire !

w doth your little sister and your brother ;
d whether you love me or any other.
LUCE. Sir, these are quickly answered.
HUMPHREY.   So they are,
here women are not cruel.   But how far
it now distant from the place we are in,
to that blessèd place, your father's warren ?
LUCE. What makes you think of that, sir ?
HUMPHREY.   Even that fa
r, stealing rabbits whilom in that place,
d Cupid, or the keeper, I know not whether,
to my cost and charges brought you thither,
d there began——
LUCE.   Your game, sir.
HUMPHREY.   Let no game,
r any thing that tendeth to the same,
e ever more remembered, thou fair killer,
or whom I sate me down, and brake my tiller.

   [WIFE. There 's a kind gentleman, I warrant you
   when will you do as much for me, George ?]

LUCE. Beshrew me, sir, I am sorry for your losses.
ut, as the proverb says, I cannot cry :
would you have not seen me !
HUMPHREY.   So would I,
nless you had more maw to do me good.
LUCE. Why, cannot this strange passion be withstood
end for a constable, and raise the town.
HUMPRHEY. Oh, no ! my valiant love will batter dow
illions of constables, and put to flight
ven that great watch of Midsummer-day at night.
LUCE. Beshrew me, sir, 'twere good I yielded, then ;
Veak women cannot hope, where valiant men
Iave no resistance.
HUMPHREY.   Yield, then ; I am full
Of pity, though I say it, and can pull

Enter LUCE.

LUCE. Why, how now, friend ? struck with my father's
   thunder ?
JASPER. Struck, and struck dead, unless the remedy
Be full of speed and virtue ; I am now,
What I expected long, no more your father's.
LUCE. But mine.
JASPER.   But yours, and only yours, I am ;   5
That 's all I have to keep me from the statute.
You dare be constant still ?
LUCE.   Oh, fear me not !
In this I dare be better than a woman :
Nor shall his anger nor his offers move me,
Were they both equal to a prince's power.   10
JASPER. You know my rival ?
LUCE.   Yes, and love him dearly :
Even as I love an ague or foul weather :
I prithee, Jasper, fear him not.
JASPER.   Oh, no !
I do not mean to do him so much kindness.
But to our own desires : you know the plot   15
We both agreed on ?
LUCE.   Yes, and will perform
My part exactly.
JASPER.   I desire no more.
Farewell, and keep my heart ; 'tis yours.
LUCE.   I take it ;
He must do miracles makes me forsake it.
                           [*Exeunt severally.*

   [CITIZEN. Fie upon 'em, little infidels ! what a   20
   matter 's here now ! Well, I'll be hanged for a half-
   penny, if there be not some abomination knavery in
   this play. Well, let 'em look to 't ; Ralph must
   come, and if there be any tricks a-brewing——

WIFE. Let 'em brew and bake too, husband, a' God's name ; Ralph will find all out, I warrant you, an they were older than they are.

Enter BOY.

—I pray, my pretty youth, is Ralph ready ?

5   BOY. He will be presently.

WIFE. Now, I pray you, make my commendations unto him, and withal carry him this stick of liquorice : tell him his mistress sent it him ; and bid him bite a piece ; 'twill open his pipes the better, say.]

[*Exit* BOY.

SCENE II.—*Another Room in the House of* VENTUREWELL.

Enter VENTUREWELL *and* HUMPHREY.

10   VENTUREWELL. Come, sir, she 's yours ; upon my faith, she 's yours ;
You have my hand : for other idle lets
Between your hopes and her, thus with a wind
They are scattered and no more.   My wanton prentice,
That like a bladder blew himself with love,
15 I have let out, and sent him to discover
New masters yet unknown.
    HUMPHREY.   I thank you, sir,
Indeed, I thank you, sir ; and, ere I stir,
It shall be known, however you do deem,
I am of gentle blood, and gentle seem.
20   VENTUREWELL.   Oh, sir, I know it certain.
    HUMPHREY.   Sir, my friend,
Although, as writers say, all things have end,
And that we call a pudding hath his two,
Oh, let it not seem strange, I pray, to you,
If in this bloody simile I put
25 My love, more endless than frail things or gut !

[WIFE. Husband, I prithee, sweet la
thing ; but tell me truly.—Stay, you
you, till I question my husband.
    CITIZEN. What is it, mouse ?
    WIFE. Sirrah, didst thou ever see a
how it behaves itself, I warrant ye, a
looks, and perts up the head !—I pray
with your favour, were you never n
Moncaster's scholars ?
    CITIZEN. Chicken, I prithee heartily,
self : the childer are pretty childer ; bu
comes, lamb——
    WIFE. Aye, when Ralph comes, cony
youth, you may proceed.]

VENTUREWELL. Well, sir, you know my
    hope,
Assured of my consent ; get but my daugh
And wed her when you please.   You must
And clap in close unto her : come, I know
You have language good enough to win a w

[WIFE. A whoreson tyrant ! h'as b
stringer in 's days, I warrant him.]

HUMPHREY. I take your gentle offer, and
Yield love again for love reciprocal.
    VENTUREWELL. What, Luce ! within there

Enter LUCE.

LUCE.   Called you
VENTUREWELL.
Give entertainment to this gentleman :
And see you be not froward.—To her, sir :
My presence will but be an eye-sore to you.
    HUMPHREY. Fair Mistress Luce, how do y
    well ?
Give me your hand, and then I pray you tell

Out of my pocket thus a pair of gloves.
Look, Lucy, look ; the dog's tooth nor the dove's
Are not so white as these ; and sweet they be,
And whipt about with silk, as you may see.
If you desire the price, shoot from your eye   5
A beam to this place, and you shall espy
F S, which is to say, my sweetest honey,
They cost me three and twopence, or no money.

  LUCE. Well, sir, I take them kindly, and I thank you :
What would you more ?
  HUMPHREY.   Nothing.
  LUCE.   Why, then, farewell. 10
  HUMPHREY. Nor so, nor so ; for, lady, I must tell,
Before we part, for what we met together :
God grant me time and patience and fair weather !
  LUCE. Speak, and declare your mind in terms so brief.
  HUMPHREY. I shall : then, first and foremost, for relief 15
I call to you, if that you can afford it ;
I care not at what price, for, on my word, it
Shall be repaid again, although it cost me
More than I'll speak of now ; for love hath tost me
In furious blanket like a tennis-ball,   20
And now I rise aloft, and now I fall.
  LUCE. Alas, good gentleman, alas the day !
  HUMPHREY. I thank you heartily ; and, as I say,
Thus do I still continue without rest,
I' the morning like a man, at night a beast,   25
Roaring and bellowing mine own disquiet,
That much I fear, forsaking of my diet
Will bring me presently to that quandary,
I shall bid all adieu.
  LUCE.   Now, by St Mary,
That were great pity !
  HUMPHREY.   So it were, beshrew me ;   30
Then, ease me, lusty Luce, and pity show me.
  LUCE. Why, sir, you know my will is nothing worth

Without my father's grant ; get his consent,
And then you may with [full]¹ assurance try me.

    HUMPHREY. The worshipful your sire will not deny me ;
For I have asked him, and he hath replied,
5 " Sweet Master Humphrey, Luce shall be thy bride ".

    LUCE. Sweet Master Humphrey, then I am content.

    HUMPHREY. And so am I, in truth.

    LUCE.   Yet take me with you ;
There is another clause must be annexed,
And this it is : I swore, and will perform it,
10 No man shall ever joy me as his wife
But he that stole me hence.   If you dare venture,
I am yours (you need not fear ; my father loves you) ;
If not, farewell for ever !

    HUMPHREY.   Stay, nymph, stay :
I have a double gelding, coloured bay,
15 Sprung by his father from Barbarian kind ;
Another for myself, though somewhat blind,
Yet true as trusty tree.

    LUCE.   I am satisfied ;
And so I give my hand.   Our course must lie
Through Waltham Forest, where I have a friend
20 Will entertain us.   So, farewell, Sir Humphrey,
And think upon your business.   [*Exit*.

    HUMPRHEY.   Though I die,
I am resolved to venture life and limb
For one so young, so fair, so kind, so trim.   [*Exit*.

    [WIFE. By my faith and troth, George, and as I am
25   virtuous, it is e'en the kindest young man that ever
trod on shoe-leather.—Well, go thy ways ; if thou
hast her not, 'tis not thy fault, i' faith.

    CITIZEN. I prithee, mouse, be patient ; 'a shall have
her, or I'll make some of 'em smoke for 't.

30   WIFE. That's my good lamb, George.—Fie, this

¹ [full] added by most editors for the metre.

stinking tobacco kills me ! would there were none in England !—Now, I pray, gentlemen, what good does this stinking tobacco do you ? nothing I warrant you : make chimneys o' your faces !]

SCENE III.—*A Grocer's Shop.*

Enter RALPH, *as a Grocer, reading "Palmerin of England", with* TIM *and* GEORGE.

[WIFE. Oh, husband, husband, now, now ! there 's   5
Ralph, there 's Ralph.
CITIZEN. Peace, fool ! let Ralph alone.—Hark you,
Ralph ; do not strain yourself too much at the first.
—Peace !—Begin, Ralph.]

RALPH [*reads*]. " Then Palmerin and Trineus, snatching   10
their lances from their dwarfs, and clasping their helmets,
galloped amain after the giant ; and Palmerin, having
gotten a sight of him, came posting amain, saying, ' Stay,
traitorous thief ! for thou mayst not so carry away her,
that is worth the greatest lord in the world ' ; and, with   15
these words, gave him a blow on the shoulder, that he
struck him besides his elephant. And Trineus, coming to
the knight that had Agricola behind him, set him soon
besides his horse, with his neck broken in the fall ; so that
the princess, getting out of the throng, between joy and   20
grief, said, ' All happy knight, the mirror of all such as
follow arms, now may I be well assured of the love thou
bearest me '."—I wonder why the kings do not raise an
army of fourteen or fifteen hundred thousand men, as big
as the army that the Prince of Portigo brought against   25
Rosicleer, and destroy these giants ; they do much hurt
to wandering damsels, that go in quest of their knights.

[WIFE. Faith, husband, and Ralph says true ; for
they say the King of Portugal cannot sit at his meat,

but the giants and the ettins will come and snatch it
from him.

    CITIZEN. Hold thy tongue.—On, Ralph !]

    RALPH. And certainly those knights are much to be
commended, who, neglecting their possessions, wander
with a squire and a dwarf through the deserts to relieve
poor ladies.

    [WIFE. Aye, by my faith, are they, Ralph ; let 'em
say what they will, they are indeed. Our knights
neglect their possessions well enough, but they do not
the rest.]

    RALPH. There are no such courteous and fair well-spoken
knights in this age : they will call one " the son of a dog ",
that Palmerin of England would have called " fair sir " ;
and one that Rosicleer would have called " right beauteous
damsel ", they will call " damned wench ".

    [WIFE. I'll be sworn will they, Ralph ; they have
called me so an hundred times about a scurvy pipe of
tobacco.]

    RALPH. But what brave spirit could be content to sit
in his shop, with a flappet of wood, and a blue apron before
him, selling mithridatum and dragon's-water to visited
houses that might pursue feats of arms, and, through his
noble achievements, procure such a famous history to be
written of his heroic prowess ?

    [CITIZEN. Well said, Ralph ; some more of those
words, Ralph !

    WIFE. They go finely, by my troth.]

    RALPH. Why should not I, then, pursue this course,
both for the credit of myself and our company ? for
amongst all the worthy books of achievements, I do not
call to mind that I yet read of a grocer-errant : I will

be the said knight.—Have you heard of any that hath
wandered unfurnished of his squire and dwarf? My
elder prentice Tim shall be my trusty squire, and little
George my dwarf. Hence, my blue apron! Yet, in
remembrance of my former trade, upon my shield shall 5
be portrayed a Burning Pestle, and I will be called the
Knight of the Burning Pestle.

[WIFE. Nay, I dare swear thou wilt not forget thy
old trade; thou wert ever meek.]

RALPH. Tim! 10
TIM. Anon.
RALPH. My beloved squire, and George my dwarf, I
charge you that from henceforth you never call me by any
other name but " the right courteous and valiant Knight
of the Burning Pestle "; and that you never call any 15
female by the name of a woman or wench, but " fair lady ",
if she have her desires, if not, " distressed damsel "; that
you call all forests and heaths, " deserts ", and all horses
" palfreys ".

[WIFE. This is very fine, faith.—Do the gentlemen 20
like Ralph, think you, husband?
CITIZEN. Aye, I warrant thee; the players would
give all the shoes in their shop for him.]

RALPH. My beloved squire Tim, stand out. Admit this
were a desert, and over it a knight-errant pricking, and I 25
should bid you inquire of his intents, what would you say?
TIM. Sir, my master sent me to know whither you are
riding?
RALPH. No, thus: " Fair sir, the right courteous and
valiant Knight of the Burning Pestle commanded me to 30
inquire upon what adventure you are bound, whether to
relieve some distressed damsel, or otherwise ".

[CITIZEN. Whoreson blockhead, cannot remember!

WIFE. I' faith, and Ralph told him on 't before : all the gentlemen heard him.—Did he not, gentlemen ? did not Ralph tell him on 't ?]

GEORGE. Right courteous and valiant Knight of the 5 Burning Pestle, here is a distressed damsel to have a half-penny-worth of pepper.

[WIFE. That 's a good boy ! see, the little boy can hit it ; by my troth, it 's a fine child.]

RALPH. Relieve her, with all courteous language. Now 10 shut up shop ; no more prentices but my trusty squire and dwarf. I must bespeak my shield and arming pestle.
                              [*Exeunt* TIM *and* GEORGE.

[CITIZEN. Go thy ways, Ralph ! As I'm a true man, thou art the best on 'em all.
WIFE. Ralph, Ralph !
15 RALPH. What say you, mistress ?
WIFE. I prithee, come again quickly, sweet Ralph.
RALPH. By and by.]   *Exit.*]

SCENE IV.—*A Room in* MERRYTHOUGHT'S *House.*

Enter MISTRESS MERRYTHOUGHT *and* JASPER.

MISTRESS MERRYTHOUGHT. Give thee my blessing ! no, I'll ne'er give thee my blessing ; I'll see thee hanged first ; 20 it shall ne'er be said I gave thee my blessing. Thou art thy father's own son, of the right blood of the Merrythoughts. I may curse the time that e'er I knew thy father ; he hath spent all his own and mine too ; and when I tell him of it, he laughs, and dances, and sings, and cries, " A merry 25 heart lives long-a ". And thou art a wastethrift, and art run away from thy master that loved thee well, and art come to me ; and I have laid up a little for my

younger son Michael, and thou thinkest to bezzle that,
but thou shalt never be able to do it.—Come hither,
Michael!

Enter MICHAEL.

Come, Michael, down on thy knees; thou shalt have my
blessing.   5

    MICHAEL [*kneels*]. I pray you, mother, pray to God to
bless me.

    MISTRESS MERRYTHOUGHT. God bless thee! but Jasper
shall never have my blessing; he shall be hanged first:
shall he not, Michael? how sayst thou?   10

    MICHAEL. Yes, forsooth, mother, and grace of God.

    MISTRESS MERRYTHOUGHT. That's a good boy!

    [WIFE. I' faith, it's a fine-spoken child.]

    JASPER. Mother, though you forget a parent's love
I must preserve the duty of a child.   15
I ran not from my master, nor return
To have your stock maintain my idleness.

    [WIFE. Ungracious child, I warrant him; hark, how
he chops logic with his mother!—Thou hadst best tell
her she lies; do, tell her she lies.   20

    CITIZEN. If he were my son, I would hang him up
by the heels, and flay him, and salt him, whoreson
halter-sack!]

    JASPER. My coming only is to beg your love,
Which I must ever, though I never gain it;   25
And, howsoever you esteem of me,
There is no drop of blood hid in these veins
But, I remember well, belongs to you
That brought me forth, and would be glad for you
To rip them all again, and let it out.   30

    MISTRESS MERRYTHOUGHT. I' faith, I had sorrow enough
for thee, God knows; but I'll hamper thee well enough.

Get thee in, thou vagabond, get thee in, and learn of thy
brother Michael.   [*Exeunt* JASPER *and* MICHAEL.

MERRYTHOUGHT [*singing within*].

> Nose, nose, jolly red nose,
> And who gave thee this jolly red nose ?

5 MISTRESS MERRYTHOUGHT. Hark, my husband ! he's
singing and hoiting ; and I'm fain to cark and care, and
all little enough.—Husband ! Charles ! Charles Merrythought !

Enter MERRYTHOUGHT.

MERRYTHOUGHT [*sings*].

> Nutmegs and ginger, cinnamon and cloves ;
10 > And they gave me this jolly red nose.

MISTRESS MERRYTHOUGHT. If you would consider your
state, you would have little list to sing, i-wis.

MERRYTHOUGHT. It should never be considered, while it
were an estate, if I thought it would spoil my singing.

15 MISTRESS MERRYTHOUGHT. But how wilt thou do,
Charles ? thou art an old man, and thou canst not work,
and thou hast not forty shillings left, and thou eatest good
meat, and drinkest good drink, and laughest.

MERRYTHOUGHT. And will do.

20 MISTRESS MERRYTHOUGHT. But how wilt thou come by
it, Charles ?

MERRYTHOUGHT. How ! why, how have I done hitherto
these forty years ? I never came into my dining room,
but, at eleven and six o'clock, I found excellent meat and
25 drink o' the table ; my clothes were never worn out, but
next morning a tailor brought me a new suit : and without
question it will be so ever ; use makes perfectness. If
all should fail, it is but a little straining myself extraordinary, and laugh myself to death.

30   [WIFE. It's a foolish old man this ; is not he,
George ?

CITIZEN. Yes, cony.

WIFE. Give me a penny i' the purse while I live, George.

CITIZEN. Aye, by Lady, cony, hold thee there.]

MISTRESS MERRYTHOUGHT. Well, Charles; you promised 5
to provide for Jasper, and I have laid up for Michael. I
pray you, pay Jasper his portion : he 's come home, and
he shall not consume Michael's stock ; he says his master
turned him away, but, I promise you truly, I think he ran
away. 10

[WIFE. No, indeed, Mistress Merrythought ; though
he be a notable gallows, yet I'll assure you his master
did turn him away, even in this place ; 'twas i' faith,
within this half-hour, about his daughter ; my
husband was by. 15

CITIZEN. Hang him, rogue ! he served him well
enough : love his master's daughter ! By my troth,
cony, if there were a thousand boys, thou wouldst spoil
them all with taking their parts ; let his mother alone
with him. 20

WIFE. Ay, George ; but yet truth is truth.]

MERRYTHOUGHT. Where is Jasper ? he 's welcome, however. Call him in ; he shall have his portion. Is he
merry ?

MISTRESS MERRYTHOUGHT. Ay, foul chive him, he is too 25
merry !—Jasper ! Michael !

Re-enter JASPER *and* MICHAEL.

MERRYTHOUGHT. Welcome, Jasper ! though thou runnest
away, welcome ! God bless thee ! 'Tis thy mother's
mind thou shouldst receive thy portion ; thou hast been
abroad, and I hope hast learned experience enough to 30
govern it ; thou art of sufficient years ; hold thy hand—
one, two, three, four, five, six, seven, eight, nine, there is

ten shillings for thee. [*Gives money*.] Thrust thyself into the world with that, and take some settled course : if fortune cross thee, thou hast a retiring place ; come home to me ; I have twenty shillings left. Be a good husband ; that is, wear ordinary clothes, eat the best meat, and drink the best drink ; be merry, and give to the poor, and, believe me, thou hast no end of thy goods.

JASPER. Long may you live free from all thought of ill, And long have cause to be thus merry still !
But, father——

MERRYTHOUGHT. No more words, Jasper ; get thee gone. Thou hast my blessing ; thy father's spirit upon thee ! Farewell, Jasper ! [*Sings*.]

> But yet, or ere you part (oh, cruel !)
> Kiss me, kiss me, sweeting, mine own dear jewel !

So, now begone ; no words.   [*Exit* JASPER.

MISTRESS MERRYTHOUGHT. So, Michael, now get thee gone too.

MICHAEL. Yes, forsooth, mother ; but I'll have my father's blessing first.

MISTRESS MERRYTHOUGHT. No, Michael ; 'tis no matter for his blessing ; thou hast my blessing ; begone. I'll fetch my money and jewels, and follow thee ; I'll stay no longer with him, I warrant thee. [*Exit* MICHAEL.]—Truly, Charles, I'll be gone too.

MERRYTHOUGHT. What ! you will not ?

MISTRESS MERRYTHOUGHT. Yes, indeed will I.

MERRYTHOUGHT [*sings*].

> Heigh-ho, farewell, Nan !
> I'll never trust wench more again, if I can.

MISTRESS MERRYTHOUGHT. You shall not think, when all your own is gone, to spend that I have been scraping up for Michael.

MERRYTHOUGHT. Farewell, good wife ; I expect it not :

all I have to do in this world, is to be merry ; which I shall,
if the ground be not taken from me ; and if it be,   [*Sings.*]

> When earth and seas from me are reft,
> The skies aloft for me are left.   [*Exeunt severally.*

[WIFE. I'll be sworn he's a merry old gentleman   5
for all that. [*Music.*]   Hark, hark, husband, hark !
fiddles, fiddles ! now surely they go finely.   They say
'tis present death for these fiddlers to tune their rebecks
before the great Turk's grace ; is 't not, George ?
[*Enter a* BOY *and dances.*]   But, look, look ! here's a   10
youth dances !—Now, good youth, do a turn o' the
toe.—Sweetheart, i' faith, I'll have Ralph come and
do some of his gambols.   He'll ride the wild mare,
gentlemen, 'twould do your hearts good to see him.—
I thank you, kind youth ; pray, bid Ralph come.   15

CITIZEN. Peace, cony !—Sirrah, you scurvy boy,
bid the players send Ralph ; or, by God's —— an they
do not, I'll tear some of their periwigs beside their
heads : this is all riff-raff.]   [*Exit* BOY.

ACT THE SECOND

SCENE I.—*A Room in the House of* VENTUREWELL.

Enter VENTUREWELL *and* HUMPHREY.

VENTUREWELL. And how, i' faith,[1] how goes it now,   20
son Humphrey ?

HUMPHREY. Right worshipful, and my belovèd friend
And father dear, this matter 's at an end.

VENTUREWELL. 'Tis well ; it should be so : I'm glad
the girl
Is found so tractable.   25

---

[1] Dyce has *faith*—Weber, for the metre, printed " *i' faith* ".

HUMPHREY.   Nay, she must whirl
From hence (and you must wink ; for so, I say,
The story tells,) to-morrow before day.

5   [WIFE. George, dost thou think in thy conscience
now 'twill be a match ? tell me but what thou think'st,
sweet rogue. Thou seest the poor gentleman, dear
heart, how it labours and throbs, I warrant you, to be
at rest ! I'll go move the father for 't.

10   CITIZEN. No, no ; I prithee, sit still, honeysuckle ;
thou'lt spoil all. If he deny him, I'll bring half a dozen
good fellows myself, and in the shutting of an evening, knock 't up, and there 's an end.

WIFE. I'll buss thee for that, i' faith, boy. Well,
George, well, you have been a wag in your days, I
15   warrant you ; but God forgive you, and I do with all
my heart.]

VENTUREWELL. How was it, son ? you told me that
to-morrow
Before daybreak, you must convey her hence.
HUMPHREY. I must, I must ; and thus it is agreed :
20 Your daughter rides upon a brown-bay steed,
I on a sorrel, which I bought of Brian,
The honest host of the Red roaring Lion,
In Waltham situate. Then, if you may,
Consent in seemly sort ; lest, by delay,
25 The Fatal Sisters come, and do the office,
And then you'll sing another song.
VENTUREWELL.   Alas !
Why should you be thus full of grief to me,
That do as willing as yourself agree
To any thing, so it be good and fair ?
30 Then, steal her when you will, if such a pleasure
Content you both ; I'll sleep and never see it,
To make your joys more full. But tell me why
You may not here perform your marriage ?

[WIFE. God's blessing o' thy soul, old man! i' faith, thou art loath to part true hearts. I see 'a has her, George; and I'm as glad on 't!—Well, go thy ways, Humphrey, for a fair-spoken man; I believe thou hast not thy fellow within the walls of London; an I should say the suburbs too, I should not lie.—Why dost not rejoice with me, George? 5

CITIZEN. If I could but see Ralph again, I were as merry as mine host, i' faith.]

HUMPHREY. The cause you seem to ask, I thus
      declare— 10
Help me, O Muses nine! Your daughter sware
A foolish oath, the more it was the pity;
Yet no one but myself within this city
Shall dare to say so, but a bold defiance
Shall meet him, were he of the noble science; 15
And yet she sware, and yet why did she swear?
Truly, I cannot tell, unless it were
For her own ease; for, sure, sometimes an oath,
Being sworn thereafter, is like cordial broth;
And this it was she swore, never to marry 20
But such a one whose mighty arm could carry
(As meaning me, for I am such a one)
Her bodily away, through stick and stone,
Till both of us arrive, at her request,
Some ten miles off, in the wild Waltham Forest. 25
      VENTUREWELL. If this be all, you shall not need to fear
Any denial in your love: proceed;
I'll neither follow, nor repent the deed.
      HUMPHREY. Good night, twenty good nights, and twenty
      more,
And twenty more good nights,—that makes three score! 30
                              [*Exeunt severally.*

Scene II.—*Waltham Forest.*

Enter MISTRESS MERRYTHOUGHT *and* MICHAEL.

MISTRESS MERRYTHOUGHT. Come, Michael; art thou not weary, boy?

MICHAEL. No, forsooth, mother, not I.

MISTRESS MERRYTHOUGHT. Where be we now, child?

5 MICHAEL. Indeed, forsooth, mother, I cannot tell, unless we be at Mile End. Is not all the world Mile End, mother?

MISTRESS MERRYTHOUGHT. No, Michael, not all the world, boy; but I can assure thee, Michael, Mile End is a goodly matter: there has been a pitch-field, my child, between 10 the naughty Spaniels and the Englishmen; and the Spaniels ran away, Michael, and the Englishmen followed: my neighbour Coxstone was there, boy, and killed them all with a birding-piece.

MICHAEL. Mother, forsooth——

15 MISTRESS MERRYTHOUGHT. What says my white boy?

MICHAEL. Shall not my father go with us too?

MISTRESS MERRYTHOUGHT. No, Michael, let thy father go snick up; let him stay at home, and sing for his supper, boy. Come, child, sit down, and I'll show my boy fine 20 knacks, indeed. [*They sit down: and she takes out a casket.*] Look here, Michael; here's a ring, and here's a brooch, and here's a bracelet, and here's two rings more, and here's money and gold by th' eye, my boy.

MICHAEL. Shall I have all this, mother?

25 MISTRESS MERRYTHOUGHT. Ay, Michael, thou shalt have all, Michael.

[CITIZEN. How lik'st thou this wench?

WIFE. I cannot tell; I would have Ralph, George; I'll see no more else, indeed, la; and I pray you, 30 let the youths understand so much by word of mouth; for, I tell you truly, I'm afraid o' my boy. Come,

come, George, let's be merry and wise : the child's a
fatherless child ; and say they should put him into a
strait pair of gaskins, 'twere worse than knot-grass ;
he would never grow after it.]

Enter RALPH, TIM, *and* GEORGE.

[CITIZEN. Here's Ralph, here's Ralph !   5
WIFE. How do you, Ralph ? you are welcome,
Ralph, as I may say ; it's a good boy, hold up thy
head, and be not afraid ; we are thy friends, Ralph ;
the gentlemen will praise thee, Ralph, if thou playest
thy part with audacity. Begin, Ralph, a' God's name!]   10

RALPH. My trusty squire, unlace my helm ; give me my
     hat.
Where are we, or what desert may this be ?
GEORGE. Mirror of knighthood, this is, as I take it, the
perilous Waltham Down ; in whose bottom stands the
enchanted valley.   15
MISTRESS MERRYTHOUGHT. Oh, Michael, we are betrayed,
we are betrayed ! here be giants ! Fly, boy ! fly, boy,
fly !   [*Exit with* MICHAEL, *leaving the casket.*
RALPH. Lace on my helm again. What noise is this ?
A gentle lady, flying the embrace   20
Of some uncourteous knight ! I will relieve her.
Go, squire, and say, the Knight, that wears this Pestle
In honour of all ladies, swears revenge
Upon that recreant coward that pursues her ;
Go, comfort her and that same gentle squire   25
That bears her company.
TIM.   I go, brave knight.   [*Exit.*
RALPH. My trusty dwarf and friend, reach me my shield;
And hold it while I swear. First, by my knighthood ;
Then by the soul of Amadis de Gaul,
My famous ancestor ; then by my sword   30
The beauteous Brionella girt about me ;

19 E

By this bright burning Pestle, of mine honour
The living trophy ; and by all respect
Due to distressèd damsels ; here I vow
Never to end the quest of this fair lady
5 And that forsaken squire till by my valour
I gain their liberty !

GEORGE.   Heaven bless the knight
That thus relieves poor errant gentlewomen !   [*Exeunt.*

[WIFE. Aye, marry, Ralph, this has some savour
in 't ; I would see the proudest of them all offer to
10 carry his books after him. But, George, I will not
have him go away so soon ; I shall be sick if he go
away, that I shall : call Ralph again, George, call
Ralph again ; I prithee, sweetheart, let him come
fight before me, and let 's ha' some drums and some
15 trumpets, and let him kill all that comes near him, an
thou lovest me, George !

CITIZEN. Peace a little, bird : he shall kill them all,
an they were twenty more on 'em than there are.]

Enter JASPER.

JASPER. Now, Fortune, if thou be'st not only ill,
20 Show me thy better face, and bring about
Thy desperate wheel, that I may climb at length,
And stand [secure].[1]   This is our place of meeting,
If love have any constancy.   Oh, age,
Where only wealthy men are counted happy !
25 How shall I please thee, how deserve thy smiles,
When I am only rich in misery ?
My father's blessing and this little coin
Is my inheritance ; a strong revénue !
From earth thou art, and to the earth I give thee:
                              [*Throws away the money.*
30 There grow and multiply, whilst fresher air

---
[1] Suggested by Dyce.

Breeds me a fresher fortune.—How! illusion!
> [*Spies the casket.*

What, hath the devil coined himself before me?
'Tis metal good, it rings well; I am waking,
And taking too, I hope. Now, God's dear blessing
Upon his heart that left it here! 'tis mine;   5
These pearls, I take it, were not left for swine.
> [*Exit with the casket.*

    [WIFE. I do not like that this unthrifty youth
should embezzle away the money; the poor gentlewoman his mother will have a heavy heart for it,
God knows.   10
    CITIZEN. And reason good, sweetheart.
    WIFE. But let him go; I'll tell Ralph a tale in 's
ear shall fetch him again with a wanion, I warrant
him, if he be above ground; and besides, George,
here are a number of sufficient gentlemen can witness,   15
and myself, and yourself, and the musicians, if we be
called in question.

SCENE III.—*Another part of the Forest.*

Enter RALPH *and* GEORGE.

    But here comes Ralph, George; thou shalt hear
him speak as he were an emperal.]

    RALPH. Comes not sir squire again?
    GEORGE.   Right courteous knight, 20
Your squire doth come, and with him comes the lady,
For and the Squire of Damsels, as I take it.

Enter TIM, MISTRESS MERRYTHOUGHT, *and* MICHAEL.

    RALPH. Madam, if any service or devoir
Of a poor errant knight may right your wrongs,

Command it ; I am prest to give you succour ;
For to that holy end I bear my armour.

MISTRESS MERRYTHOUGHT. Alas, sir ! I am a poor
gentlewoman, and I have lost my money in this forest !

5   RALPH. Desert, you would say, lady ; and not lost
Whilst I have sword and lance. Dry up your tears,
Which ill befit the beauty of that face,
And tell the story, if I may request it,
Of your disastrous fortune.

10   MISTRESS MERRYTHOUGHT. Out, alas ! I left a thousand
pound, a thousand pound, e'en all the money I had laid up
for this youth, upon the sight of your mastership, you
looked so grim, and, as I may say it, saving your presence,
more like a giant than a mortal man.

15   RALPH. I am as you are, lady ; so are they ;
All mortal. But why weeps this gentle squire ?

MISTRESS MERRYTHOUGHT. Has he not cause to weep,
do you think, when he hath lost his inheritance ?

RALPH. Young hope of valour, weep not ; I am here
20 That will confound thy foe, and pay it dear
Upon his coward head, that dares deny
Distressèd squires and ladies equity.
I have but one horse, [up]on [1] which shall ride
This lady fair behind me, and before
25 This courteous squire : fortune will give us more
Upon our next adventure. Fairly speed
Beside us, squire and dwarf, to do us need !   [*Exeunt.*

[CITIZEN. Did not I tell you, Nell, what your man
would do ? by the faith of my body, wench, for clean
30 action and good delivery, they may all cast their caps
at him.

WIFE. And so they may, i' faith ; for I dare speak
it boldly, the twelve companies of London cannot

---

[1] Dyce has " on "—" upon " suggested by other Editors for the
metre.

match him, timber for timber. Well, George, an he
be not inveigled by some of these paltry players, I ha'
much marvel : but, George, we ha' done our parts, if
the boy have any grace to be thankful.

    CITIZEN. Yes, I warrant thee, duckling.]   5

SCENE IV.—*Another part of the Forest.*

Enter HUMPHREY *and* LUCE.

    HUMPHREY. Good Mistress Luce, however I in fault am
For your lame horse, you're welcome unto Waltham ;
But which way now to go, or what to say,
I know not truly, till it be broad day.

    LUCE. Oh, fear not, Master Humphrey ; I am guide   10
For this place good enough.

    HUMPHREY.   Then, up and ride ;
Or, if it please you, walk for your repose ;
Or sit, or, if you will, go pluck a rose ;
Either of which shall be indifferent
To your good friend and Humphrey, whose consent   15
Is so entangled ever to your will,
As the poor harmless horse is to the mill.

    LUCE. Faith, an you say the word, we'll e'en sit down
And take a nap.

    HUMPHREY.   'Tis better in the town,
Where we may nap together ; for, believe me,   20
To sleep without a snatch would mickle grieve me.

    LUCE. You're merry, Master Humphrey.

    HUMPHREY.   So I am,
And have been ever merry from my dam.

    LUCE. Your nurse had the less labour.

    HUMPHREY.   Faith, it may be,
Unless it were by chance I did beray me.   25

Enter JASPER.

JASPER. Luce ! dear friend Luce !

LUCE. Here, Jasper.

JASPER. You are mine.

HUMPHREY. If it be so, my friend, you use me fine :
What do you think I am ?

JASPER. An arrant noddy.

HUMPHREY. A word of obloquy ! Now, by God's body,
5 I'll tell thy master ; for I know thee well.

JASPER. Nay, an you be so forward for to tell,
Take that, and that ; and tell him, sir, I gave it :
And say, I paid you well. [*Beats him.*

HUMPHREY. Oh, sir, I have it
And do confess the payment ! Pray, be quiet.

10 JASPER. Go, get you to your nightcap and the diet,
To cure your beaten bones.

LUCE. Alas, poor Humphrey ;
Get thee some wholesome broth, with sage and comfrey ;
A little oil of roses and a feather
To 'noint thy back withal.

HUMPHREY. When I came hither,
15 Would I had gone to Paris with John Dory !

LUCE. Farewell, my pretty nump ; I am very sorry
I cannot bear thee company.

HUMPHREY. Farewell :
The devil's dam was ne'er so banged in hell.

[*Exeunt* LUCE *and* JASPER.

[WIFE. This young Jasper will prove me another
20 thing, o' my conscience, an he may be suffered. George,
dost not see, George, how 'a swaggers, and flies at the
very heads o' folks, as he were a dragon ? Well, if I
do not do his lesson for wronging the poor gentleman,
I am no true woman. His friends that brought him
25 up might have been better occupied, i-wis, than have

taught him these fegaries : he 's e'en in the high way to the gallows, God bless him !

CITIZEN. You're too bitter, cony ; the young man may do well enough for all this.

WIFE. Come hither, Master Humphrey ; has he hurt 5 you ? now, beshrew his fingers for 't ! Here, sweetheart, here 's some green ginger for thee. Now, beshrew my heart, but 'a has peppernel in 's head, as big as a pullet's egg ! Alas, sweet lamb, how thy temples beat ! Take the peace on him, sweetheart, 10 take the peace on him.

CITIZEN. No, no ; you talk like a foolish woman : I'll ha' Ralph fight with him, and swinge him up well-favouredly.—Sirrah boy, come hither. [*Enter* BOY.] Let Ralph come in and fight with Jasper. 15

WIFE. Ay, and beat him well ; he 's an unhappy boy.

BOY. Sir, you must pardon us ; the plot of our play lies contrary ; and 'twill hazard the spoiling of our play. 20

CITIZEN. Plot me no plots ! I'll ha' Ralph come out ; I'll make your house too hot for you else.

BOY. Why, sir, he shall ; but if any thing fall out of order, the gentlemen must pardon us.

CITIZEN. Go your ways, goodman boy ! [*Exit* BOY.] 25 I'll hold him a penny, he shall have his bellyful of fighting now. Ho, here comes Ralph ! no more !]

SCENE V.—*Another part of the Forest.*

Enter RALPH, MISTRESS MERRYTHOUGHT, MICHAEL, TIM, *and* GEORGE.

RALPH. What knight is that, squire ? ask him if he keep
The passage, bound by love of lady fair,

Or else but prickant.

     HUMPHREY.   Sir, I am no knight,
But a poor gentleman, that this same night
Had stolen from me, on yonder green,
My lovely wife, and suffered (to be seen
5 Yet extant on my shoulders) such a greeting,
That whilst I live I shall think of that meeting.

     [WIFE. Ay, Ralph, he beat him unmercifully
Ralph ; an thou sparest him, Ralph, I would thou
wert hanged.
10   CITIZEN. No more, wife, no more.]

     RALPH. Where is the caitiff-wretch hath done this deed ?
Lady, your pardon ; that I may proceed
Upon the quest of this injurious knight.—
And thou, fair squire, repute me not the worse,
15 In leaving the great venture of the purse
And the rich casket, till some better leisure.

     HUMPHREY. Here comes the broker hath purloined my
        treasure.

              Enter JASPER *and* LUCE.

     RALPH. Go, [trusty] squire, and tell him I am here,
An errant knight-at-arms, to crave delivery
20 Of that fair lady to her own knight's arms.
If he deny, bid him take choice of ground,
And so defy him.

     TIM.   From the Knight that bears
The Golden Pestle, I defy thee, knight,
Unless thou make fair restitution
25 Of that bright lady.

     JASPER.   Tell the knight that sent thee,
He is an ass ; and I will keep the wench,
And knock his head-piece.

     RALPH.   Knight, thou art but dead,
If thou recall not thy uncourteous terms.

[WIFE. Break 's pate, Ralph ; break 's pate, Ralph, soundly !]

JASPER. Come, knight ; I am ready for you. Now
     your Pestle   [*Snatches away his pestle.*
Shall try what temper, sir, your mortar 's of.
With that he stood upright in his stirrups,   5
And gave the Knight of the calf-skin such a knock,
                     [*Knocks* RALPH *down.*
That he forsook his horse, and down he fell ;
And then he leaped upon him, and plucking off
His helmet——
    HUMPHREY. Nay, an my noble knight be down so soon, 10
Though I can scarcely go, I needs must run.   [*Exit.*

[WIFE. Run, Ralph, run, Ralph ; run for thy life,
boy ; Jasper comes, Jasper comes !]   [*Exit* RALPH.

JASPER. Come Luce, we must have other arms for you :
Humphrey, and Golden Pestle, both adieu !   [*Exeunt.* 15

[WIFE. Sure the devil (God bless us !) is in this
springald ! Why, George, didst ever see such a fire-
drake ? I am afraid my boy 's miscarried : if he be,
though he were Master Merrythought's son a thousand
times, if there be any law in England, I'll make some   20
of them smart for 't.
    CITIZEN. No, no ; I have found out the matter,
sweetheart ; Jasper is enchanted ; as sure as we are
here, he is enchanted : he could no more have stood
in Ralph's hands than I can stand in my lord mayor's.   25
I'll have a ring to discover all enchantments, and
Ralph shall beat him yet : be no more vexed, for it
shall be so.]

Scene VI.—*Before the Bell-Inn, Waltham.*

Enter RALPH, MISTRESS MERRYTHOUGHT, MICHAEL, TIM, *and* GEORGE.

[WIFE. Oh, husband, here's Ralph again!—Stay, Ralph, again, let me speak with thee. How dost thou, Ralph? art thou not shrewdly hurt? the foul great lungies laid unmercifully on thee: there's some
5 sugar-candy for thee. Proceed; thou shalt have another bout with him.

CITIZEN. If Ralph had him at the fencing-school, if he did not make a puppy of him, and drive him up and down the school, he should ne'er come in my
10 shop more.]

MISTRESS MERRYTHOUGHT. Truly, Master Knight of the Burning Pestle, I am weary.

MICHAEL. Indeed, la, mother, and I am very hungry.

RALPH. Take comfort, gentle dame, and you, fair squire;
15 For in this desert there must needs be placed
Many strong castles, held by courteous knights;
And till I bring you safe to one of those,
I swear by this my order ne'er to leave you.

[WIFE. Well said, Ralph!—George, Ralph was ever
20 comfortable, was he not?

CITIZEN. Yes, duck.

WIFE. I shall ne'er forget him. When we had lost our child (you know it was strayed almost alone to Puddle Wharf, and the criers were abroad for it, and
25 there it had drowned itself but for a sculler), Ralph was the most comfortablest to me: "Peace, mistress," says he, "let it go; I'll get you another as good." Did he not, George, did he not say so?

CITIZEN. Yes, indeed did he, mouse.]

GEORGE. I would we had a mess of pottage and a pot of drink, squire, and were going to bed!

TIM. Why, we are at Waltham-town's end, and that's the Bell Inn.

GEORGE. Take courage, valiant knight, damsel, and
      squire!   5
I have discovered, not a stone's cast off,
An ancient castle, held by the old knight
Of the most holy order of the Bell,
Who gives to all knights-errant entertain:
There plenty is of food, and all prepared   10
By the white hands of his own lady dear.
He hath three squires that welcome all his guests:
The first, hight Chamberlino, who will see
Our beds prepared, and bring us snowy sheets
Where never footman stretched his buttered hams;   15
The second, hight Tapstero, who will see
Our pots full fillèd, and no froth therein;
The third, a gentle squire, Ostlero hight,
Who will our palfreys slick with wisps of straw,
And in the manger put them oats enough,   20
And never grease their teeth with candle-snuff.

[WIFE. That same dwarf's a pretty boy, but the squire's a groutnol.]

RALPH. Knock at the gates, my squire, with stately lance.   [TIM *knocks at the door.* 25

Enter TAPSTER.

TAPSTER. Who's there?—You're welcome, gentlemen: will you see a room?

GEORGE. Right courteous and valiant Knight of the Burning Pestle, this is the Squire Tapstero.

RALPH. Fair Squire Tapstero, I a wandering knight,   30
Hight of the Burning Pestle, in the quest
Of this fair lady's casket and wrought purse,
Losing myself in this vast wilderness,

Am to this castle well by fortune brought ;
Where, hearing of the goodly entertain
Your knight of holy order of the Bell
Gives to all damsels and all errant knights,
5 I thought to knock, and now am bold to enter.

    TAPSTER. An 't please you see a chamber, you are very
welcome.   [*Exeunt.*

    [WIFE. George, I would have something done, and
I cannot tell what it is.
10   CITIZEN. What is it, Nell ?

    WIFE. Why, George, shall Ralph beat nobody
again ? prithee, sweetheart, let him.

    CITIZEN. So he shall, Nell ; and if I join with him,
we'll knock them all.]

SCENE VII.—*A Room in the House of* VENTUREWELL.

Enter HUMPHREY *and* VENTUREWELL.

15   [WIFE. Oh, George, here 's Master Humphrey again
now that lost Mistress Luce, and Mistress Luce's
father. Master Humphrey will do somebody's errand,
I warrant him.]

    HUMPHREY. Father, it 's true in arms I ne'er shall clasp
her ;
20 For she is stoln away by your man Jasper.

    [WIFE. I thought he would tell him.]

    VENTUREWELL. Unhappy that I am, to lose my child !
Now I begin to think on Jasper's words,
Who oft hath urged to me thy foolishness :
25 Why didst thou let her go ? thou lov'st her not,
That wouldst bring home thy life, and not bring her.

    HUMPHREY. Father, forgive me. Shall I tell you true ?
Look on my shoulders, they are black and blue :

Whilst to and fro fair Luce and I were winding,
He came and basted me with a hedge-binding.

VENTUREWELL. Get men and horses straight : we will
be there
Within this hour. You know the place again ?

HUMPHREY. I know the place where he my loins did
swaddle ;   5
I'll get six horses, and to each a saddle.

VENTUREWELL. Mean time I will go talk with Jasper's
father.   [*Exeunt severally.*

[WIFE. George, what wilt thou lay with me now,
that Master Humphrey has not Mistress Luce yet ?
speak, George, what wilt thou lay with me ?   10

CITIZEN. No, Nell ; I warrant thee, Jasper is at
Puckeridge with her by this.

WIFE. Nay, George, you must consider Mistress
Luce's feet are tender ; and besides 'tis dark ; and,
I promise you truly, I do not see how he should get   15
out of Waltham-forest with her yet.

CITIZEN. Nay, cony, what wilt thou lay with me,
that Ralph has her not yet ?

WIFE. I will not lay against Ralph, honey, because
I have not spoken with him.]   20

SCENE VIII.—*A Room in* MERRYTHOUGHT'S *House.*

Enter MERRYTHOUGHT.

[WIFE. But look, George, peace ! here comes the
merry old gentleman again.]

MERRYTHOUGHT [*sings*].

When it was grown to dark midnight,
And all were fast asleep,
In came Margaret's grimly ghost,   25
And stood at William's feet.

I have money, and meat, and drink beforehand, till to-
morrow at noon ; why should I be sad ? methinks I have
half a dozen jovial spirits within me ! [*Sings.*]

I am three merry men, and three merry men !

5 To what end should any man be sad in this world ? give
me a man that when he goes to hanging cries,

Troul the black bowl to me !

and a woman that will sing a catch in her travail ! I have
seen a man come by my door with a serious face, in a
10 black cloak, without a hat-band, carrying his head as if
he looked for pins in the street ; I have looked out of my
window half a year after, and have spied that man's head
upon London Bridge. 'Tis vile : never trust a tailor that
does not sing at his work ; his mind is of nothing but
15 filching.

[WIFE. Mark this, George ; 'tis worth noting ;
Godfrey my tailor, you know, never sings, and he had
fourteen yards to make this gown : and I'll be sworn,
Mistress Penistone the draper's wife had one made
20 with twelve.]

MERRYTHOUGHT [*sings*].

'Tis mirth that fills the veins with blood,
More than wine, or sleep, or food ;
Let each man keep his heart at ease
No man dies of that disease.
25 He that would his body keep
From diseases, must not weep ;
But whoever laughs and sings,
Never he his body brings
Into fevers, gouts, or rheums,
30 Or lingeringly his lungs consumes,

> Or meets with achès in the bone,
> Or catarrhs or griping stone ;
> But contented lives for aye ;
> The more he laughs, the more he may.

[WIFE. Look, George ; how sayst thou by this,   5
George ? is 't not a fine old man ?—Now, God's
blessing o' thy sweet lips !—When wilt thou be so
merry, George ? faith, thou art the frowningest little
thing, when thou art angry, in a country.

CITIZEN. Peace, cony ; thou shalt see him taken   10
down too, I warrant thee.

Enter VENTUREWELL.

Here 's Luce's father come now.]

MERRYTHOUGHT [*sings*].

> As you came from Walsingham,
>   From that holy land,
> There met you not with my true love   15
>   By the way as you came ?

VENTUREWELL. Oh, Master Merrythought, my daughter's
  gone !
This mirth becomes you not ; my daughter 's gone !

MERRYTHOUGHT [*sings*].

> Why, an if she be, what care I ?
> Or let her come, or go, or tarry.   20

VENTUREWELL. Mock not my misery ; it is your son
(Whom I have made my own, when all forsook him)
Has stolen my only joy, my child, away.

MERRYTHOUGHT [*sings*].

> He set her on a milk-white steed,
>   And himself upon a grey ;   25
> He never turned his face again,
>   But he bore her quite away.

VENTUREWELL. Unworthy of the kindness I have shown
To thee and thine ! too late I well perceive
Thou art consenting to my daughter's loss.

MERRYTHOUGHT. Your daughter ! what a stir 's here wi'
5 your daughter ? Let her go, think no more on her, but
sing loud. If both my sons were on the gallows, I would
sing,

> [*Sings.*] Down, down, down they fall ;
> Down, and arise they never shall.

10 VENTUREWELL. Oh, might I behold [1] her once again,
And she once more embrace her agèd sire !

MERRYTHOUGHT. Fie, how scurvily this goes ! " And
she once more embrace her agèd sire " ? You'll make a
dog on her, will ye ? she cares much for her agèd sire, I
15 warrant you.

> [*Sings.*] She cares not for her daddy, nor
> She cares not for her mammy,
> For she is, she is, she is, she is
> My lord of Lowgave's lassy.

20 VENTUREWELL. For this thy scorn I will pursue that
son
Of thine to death.

MERRYTHOUGHT. Do ; and when you ha' killed him,

> [*Sings.*] Give him flowers enow, palmer, give him flowers
> enow ;
> Give him red, and white, and blue, green and
> yellow.

25 VENTUREWELL. I'll fetch my daughter——

MERRYTHOUGHT. I'll hear no more o' your daughter ; it
spoils my mirth.

VENTUREWELL. I say, I'll fetch my daughter.

---

[1] Weber suggests " I but behold " for the metre.

MERRYTHOUGHT [*sings*].

> Was never man for lady's sake,
>> Down, down,
> Tormented as I poor Sir Guy,
>> De derry down,
> For Lucy's sake, that lady bright,   5
>> Down, down,
> As ever men beheld with eye,
>> De derry down.

VENTUREWELL. I'll be revenged, by Heaven !

[*Exeunt severally.*

[WIFE. How dost thou like this, George ?   10

CITIZEN. Why, this is well, cony ; but if Ralph were hot once, thou shouldst see more.   [*Music.*

WIFE. The fiddlers go again, husband.

CITIZEN. Ay, Nell ; but this is scurvy music. I gave the whoreson gallows money, and I think he has   15 not got me the waits of Southwark : if I hear 'em not anon, I'll twinge him by the ears.—You musicians, play Baloo !

WIFE. No, good George, let 's ha' Lachrymae !

CITIZEN. Why, this is it, cony.   20

WIFE. It 's all the better, George. Now, sweet lamb, what story is that painted upon the cloth ? the Confutation of St Paul ?

CITIZEN. No, lamb ; that 's Ralph and Lucrece.

WIFE. Ralph and Lucrece ! which Ralph ? our   25 Ralph ?

CITIZEN. No, mouse ; that was a Tartarian.

WIFE. A Tartarian ! Well, I would the fiddlers had done, that we might see our Ralph again !]

ACT THE THIRD

Scene I.—*Waltham Forest.*

Enter JASPER AND LUCE.

JASPER. Come, my dear dear ; though we have lost our
    way,
We have not lost ourselves.   Are you not weary
With this night's wandering, broken from your rest,
And frighted with the terror that attends
5 The darkness of this wild unpeopled place ?
    LUCE. No, my best friend : I cannot either fear,
Or entertain a weary thought, whilst you
(The end of all my full desires) stand by me :
Let them that lose their hopes, and live to languish
10 Amongst the number of forsaken lovers,
Tell the long weary steps, and number time,
Start at a shadow, and shrink up their blood,
Whilst I (possessed with all content and quiet)
Thus take my pretty love, and thus embrace him.
15   JASPER. You have caught me, Luce, so fast, that, whilst
      I live,
I shall become your faithful prisoner,
And wear these chains for ever.   Come, sit down,
And rest your body, too, too delicate
For these disturbances.—[*They sit down.*]   So : will you
    sleep ?
20 Come, do not be more able than you are ;
I know you are not skilful in these watches,
For women are no soldiers : be not nice,
But take it ; sleep, I say.
    LUCE.   I cannot sleep ;
Indeed, I cannot, friend.
    JASPER.   Why, then, we'll sing,
25 And try how that will work upon our senses.

LUCE. I'll sing, or say, or any thing but sleep.

JASPER. Come, little mermaid, rob me of my heart
With that enchanting voice.

LUCE. You mock me, Jasper. [*They sing.*

JASPER. Tell me, dearest, what is love ?

LUCE. 'Tis a lightning from above ; 5
    'Tis an arrow, 'tis a fire,
    'Tis a boy they call Desire ;
       'Tis a smile
       Doth beguile

JASPER. The poor hearts of men that prove. 10

    Tell me more, are women true ?

LUCE. Some love change, and so do you.

JASPER. Are they fair and never kind ?

LUCE. Yes, when men turn with the wind.

JASPER.   Are they froward ? 15

LUCE.   Ever toward
    Those that love, to love anew.

JASPER. Dissemble it no more ; I see the god
Of heavy sleep lay on his heavy mace
Upon your eyelids.

LUCE. I am very heavy. [*Sleeps.* 20

JASPER. Sleep, sleep ; and quiet rest crown thy sweet
   thoughts !
Keep from her fair blood distempers, startings,
Horrors, and fearful shapes ! let all her dreams
Be joys, and chaste delights, embraces, wishes,
And such new pleasures as the ravished soul 25
Gives to the senses !—So ; my charms have took.—
Keep her, you powers divine, whilst I contemplate
Upon the wealth and beauty of her mind !
She is only fair and constant, only kind,
And only to thee, Jasper. Oh, my joys ! 30
Whither will you transport me ? let not fullness

Of my poor buried hopes come up together
And overcharge my spirits ! I am weak.
Some say (however ill) the sea and women
Are governed by the moon ; both ebb and flow,
5 Both full of changes ; yet to them that know,
And truly judge, these but opinions are,
And heresies, to bring on pleasing war
Between our tempers, that without these were
Both void of after-love and present fear ;
10 Which are the best of Cupid. Oh, thou child
Bred from despair, I dare not entertain thee,
Having a love without the faults of women,
And greater in her perfect goods than men !
Which to make good, and please myself the stronger,
15 Though certainly I am certain of her love,
I'll try her, that the world and memory
May sing to after-times her constancy.— *[Draws his sword.*
Luce ! Luce ! awake !

    LUCE.   Why do you fright me, friend,
With those distempered looks ? what makes your sword
Drawn in your hand ? who hath offended you ?
20 I prithee, Jasper, sleep ; thou art wild with watching.

    JASPER. Come, make your way to Heaven, and bid the
       world,
With all the villainies that stick upon it,
Farewell ; you're for another life.

    LUCE.   Oh, Jasper,
How have my tender years committed evil,
25 Especially against the man I love,
Thus to be cropped untimely ?

    JASPER.   Foolish girl,
Canst thou imagine I could love his daughter
That flung me from my fortune into nothing ?
Dischargèd me his service, shut the doors
30 Upon my poverty, and scorned my prayers,
Sending me, like a boat without a mast,

To sink or swim ?   Come ; by this hand you die ;
I must have life and blood, to satisfy
Your father's wrongs.

> [WIFE. Away, George, away ! raise the watch at
> Ludgate, and bring a mittimus from the justice for   5
> this desperate villain !—Now, I charge you, gentle-
> men, see the king's peace kept !—Oh, my heart, what
> a varlet 's this, to offer manslaughter upon the harm-
> less gentlewoman !
>   CITIZEN. I warrant thee, sweetheart, we'll have him   10
> hampered.]

LUCE.   Oh, Jasper, be not cruel !
If thou wilt kill me, smile, and do it quickly,
And let not many deaths appear before me ;
I am a woman, made of fear and love,
A weak, weak woman ; kill not with thy eyes,   15
They shoot me through and through : strike, I am ready ;
And, dying, still I love thee.

Enter VENTUREWELL, HUMPHREY, *and* ATTENDANTS.

VENTUREWELL.   Whereabouts ?
JASPER [*aside*]. No more of this ; now to myself again.
HUMPHREY. There, there he stands, with sword, like
    martial knight,
Drawn in his hand ; therefore beware the fight,   20
You that be wise ; for, were I good Sir Bevis,
I would not stay his coming, by your leavès.
VENTUREWELL. Sirrah, restore my daughter !
JASPER.   Sirrah, no.
VENTUREWELL. Upon him, then !
        [*They attack* JASPER, *and force* LUCE *from him.*

> [WIFE. So ; down with him, down with him, down   25
> with him ! cut him i' the leg, boys, cut him i' the
> leg !]

VENTUREWELL. Come your ways, minion : I'll provide
  a cage
For you, you're grown so tame.—Horse her away.
  HUMPHREY. Truly, I'm glad your forces have the day
                   [*Exeunt all except* JASPER.
  JASPER. They are gone, and I am hurt ; my love is lost,
5 Never to get again. Oh, me unhappy !
Bleed, bleed and die ! I cannot. Oh, my folly,
Thou hast betrayed me ! Hope, where art thou fled ?
Tell me, if thou be'st anywhere remaining,
Shall I but see my love again ? Oh, no !
10 She will not deign to look upon her butcher,
Nor is it fit she should ; yet I must venture.
Oh, Chance, or Fortune, or whate'er thou art,
That men adore for powerful, hear my cry,
And let me loving live, or losing die !   [*Exit.*

15   [WIFE. Is 'a gone, George ?
    CITIZEN. Ay, cony.
    WIFE. Marry, and let him go, sweetheart. By the
faith o' my body, 'a has put me into such a fright,
that I tremble (as they say) as 'twere an aspen-leaf.
20 Look o' my little finger, George, how it shakes. Now,
in truth, every member of my body is the worse for 't.
    CITIZEN. Come, hug in mine arms, sweet mouse ;
he shall not fright thee any more. Alas, mine own
dear heart, how it quivers !]

SCENE II.—*A Room in the Bell Inn, Waltham.*

Enter MISTRESS MERRYTHOUGHT, RALPH, MICHAEL, TIM,
GEORGE, HOST, *and* TAPSTER.

25   [WIFE. Oh, Ralph ! how dost thou, Ralph ? How
hast thou slept to-night ? has the knight used thee well ?
    CITIZEN. Peace, Nell ; let Ralph alone.]

TAPSTER. Master, the reckoning is not paid.

RALPH. Right courteous Knight, who, for the order's
sake
Which thou hast ta'en, hang'st out the holy Bell,
As I this flaming Pestle bear about,
We render thanks to your puissant self,   5
Your beauteous lady, and your gentle squires,
For thus refreshing of our wearied limbs,
Stiffened with hard achievements in wild desert.

TAPSTER. Sir, there is twelve shillings to pay.

RALPH. Thou merry Squire Tapstero, thanks to thee   10
For comforting our souls with double jug :
And, if adventurous fortune prick thee forth,
Thou jovial squire, to follow feats of arms,
Take heed thou tender every lady's cause,
Every true knight, and every damsel fair ;   15
But spill the blood of treacherous Saracens,
And false enchanters that with magic spells
Have done to death full many a noble knight.

HOST. Thou valiant Knight of the Burning Pestle, give
ear to me ; there is twelve shillings to pay, and, as I am a 20
true knight, I will not bate a penny.

[WIFE. George, I prithee, tell me, must Ralph pay
twelve shillings now ?

CITIZEN. No, Nell, no ; nothing but the old knight is
merry with Ralph.   25

WIFE. Oh, is 't nothing else ?   Ralph will be as merry
as he.]

RALPH. Sir Knight, this mirth of yours becomes you
well ;
But, to requite this liberal courtesy,
If any of your squires will follow arms,   30
He shall receive from my heroic hand
A knighthood, by the virtue of this Pestle.

HOST. Fair Knight, I thank you for your noble offer :

[But here 's the reckoning,]¹ therefore, gentle Knight,
Twelve shillings you must pay, or I must cap you.

[WIFE. Look, George! did not I tell thee as much?
the Knight of the Bell is in earnest. Ralph shall not
5 be beholding to him : give him his money, George, and
let him go snick up.

CITIZEN. Cap Ralph! no!—Hold your hand, Sir
Knight of the Bell; there 's your money: [*gives
money*] have you any thing to say to Ralph now?
10 Cap Ralph!

WIFE. I would you should know it, Ralph has
friends that will not suffer him to be capt for ten
times so much, and ten times to the end of that.—
Now take thy course, Ralph.]

15 MISTRESS MERRYTHOUGHT. Come, Michael; thou and I
will go home to thy father; he hath enough left to keep
us a day or two, and we'll set fellows abroad to cry our
purse and casket : shall we, Michael?

MICHAEL. Ay, I pray, mother; in truth my feet are full
20 of chilblains with travelling.

[WIFE. Faith, and those chilblains are a foul trouble.
Mistress Merrythought, when your youth comes home,
let him rub all the soles of his feet, and his heels,
and his ankles, with a mouse-skin; or, if none of
25 your people can catch a mouse, when he goes to bed,
let him roll his feet in the warm embers, and, I
warrant you, he shall be well; and you may make
him put his fingers between his toes, and smell to
them; it 's very sovereign for his head, if he be
30 costive.]

MISTRESS MERRYTHOUGHT. Master Knight of the Burn-

¹ [But here's the reckoning] added by C. B. Wheeler in his
edition of the play (Six Elizabethan Plays, World's Classics,
O.U.P.) to fill an obvious gap.

ing Pestle, my son Michael and I bid you farewell : I thank
your worship heartily for your kindness.

RALPH. Farewell, fair lady, and your tender squire.
If pricking through these deserts, I do hear
Of any traitorous knight, who through his guile 5
Hath light upon your casket and your purse,
I will despoil him of them, and restore them.

MISTRESS MERRYTHOUGHT. I thank your worship.

[*Exit with* MICHAEL.

RALPH. Dwarf, bear my shield; squire, elevate my
lance :—
And now farewell, you Knight of holy Bell. 10

[CITIZEN. Ay, ay, Ralph, all is paid.]

RALPH. But yet, before I go, speak, worthy knight,
If aught you do of sad adventures know,
Where errant knight may through his prowess win
Eternal fame, and free some gentle souls 15
From endless bonds of steel and lingering pain.

HOST. Sirrah, go to Nick the barber, and bid him prepare himself, as I told you before, quickly.

TAPSTER. I am gone, sir. [*Exit.*

HOST. Sir Knight, this wilderness affordeth none 20
But the great venture, where full many a knight
Hath tried his prowess, and come off with shame ;
And where I would not have you lose your life
Against no man, but furious fiend of hell.

RALPH. Speak on, Sir Knight; tell what he is and where: 25
For here I vow, upon my blazing badge,
Never to blaze a day in quietness,
But bread and water will I only eat,
And the green herb and rock shall be my couch,
Till I have quelled that man, or beast, or fiend, 30
That works such damage to all errant knights.

HOST. Not far from hence, near to a craggy cliff,
At the north end of this distressèd town,

There doth stand a lowly house,[1]
Ruggedly builded, and in it a cave
In which an ugly giant now doth won,
Yclepèd Barbaroso : in his hand
5 He shakes a naked lance of purest steel,
With sleeves turned up ; and him before he wears
A motley garment, to preserve his clothes
From blood of those knights which he massacres
And ladies gent : without his door doth hang
10 A copper basin on a prickant spear ;
At which no sooner gentle knights can knock,
But the shrill sound fierce Barbaroso hears,
And rushing forth, brings in the errant knight,
And sets him down in an enchanted chair ;
15 Then with an engine, which he hath prepared,
With forty teeth, he claws his courtly crown ;
Next makes him wink, and underneath his chin
He plants a brazen piece of mighty bord,
And knocks his bullets round about his cheeks ;
20 Whilst with his fingers, and an instrument
With which he snaps his hair off, he doth fill
The wretch's ears with a most hideous noise :
Thus every knight-adventurer he doth trim,
And now no creature dares encounter him.

25   RALPH. In God's name, I will fight with him.   Kind sir,
Go but before me to this dismal cave,
Where this huge giant Barbaroso dwells,
And, by that virtue that brave Rosicleer
That damnèd brood of ugly giants slew,
30 And Palmerin Frannarco overthrew,
I doubt not but to curb this traitor foul,
And to the devil send his guilty soul.

    HOST. Brave-sprighted Knight, thus far I will perform
This your request ; I'll bring you within sight

---

[1] Dyce suggests a misprint here, and quotes the proposed line :
    " A mansion there doth stand a lonely house."

Of this most loathsome place, inhabited
By a more loathsome man ; but dare not stay,
For his main force swoops all he sees away.

RALPH. Saint George, set on before ! march squire and
page ! [*Exeunt.*

[WIFE. George, dost think Ralph will confound the 5
giant ?

CITIZEN. I hold my cap to a farthing he does : why,
Nell, I saw him wrestle with the great Dutchman, and
hurl him.

WIFE. Faith, and that Dutchman was a goodly 10
man, if all things were answerable to his bigness.
And yet they say there was a Scotchman higher than
he, and that they two and a knight met, and saw one
another for nothing. But of all the sights that ever
were in London, since I was married, methinks the 15
little child that was so fair grown was the prettiest ;
that and the hermaphrodite.

CITIZEN. Nay, by your leave, Nell, Ninivie was better.

WIFE. Ninivie ! oh, that was the story of Jone and
the wall, was it not, George ? 20

CITIZEN. Yes, lamb.]

SCENE III.—*Street before* MERRYTHOUGHT'S *House.*

Enter MISTRESS MERRYTHOUGHT.

[WIFE. Look, George, here comes Mistress Merrythought again ! and I would have Ralph come and
fight with the giant ; I tell you true, I long to see 't.

CITIZEN. Good Mistress Merrythought, begone, I 25
pray you, for my sake ; I pray you, forbear a little ;
you shall have audience presently ; I have a little
business.

WIFE. Mistress Merrythought, if it please you to

refrain your passion a little, till Ralph have despatched the giant out of the way, we shall think ourselves much bound to you. [*Exit* MISTRESS MERRYTHOUGHT.] I thank you, good Mistress Merrythought.

5   CITIZEN. Boy, come hither. [*Enter* BOY.] Send away Ralph and this whoreson giant quickly.

BOY. In good faith, sir, we cannot ; you'll utterly spoil our play, and make it to be hissed ; and it cost money ; you will not suffer us to go on with our plot.—

10   I pray, gentlemen, rule him.

CITIZEN. Let him come now and despatch this, and I'll trouble you no more.

BOY. Will you give me your hand of that ?

WIFE. Give him thy hand, George, do ; and I'll kiss

15   him. I warrant thee, the youth means plainly.

BOY. I'll send him to you presently.

WIFE [*kissing him*]. I thank you, little youth. [*Exit* BOY.] Faith, the child hath a sweet breath, George ; but I think it be troubled with the worms ;

20   carduus benedictus and mare's milk were the only thing in the world for 't.

SCENE IV.—*Before a Barber's Shop, Waltham.*

Enter RALPH, HOST, TIM, *and* GEORGE.

WIFE. Oh, Ralph 's here, George !—God send thee good luck, Ralph !]

HOST. Puissant knight, yonder his mansion is.

25 Lo, where the spear and copper basin are !
Behold that string, on which hangs many a tooth,
Drawn from the gentle jaw of wandering knights !
I dare not stay to sound ; he will appear.   [*Exit.*

RALPH. Oh, faint not, heart ! Susan, my lady dear,

30 The cobbler's maid in Milk-street, for whose sake

I take these arms, oh, let the thought of thee
Carry thy knight through all adventurous deeds ;
And, in the honour of thy beauteous self,
May I destroy this monster Barbaroso !—
Knock, squire, upon the basin, till it break   5
With the shrill strokes, or till the giant speak.
                        [TIM *knocks upon the basin.*

Enter BARBER.

[WIFE. Oh, George, the giant, the giant !—Now,
Ralph, for thy life !]

BARBER. What fond unknowing wight is this, that dares
So rudely knock at Barbaroso's cell,   10
Where no man comes but leaves his fleece behind ?
RALPH. I, traitorous caitiff, who am sent by fate
To punish all the sad enormities
Thou hast committed against ladies gent
And errant knights. Traitor to God and men,   15
Prepare thyself ; this is the dismal hour
Appointed for thee to give strict account
Of all thy beastly treacherous villainies.
BARBER. Fool-hardy knight, full soon thou shalt aby
This fond reproach : thy body will I bang ;   20
                        [*Takes down his pole.*
And, lo, upon that string thy teeth shall hang !
Prepare thyself, for dead soon shalt thou be.
RALPH. Saint George for me !   [*They fight.*
BARBER.   Gargantua for me !

[WIFE. To him, Ralph, to him ! hold up the giant ;
set out thy leg before, Ralph !   25
CITIZEN. Falsify a blow, Ralph, falsify a blow ! the
giant lies open on the left side.
WIFE. Bear 't off, bear 't off still ! there, boy !—
Oh, Ralph's almost down, Ralph's almost down !]

RALPH. Susan, inspire me ! now have up again.   30

[WIFE. Up, up, up, up, up! so, Ralph, down with him, down with him, Ralph!

CITIZEN. Fetch him o'er the hip, boy!

[RALPH *knocks down the* BARBER.

WIFE. There, boy! kill, kill, kill, kill, kill, Ralph!

5   CITIZEN. No, Ralph; get all out of him first.]

RALPH. Presumptuous man, see to what desperate end
Thy treachery hath brought thee! The just gods,
Who never prosper those that do despise them,
For all the villainies which thou hast done
10 To knights and ladies, now have paid thee home
By my stiff arm, a knight adventurous.
But say, vile wretch, before I send thy soul
To sad Avernus (whither it must go),
What captives holdst thou in thy sable cave?

15   BARBER. Go in, and free them all; thou hast the day.

RALPH. Go, squire and dwarf, search in this dreadful cave,
And free the wretched prisoners from their bonds.

[*Exeunt* TIM *and* GEORGE.

BARBER. I crave for mercy, as thou art a knight,
And scorn'st to spill the blood of those that beg.

20   RALPH. Thou show'd'st no mercy, nor shalt thou have any;
Prepare thyself, for thou shalt surely die.

Re-enter TIM *leading a* MAN *winking, with a Basin
under his Chin.*

TIM. Behold, brave knight, here is one prisoner,
Whom this vild man hath used as you see.

[WIFE. This is the first wise word I heard the squire
25   speak.]

RALPH. Speak what thou art, and how thou hast been used,

That I may give him condign punishment.

MAN. I am a knight that took my journey post
Northward from London ; and in courteous wise
This giant trained me to his loathsome den,
Under pretence of killing of the itch ;   5
And all my body with a powder strewed,
That smarts and stings ; and cut away my beard,
And my curled locks wherein were ribands tied ;
And with a water washed my tender eyes,
(Whilst up and down about me still he skipt,)   10
Whose virtue is, that, till my eyes be wiped
With a dry cloth, for this my foul disgrace,
I shall not dare to look a dog i' the face.

    [WIFE. Alas, poor knight ! — Relieve him, Ralph ;
    relieve poor knights, whilst you live.]   15

RALPH. My trusty squire, convey him to the town,
Where he may find relief.—Adieu, fair knight.
              [*Exit* MAN *with* TIM, *who presently re-enters.*

    Re-enter GEORGE, *leading a* SECOND MAN, *with a
    patch over his nose.*

GEORGE. Puissant Knight, of the Burning Pestle hight,
See here another wretch, whom this foul beast
Hath scorched and scored in this inhuman wise.   20

RALPH. Speak me thy name, and eke thy place of birth,
And what hath been thy usage in this cave.

SECOND MAN. I am a knight, Sir Pockhole is my name,
And by my birth I am a Londoner,
Free by my copy, but my ancestors   25
Were Frenchmen all ; and riding hard this way
Upon a trotting horse, my bones did ache ;
And I, faint knight, to ease my weary limbs,
Light at this cave ; when straight this furious fiend,
With sharpest instrument of purest steel,   30
Did cut the gristle of my nose away,

And in the place this velvet plaster stands :
Relieve me, gentle knight, out of his hands !

[WIFE. Good Ralph, relieve Sir Pockhole, and send him away ; for in truth his breath stinks.]

5 RALPH. Convey him straight after the other knight.—
Sir Pockhole, fare you well.   Kind sir, good night.
SECOND MAN.
                [*Exit with* GEORGE, *who presently re-enters.*

[CITIZEN. Cony, I can tell thee, the gentlemen like Ralph.
WIFE. Ay, George, I see it well enough.—Gentle-
10 men, I thank you all heartily for gracing my man Ralph ; and I promise you, you shall see him oftener.]

BARBER. Mercy, great knight ! I do recant my ill,
And henceforth never gentle blood will spill.
RALPH. I give thee mercy ; but yet shalt thou swear
15 Upon my Burning Pestle, to perform
Thy promise utterèd.
BARBER.   I swear and kiss.   [*Kisses the pestle.*
RALPH. Depart, then, and amend.—   [*Exit* BARBER.
Come, squire and dwarf ; the sun grows towards his set,
And we have many more adventures yet.   [*Exeunt.*

20 [CITIZEN. Now Ralph is in this humour, I know he would ha' beaten all the boys in the house, if they had been set on him.
WIFE. Aye, George, but it is well as it is : I warrant you, the gentlemen do consider what it is to over-
25 throw a giant.]

SCENE V.—*Street before* MERRYTHOUGHT'S *House.*

Enter MISTRESS MERRYTHOUGHT *and* MICHAEL.

[WIFE. But, look, George; here comes Mistress Merrythought, and her son Michael.—Now you are welcome, Mistress Merrythought; now Ralph has done, you may go on.]

MISTRESS MERRYTHOUGHT. Mick, my boy—   5
MICHAEL. Aye, forsooth, mother.
MISTRESS MERRYTHOUGHT. Be merry, Mick; we are at home now; where, I warrant you, you shall find the house flung out of the windows. [*Music within.*]   Hark! hey, dogs, hey! this is the old world, i' faith, with my husband. 10 If I get in among them, I'll play them such a lesson, that they shall have little list to come scraping hither again— Why, Master Merrythought! husband! Charles Merry-thought!
MERRYTHOUGHT [*appearing above, and singing*].

If you will sing, and dance, and laugh,   15
    And hollow, and laugh again,
And then cry, " there, boy, there ! " why, then,
    One, two, three, and four,
    We shall be merry within this hour.

MISTRESS MERRYTHOUGHT. Why, Charles, do you not 20 know your own natural wife ?   I say, open the door, and turn me out those mangy companions; 'tis more than time that they were fellow and fellow-like with you. You are a gentleman, Charles, and an old man, and father of two children ; and I myself (though I say it) by my 25 mother's side niece to a worshipful gentleman and a con-ductor ; he has been three times in his majesty's service at Chester, and is now the fourth time, God bless him and his charge, upon his journey.

19 G

MERRYTHOUGHT [*sings*].

> Go from my window, love, go ;
> Go from my window, my dear !
> The wind and the rain
> Will drive you back again ;
> 5   You cannot be lodged here.

Hark you, Mistress Merrythought, you that walk upon adventures, and forsake your husband, because he sings with never a penny in his purse ; what, shall I think myself the worse ? Faith, no, I'll be merry. You come not here ; 10 here's none but lads of mettle, lives of a hundred years and upwards ; care never drunk their bloods, nor want made them warble " Heigh-ho, my heart is heavy."

MISTRESS MERRYTHOUGHT. Why, Master Merrythought, what am I, that you should laugh me to scorn thus 15 abruptly ? am I not your fellow-feeler, as we may say, in all our miseries ? your comforter in health and sickness ? have I not brought you children ? are they not like you, Charles ? look upon thine own image, hard-hearted man ! and yet for all this——

MERRYTHOUGHT [*sings*].

> 20   Begone, begone, my juggy, my puggy,
> Begone, my love, my dear !
> The weather is warm,
> 'Twill do thee no harm :
> Thou canst not be lodged here.——

25 Be merry, boys ! some light music, and more wine !

[Exit above.

[WIFE. He's not in earnest, I hope, George, is he ?

CITIZEN. What if he be, sweetheart ?

WIFE. Marry, if he be, George, I'll make bold to tell 30 him he's an ingrant old man to use his bed-fellow so scurvily.

CITIZEN. What! how does he use her, honey?

WIFE. Marry, come up, sir saucebox! I think you'll take his part, will you not? Lord, how hot you are grown! you are a fine man, an' you had a fine dog; it becomes you sweetly! 5

CITIZEN. Nay, prithee, Nell, chide not; for, as I am an honest man and a true Christian grocer, I do not like his doings.

WIFE. I cry you mercy, then, George! you know we are all frail and full of infirmities.—D'ye hear, 10 Master Merrythought? may I crave a word with you?]

MERRYTHOUGHT [*appearing above*]. Strike up lively, lads!

[WIFE. I had not thought, in truth, Master Merry- 15 thought, that a man of your age and discretion, as I may say, being a gentleman, and therefore known by your gentle conditions, could have used so little respect to the weakness of his wife; for your wife is your own flesh, the staff of your age, your yoke-fellow, 20 with whose help you draw through the mire of this transitory world; nay, she 's your own rib: and again——]

MERRYTHOUGHT [*sings.*]

I come not hither for thee to teach,
I have no pulpit for thee to preach, 25
I would thou hadst kissed me under the breech,
    As thou art a lady gay.

[WIFE. Marry, with a vengeance! I am heartily sorry for the poor gentlewoman: but if I were thy wife, i' faith, greybeard, i' faith—— 30

CITIZEN. I prithee, sweet honeysuckle, be content.

WIFE. Give me such words, that am a gentlewoman born! hang him, hoary rascal! Get me some drink,

George; I am almost molten with fretting: now, beshrew his knave's heart for it !] [*Exit* CITIZEN.

MERRYTHOUGHT. Play me a light lavolta. Come, be frolic.
Fill the good fellows wine.

5 MISTRESS MERRYTHOUGHT. Why, Master Merrythought, are you disposed to make me wait here ? You'll open, I hope ; I'll fetch them that shall open else.

MERRYTHOUGHT. Good woman, if you will sing, I'll give you something ; if not— [*Sings.*]

10   You are no love for me, Margaret,
          I am no love for you.—

Come aloft, boys, aloft !   [*Exit above.*

MISTRESS MERRYTHOUGHT. Now a churl's —— in your teeth, sir !—Come, Mick, we'll not trouble him ; 'a shall
15 not ding us i' the teeth with his bread and his broth, that he shall not. Come, boy; I'll provide for thee, I warrant thee. We'll go to Master Venturewell's, the merchant : I'll get his letter to mine host of the Bell in Waltham ; there I'll place thee with the tapster : will not that do well for
20 thee, Mick ? and let me alone for that old cuckoldly knave your father ; I'll use him in his kind, I warrant ye.
                                                      [*Exeunt.*

          Re-enter CITIZEN *with Beer.*

[WIFE. Come, George, where 's the beer ?
CITIZEN. Here, love.
WIFE. This old fellow will not out of my mind yet.—
25 Gentlemen, I'll begin to you all ; and I desire more of your acquaintance with all my heart. [*Drinks.*] Fill the gentlemen some beer, George. [*Enter* BOY.] Look, George, the little boy 's come again : methinks he looks something like the Prince of Orange in his
30 long stocking, if he had a little harness about his neck. George, I will have him dance Fading. Fading is a fine

jig, I'll assure you, gentlemen.—Begin, brother. [BOY *dances*.]   Now 'a capers, sweetheart!—Now a turn o' the toe, and then tumble! cannot you tumble, youth?

BOY. No, indeed, forsooth.

WIFE. Nor eat fire?   5

BOY. Neither.

WIFE. Why, then, I thank you heartily; there's twopence to buy you points withal.]

ACT THE FOURTH

SCENE I.—*A Street.*

Enter JASPER *and* BOY.

JASPER. There, boy, deliver this; [*Gives a letter.*]
    but do it well.
Hast thou provided me four lusty fellows,   10
Able to carry me? and art thou perfect
In all thy business?

BOY.   Sir, you need not fear;
I have my lesson here, and cannot miss it:
The men are ready for you, and what else
Pertains to this employment.

JASPER.   There, my boy; [*Gives money.* 15
Take it, but buy no land.

BOY.   Faith, sir, 'twere rare
To see so young a purchaser. I fly,
And on my wings carry your destiny.

JASPER. Go, and be happy! [*Exit* BOY.] Now, my
    latest hope,
Forsake me not, but fling thy anchor out,   20
And let it hold! Stand fixed, thou rolling stone,
Till I enjoy my dearest! Hear me, all
You powers, that rule in men, celestial!   [*Exit.*

[WIFE. Go thy ways ; thou art as crooked a sprig
as ever grew in London. I warrant him, he'll come
to some naughty end or other ; for his looks say no
less : besides, his father (you know, George) is none
5   of the best ; you heard him take me up like a flirt-gill,
and sing bawdy songs upon me ; but, i' faith, if I live,
George——

CITIZEN. Let me alone, sweetheart : I have a trick
in my head shall lodge him in the Arches for one year,
10 and make him sing peccavi ere I leave him ; and yet
he shall never know who hurt him neither.

WIFE. Do, my good George, do !

CITIZEN. What shall we have Ralph do now, boy ?

BOY. You shall have what you will, sir.

15 CITIZEN. Why, so, sir ; go and fetch me him then,
and let the Sophy of Persia come and christen him a
child.

BOY. Believe me, sir, that will not do so well ; 'tis
stale ; it has been had before at the Red Bull.

20 WIFE. George, let Ralph travel over great hills, and
let him be very weary, and come to the King of
Cracovia's house, covered with [black] velvet ; and
there let the king's daughter stand in her window, all
in beaten gold, combing her golden locks with a comb
25 of ivory ; and let her spy Ralph, and fall in love with
him, and come down to him, and carry him into her
father's house ; and then let Ralph talk with her.

CITIZEN. Well said, Nell ; it shall be so.—Boy, let 's
ha't done quickly.

30 BOY. Sir, if you will imagine all this to be done
already, you shall hear them talk together ; but we
cannot present a house covered with black velvet,
and a lady in beaten gold.

CITIZEN. Sir boy, let 's ha't as you can, then.

35 BOY. Besides, it will show ill-favouredly to have a
grocer's prentice to court a king's daughter.

CITIZEN. Will it so sir? you are well read in histories! I pray you, what was Sir Dagonet? was not he prentice to a grocer in London? Read the play of "The Four Prentices of London", where they toss their pikes so. I pray you, fetch him in, sir, fetch him in.   5

BOY. It shall be done.—It is not our fault, gentle-men.   *Exit.*

WIFE. Now we shall see fine doings, I warrant thee, George.]   10

SCENE II.—*A Hall in the King of Moldavia's Court.*

Enter POMPIONA, RALPH, TIM, *and* GEORGE.

[WIFE. Oh, here they come! how prettily the King of Cracovia's daughter is dressed!

CITIZEN. Ay, Nell, it is the fashion of that country, I warrant thee.]

POMPIONA. Welcome, Sir Knight, unto my father's court,   15
King of Moldavia; unto me Pompiona,
His daughter dear! But, sure, you do not like
Your entertainment, that will stay with us
No longer but a night.
    RALPH.   Damsel right fair,
I am on many sad adventures bound,   20
That call me forth into the wilderness;
Besides, my horse's back is something galled,
Which will enforce me ride a sober pace.
But many thanks, fair lady, be to you
For using errant knight with courtesy!   25
    POMPIONA. But say, brave knight, which is your name and birth?
    RALPH. My name is Ralph; I am an Englishman,

(As true as steel, a hearty Englishman,)
And prentice to a grocer in the Strand
By deed indent, of which I have one part :
But fortune calling me to follow arms,
5 On me this holy order I did take
Of Burning Pestle, which in all men's eyes
I bear, confounding ladies' enemies.

POMPIONA. Oft have I heard of your brave countrymen,
And fertile soil and store of wholesome food ;
10 My father oft will tell me of a drink
In England found, and nipitato called,
Which driveth all the sorrow from your hearts.

RALPH. Lady, 'tis true ; you need not lay your lips
To better nipitato than there is.

15 POMPIONA. And of a wild fowl he will often speak,
Which powdered-beef-and-mustard callèd is :
For there have been great wars 'twixt us and you ;
But truly, Ralph, it was not 'long of me.
Tell me then, Ralph, could you contented be
20 To wear a lady's favour in your shield ?

RALPH. I am a knight of [a] religious order,
And will not wear a favour of a lady
That trusts in Antichrist and false traditions.

[CITIZEN. Well said, Ralph ! convert her, if thou
25 canst.]

RALPH. Besides, I have a lady of my own
In merry England, for whose virtuous sake
I took these arms ; and Susan is her name,
A cobbler's maid in Milk Street ; whom I vow
30 Ne'er to forsake whilst life and Pestle last.

POMPIONA. Happy that cobbling dame, whoe'er she be,
That for her own, dear Ralph, hath gotten thee !
Unhappy I, that ne'er shall see the day
To see thee more, that bear'st my heart away !

35 RALPH. Lady, farewell ; I needs must take my leave.

POMPIONA. Hard-hearted Ralph, that ladies dost deceive !

[CITIZEN. Hark thee, Ralph : there 's money for thee [*gives money*] ; give something in the King of Cracovia's house ; be not beholding to him.]   5

RALPH. Lady, before I go, I must remember
Your father's officers, who, truth to tell,
Have been about me very diligent :
Hold up thy snowy hand, thou princely maid !
There 's twelve-pence for your father's chamberlain ;   10
And [there 's] [1] another shilling for his cook,
For, by my troth, the goose was roasted well ;
And twelve-pence for your father's horse-keeper,
For 'nointing my horse-back, and for his butter
There is another shilling ; to the maid   15
That washed my boot-hose there 's an English groat ;
And two-pence to the boy that wiped my boots ;
And last, fair lady, there is for yourself
Three-pence, to buy you pins at Bumbo Fair.
POMPIONA. Full many thanks ; and I will keep them safe   20
Till all the heads be off, for thy sake, Ralph.
RALPH. Advance, my squire and dwarf ! I cannot stay.
POMPIONA. Thou kill'st my heart in parting thus away.   [*Exeunt.*

[WIFE. I commend Ralph yet, that he will not stoop to a Cracovian ; there 's properer women in   25 London than any are there, I-wis.

---

[1] *there 's*—inserted by modern Editors for the metre (Dyce).

SCENE III.—*A Room in the House of* VENTUREWELL.

Enter VENTUREWELL, HUMPHREY, LUCE, *and* BOY.

WIFE. But here comes Master Humphrey and his
love again now, George.

CITIZEN. Ay, cony ; peace.]

VENTUREWELL. Go, get you up ; I will not be en-
treated ;

5 And, gossip mine, I'll keep you sure hereafter
From gadding out again with boys and unthrifts :
Come, they are women's tears ; I know your fashion.—
Go, sirrah, lock her in, and keep the key
Safe as you love your life.　　　*[Exeunt* LUCE *and* BOY.
　　　　　　　　　　　Now, my son Humphrey,

10 You may both rest assurèd of my love
In this, and reap your own desire.

HUMPHREY. I see this love you speak of, through your
daughter,
Although the hole be little ; and hereafter
Will yield the like in all I may or can,

15 Fitting a Christian and a gentleman.

VENTUREWELL. I do believe you, my good son, and
thank you ;
For 'twere an impudence to think you flattered.

HUMPHREY. It were, indeed ; but shall I tell you why ?
I have been beaten twice about the lie.

20 VENTUREWELL. Well, son, no more of compliment. My
daughter
Is yours again : appoint the time and take her ;
We'll have no stealing for it ; I myself
And some few of our friends will see you married.

HUMPHREY. I would you would, i' faith ! for, be it
known,

25 I ever was afraid to lie alone.

VENTUREWELL. Some three days hence, then.

HUMPHREY.   Three days ! let me see :
'Tis somewhat of the most ; yet I agree,
Because I mean against the appointed day
To visit all my friends in new array.

Enter SERVANT.

SERVANT. Sir, there's a gentlewoman without would 5
speak with your worship.

VENTUREWELL. What is she ?

SERVANT. Sir, I asked her not.

VENTUREWELL. Bid her come in.   [*Exit* SERVANT.

Enter MISTRESS MERRYTHOUGHT *and* MICHAEL.

MISTRESS MERRYTHOUGHT. Peace be to your worship ! 10
I come as a poor suitor to you, sir, in the behalf of this
child.

VENTUREWELL. Are you not wife to Merrythought ?

MISTRESS MERRYTHOUGHT. Yes, truly. Would I had
ne'er seen his eyes ! he has undone me and himself and 15
his children ; and there he lives at home, and sings and
hoits and revels among his drunken companions ! but, I
warrant you, where to get a penny to put bread in his
mouth he knows not : and therefore, if it like your worship,
I would entreat your letter to the honest host of the Bell 20
in Waltham, that I may place my child under the protection of his tapster, in some settled course of life.

VENTUREWELL. I'm glad the heavens have heard my
       prayers.   Thy husband,
When I was ripe in sorrows, laughed at me ;
Thy son, like an unthankful wretch, I having   25
Redeemed him from his fall, and made him mine,
To show his love again, first stole my daughter,
Then wronged this gentleman, and, last of all,
Gave me that grief had almost brought me down
Unto my grave, had not a stronger hand   30

Relieved my sorrows.   Go, and weep as I did,
And be unpitied ; for I here profess
An everlasting hate to all thy name.

    MISTRESS MERRYTHOUGHT. Will you so, sir ? how say
5 you by that ?—Come, Mick ; let him keep his wind to
cool his pottage.   We'll go to thy nurse's, Mick : she
knits silk stockings, boy ; and we'll knit too, boy, and be
beholding to none of them all.   [*Exit with* MICHAEL.

Enter BOY.

    BOY. Sir, I take it you are the master of this house.
10 VENTUREWELL. How then, boy ?
    BOY.   Then to yourself, sir, comes this letter.
                                    [*Gives letter.*
    VENTUREWELL. From whom, my pretty boy ?
    BOY. From him that was your servant ; but no more
Shall that name ever be, for he is dead :
Grief of your purchased anger broke his heart.
15 I saw him die, and from his hand received
This paper, with a charge to bring it hither :
Read it, and satisfy yourself in all.
    VENTUREWELL [*reads*]. Sir, that I have wronged your
love I must confess ; in which I have purchased to myself,
20 besides mine own undoing, the ill opinion of my friends.
Let not your anger, good sir, outlive me, but suffer me to
rest in peace with your forgiveness : let my body (if a
dying man may so much prevail with you) be brought to
your daughter, that she may truly know my hot flames
25 are now buried, and withal receive a testimony of the zeal
I bore her virtue.   Farewell for ever, and be ever happy !
                                      JASPER.

God's hand is great in this : I do forgive him ;
Yet I am glad he 's quiet, where I hope
He will not bite again.—Boy, bring the body,
30 And let him have his will, if that be all.
    BOY. 'Tis here without, sir.

VENTUREWELL. So, sir ; if you please,
You may conduct it in ; I do not fear it.
   HUMPHREY. I'll be your usher, boy ; for, though I
     say it,
He owed me something once, and well did pay it.

                               [Exeunt.

SCENE IV.—*Another Room in the House of* VENTUREWELL.

Enter LUCE.

   LUCE. If there be any punishment inflicted   5
Upon the miserable, more than yet I feel,
Let it together seize me, and at once
Press down my soul ! I cannot bear the pain
Of these delaying tortures.—Thou that art
The end of all, and the sweet rest of all,   10
Come, come, O Death ! bring me to thy peace ;
And blot out all the memory I nourish
Both of my father and my cruel friend !—
Oh, wretched maid, still living to be wretched,
To be a say to Fortune in her changes,   15
And grow to number times and woes together !
How happy had I been, if, being born,
My grave had been my cradle !

Enter SERVANT.

   SERVANT. By your leave,
Young mistress, here 's a boy hath brought a coffin :
What 'a would say, I know not ; but your father   20
Charged me to give you notice. Here they come. *[Exit.*

Enter BOY *and two* MEN *bearing a Coffin.*

   LUCE. For me I hope 'tis come, and 'tis most welcome.
   BOY. Fair mistress, let me not add greater grief
To that great store you have already. Jasper
(That whilst he lived was yours,[1] now dead   25

        [1] Dyce suggests " only yours " for the metre.

And here enclosed) commanded me to bring
His body hither, and to crave a tear
From those fair eyes (though he deserved not pity),
To deck his funeral ; for so he bid me
5 Tell her for whom he died.
     LUCE.   He shall have many.—
Good friends, depart a little, whilst I take
My leave of this dead man, that once I loved.—

                        [*Exeunt* BOY *and* MEN.

Hold yet a little, life ! and then I give thee
To thy first heavenly being.   Oh, my friend !
10 Hast thou deceived me thus, and got before me ?
I shall not long be after.   But, believe me,
Thou wert too cruel, Jasper, 'gainst thyself,
In punishing the fault I could have pardoned,
With so untimely death : thou didst not wrong me,
15 But ever wert most kind, most true, most loving ;
And I the most unkind, most false, most cruel !
Didst thou but ask a tear ? I'll give thee all,
Even all my eyes can pour down, all my sighs,
And all myself, before thou goest from me.
20 These are but sparing rites ; but if thy soul
Be yet about this place, and can behold
And see what I prepare to deck thee with,
It shall go up, borne on the wings of peace,
And satisfied.   First will I sing thy dirge,
25 Then kiss thy pale lips, and then die myself,
And fill one coffin and one grave together.

[*Sings.*]   Come, you whose loves are dead,
            And, whiles I sing,
            Weep, and wring
30   Every hand, and every head
            Bind with cypress and sad yew,
            Ribands black and candles blue
            For him that was of men most true !

    Come with heavy moaning,
      And on his grave
      Let him have
    Sacrifice of sighs and groaning ;
    Let him have fair flowers enow,   5
    White and purple, green and yellow,
    For him that was of men most true !

Thou sable cloth, sad cover of my joys,
I lift thee up, and thus I meet with death.
   [Removes the Cloth, and JASPER *rises out of the Coffin.*
  JASPER. And thus you meet the living.
   LUCE.   Save me, Heaven ! 10
  JASPER. Nay, do not fly me, fair ; I am no spirit :
Look better on me ; do you know me yet ?
  LUCE. Oh, thou dear shadow of my friend !
  JASPER.   Dear substance !
I swear I am no shadow ; feel my hand,
It is the same it was ; I am your Jasper,   15
Your Jasper that 's yet living, and yet loving.
Pardon my rash attempt, my foolish proof
I put in practice of your constancy ;
For sooner should my sword have drunk my blood,
And set my soul at liberty, than drawn   20
The least drop from that body : for which boldness
Doom me to any thing ; if death, I take it,
And willingly.
  LUCE.   This death I'll give you for it ;
              [Kisses him.
So ; now I am satisfied you are no spirit,
But my own truest, truest, truest friend,   25
Why do you come thus to me ?
  JASPER.   First, to see you ;
Then to convey you hence.
  LUCE.   It cannot be ;
For I am locked up here, and watched at all hours,

That 'tis impossible for me to 'scape.

JASPER. Nothing more possible.   Within this coffin
Do you convey yourself : let me alone
I have the wits of twenty men about me ;
5 Only I crave the shelter of your closet
A little, and then fear me not.   Creep in,
That they may presently convey you hence.
Fear nothing, dearest love ; I'll be your second ;

> [LUCE *lies down in the Coffin and* JASPER
> *covers her with the cloth.*

Lie close : so ; all goes well yet.—Boy !

Re-enter BOY *and* MEN.

BOY.   At hand, sir.
10 JASPER. Convey away the coffin, and be wary.
BOY. 'Tis done already.   [*Exeunt* MEN *with the Coffin.*
JASPER.   Now must I go conjure.

> [*Exit into a Closet.*

Enter VENTUREWELL.

VENTUREWELL. Boy, boy !
BOY.   Your servant, sir.
VENTUREWELL. Do me this kindness, boy (hold, here's
   a crown) ;
Before thou bury the body of this fellow,
15 Carry it to his old merry father, and salute him
From me, and bid him sing ; he hath cause.
BOY.   I will, sir.
VENTUREWELL. And then bring me word what tune he
   is in,
And have another crown ; but do it truly.
I have fitted him a bargain now will vex him.
20   BOY. God bless your worship's health, sir !
VENTUREWELL. Farewell, boy.   [*Exeunt severally.*

SCENE V.—*Street before* MERRYTHOUGHT'S *House.*

Enter MERRYTHOUGHT.

[WIFE. Ah, old Merrythought, art thou there again?
let 's hear some of thy songs.]

MERRYTHOUGHT [*sings*].

> Who can sing a merrier note
> Than he that cannot change a groat?

Not a denier left, and yet my heart leaps: I do wonder 5
yet, as old as I am, that any man will follow a trade, or
serve, that may sing and laugh, and walk the streets. My
wife and both my sons are I know not where; I have
nothing left, nor know I how to come by meat to supper;
yet am I merry still, for I know I shall find it upon the 10
table at six o'clock; therefore, hang thought!

[*Sings.*] I would not be a serving-man
> To carry the cloak-bag still,
> Nor would I be a falconer
> The greedy hawks to fill;   15
> But I would be in a good house,
> And have a good master too;
> But I would eat and drink of the best,
> And no work would I do.

This is it that keeps life and soul together, mirth; this 20
is the philosopher's stone that they write so much on,
that keeps a man ever young.

Enter BOY.

BOY. Sir, they say they know all your money is gone,
and they will trust you for no more drink.

MERRYTHOUGHT. Will they not? let 'em choose! The 25
best is, I have mirth at home, and need not send abroad
for that; let them keep their drink to themselves. [*Sings.*]

19 H

For Jillian of Berry, she dwells on a hill,
And she hath good beer and ale to sell,
And of good fellows she thinks no ill ;
    And thither will we go now, now, now, now,
5   And thither will we go now.

And when you have made a little stay,
You need not ask what is to pay,
But kiss your hostess, and go your way ;
    And thither will we go now, now, now, now,
10   And thither will we go now.

Enter another BOY.

SECOND BOY. Sir, I can get no bread for supper.

MERRYTHOUGHT. Hang bread and supper ! let 's preserve our mirth, and we shall never feel hunger, I'll
warrant you. Let 's have a catch, boys ; follow me,
15 come.

[*They sing.*]   Ho, ho, nobody at home !
    Meat, nor drink, nor money ha' we none.
      Fill the pot, Eedy,
      Never more need I.

20 MERRYTHOUGHT. So, boys ; enough. Follow me : let 's
change our place, and we shall laugh afresh.   [*Exeunt.*

[WIFE. Let him go, George ; 'a shall not have any
countenance from us, nor a good word from any i'
the company, if I may strike stroke in 't.

25 CITIZEN. No more 'a sha' not, love. But, Nell, I
will have Ralph do a very notable matter now, to the
eternal honour and glory of all grocers.—Sirrah ! you
there, boy ! Can none of you hear ?

Enter BOY.

30 BOY. Sir, your pleasure ?

CITIZEN. Let Ralph come out on May-day in the
morning, and speak upon a conduit, with all his scarfs

about him, and his feathers, and his rings, and his knacks.

BOY. Why, sir, you do not think of our plot ; what will become of that, then ?

CITIZEN. Why, sir, I care not what become on 't :   5
I'll have him come out, or I'll fetch him out myself ;
I'll have something done in honour of the city ; besides,
he hath been long enough upon adventures.   Bring
him out quickly ; or, if I come in amongst you——

BOY. Well, sir, he shall come out ; but if our play   10
miscarry, sir, you are like to pay for 't.

CITIZEN. Bring him away, then !   [*Exit* BOY.

WIFE. This will be brave, i' faith !   George, shall
not he dance the morris too, for the credit of the
Strand ?   15

CITIZEN. No, sweetheart, it will be too much for the
boy.

Enter RALPH, *dressed as a May-lord.*

Oh, there he is, Nell ! he 's reasonable well in reparel :
but he has not rings enough.]

RALPH. London, to thee I do present the merry month
of May ;   20
Let each true subject be content to hear me what I say :
For from the top of conduit-head, as plainly may appear,
I will both tell my name to you, and wherefore I came
here.
My name is Ralph, by due descent, though not ignoble I,
Yet far inferior to the stock of gracious grocery ;   25
And by the common counsel of my fellows in the Strand,
With gilded staff and crossèd scarf, the May-lord here I
stand,
Rejoice, O English hearts, rejoice ! rejoice, O lovers
dear !
Rejoice, O city, town, and country ! rejoice, eke every
shire !

For now the fragrant flowers do spring and sprout in
    seemly sort,
The little birds do sit and sing, the lambs do make fine
    sport;
And now the birchen tree doth bud, that makes the
    schoolboy cry;
The morris rings, while hobby-horse doth foot it
    feateously;
5 The lords and ladies now abroad, for their disport and play,
Do kiss sometimes upon the grass, and sometimes in the
    hay;
Now butter with a leaf of sage is good to purge the
    blood;
Fly Venus and phlebotomy, for they are neither good;
Now little fish on tender stone begin to cast their bellies,
10 And sluggish snails, that erst were mewed, do creep out
    of their shellies;
The rumbling rivers now do warm, for little boys to
    paddle;
The sturdy steed now goes to grass, and up they hang his
    saddle;
The heavy hart, the bellowing buck, the rascal, and the
    pricket,
Are now among the yeoman's peas, and leave the fearful
    thicket:
15 And be like them, O you, I say, of this same noble town,
And lift aloft your velvet heads, and slipping off your
    gown,
With bells on legs, and napkins clean unto your shoulders
    tied,
With scarfs and garters as you please, and " Hey for our
    town!" cried,
March out, and show your willing minds, by twenty and
    by twenty,
20 To Hogsdon or to Newington, where ale and cakes are
    —— plenty;

And let it ne'er be said for shame, that we the youths of
    London
Lay thrumming of our caps at home, and left our custom
    undone.
Up, then, I say, both young and old, both man and maid
    a-maying,
With drums, and guns that bounce aloud, and merry
    tabor playing!
Which to prolong, God save our king, and send his country
    peace,   5
And root out treason from the land! and so, my friends,
    I cease.   *[Exit.*

ACT THE FIFTH

SCENE I.—*A Room in the House of* VENTUREWELL.

Enter VENTUREWELL.

VENTUREWELL. I will have no great store of company
at the wedding; a couple of neighbours and their wives;
and we will have a capon in stewed broth, with marrow,
and a good piece of beef stuck with rosemary.   10

Enter JASPER, *with his Face mealed.*

JASPER. Forbear thy pains, fond man! it is too late.
VENTUREWELL. Heaven bless me! Jasper!
JASPER.   Ay, I am his ghost,
Whom thou hast injured for his constant love;
Fond worldly wretch! who dost not understand
In death that true hearts cannot parted be.   15
First know, thy daughter is quite borne away
On wings of angels, through the liquid air,
To far out of thy reach, and never more
Shalt thou behold her face: but she and I
Will in another world enjoy our loves;   20

Where neither father's anger, poverty,
Nor any cross that troubles earthly men,
Shall make us sever our united hearts.
And never shalt thou sit or be alone
5 In any place, but I will visit thee
With ghastly looks, and put into thy mind
The great offences which thou didst to me.
When thou art at thy table with thy friends,
Merry in heart, and filled with swelling wine,
10 I'll come in midst of all thy pride and mirth,
Invisible to all men but thyself,
And whisper such a sad tale in thine ear
Shall make thee let the cup fall from thy hand,
And stand as mute and pale as death itself.

15 VENTUREWELL. Forgive me, Jasper! Oh, what might I do,
  Tell me, to satisfy thy troubled ghost?

  JASPER. There is no means; too late thou think'st of this.

  VENTUREWELL. But tell me what were best for me to do?

  JASPER. Repent thy deed, and satisfy my father,
20 And beat fond Humphrey out of thy doors.   [*Exit.*

  [WIFE. Look, George; his very ghost would have folks beaten.]

Enter HUMPHREY.

  HUMPHREY. Father, my bride is gone, fair Mistress Luce:
  My soul's the fount of vengeance, mischief's sluice.

25 VENTUREWELL. Hence, fool, out of my sight with thy fond passion!
  Thou hast undone me.   [*Beats him.*

  HUMPHREY.   Hold, my father dear,
  For Luce thy daughter's sake, that had no peer!

  VENTUREWELL. Thy father, fool? there's some blows more; begone.—   [*Beats him.*
  Jasper, I hope thy ghost be well appeased

To see thy will performed.   Now will I go
To satisfy thy father for thy wrongs.   [*Aside and exit.*
  HUMPHREY. What shall I do ? I have been beaten
    twice,
And Mistress Luce is gone.   Help me, device !
Since my true-love is gone, I never more,   5
Whilst I do live, upon the sky will pore ;
But in the dark will wear out my shoe-soles
In passion in Saint Faith's church under Paul's.   [*Exit.*

    [WIFE. George, call Ralph hither ; if you love me,
call Ralph hither : I have the bravest thing for him   10
to do, George ; prithee, call him quickly.
    CITIZEN. Ralph ! why, Ralph, boy !

Enter RALPH.

    RALPH. Here, sir.
    CITIZEN. Come hither, Ralph ; come to thy mistress,
boy.   15
    WIFE. Ralph, I would have thee call all the youths
together in battle-ray, with drums, and guns, and
flags, and march to Mile End in pompous fashion, and
there exhort your soldiers to be merry and wise, and
to keep their beards from burning, Ralph ; and then   20
skirmish, and let your flags fly, and cry, " Kill, kill,
kill ! "   My husband shall lend you his jerkin, Ralph,
and there 's a scarf ; for the rest, the house shall
furnish you, and we'll pay for 't.   Do it bravely, Ralph ;
and think before whom you perform, and what person   25
you represent.
    RALPH. I warrant you, mistress ; if I do it not, for
the honour of the city and the credit of my master,
let me never hope for freedom !
    WIFE. 'Tis well spoken, i' faith.   Go thy ways ;   30
thou art a spark indeed.
    CITIZEN. Ralph, Ralph, double your files bravely,
Ralph !

RALPH. I warrant you, sir.   [*Exit.*

CITIZEN. Let him look narrowly to his service ; I
shall take him else. I was there myself a pikeman
once, in the hottest of the day, wench ; had my
feather shot sheer away, the fringe of my pike burnt
off with powder, my pate broken with a scouring-
stick, and yet, I thank God, I am here.
                              [*Drums within.*

WIFE. Hark, George, the drums !

CITIZEN. Ran, tan, tan, tan ; ran, tan ! Oh,
wench, an thou hadst but seen little Ned of Aldgate,
Drum-Ned, how he made it roar again, and laid on
like a tyrant, and then struck softly till the ward
came up, and then thundered again, and together we
go! "Sa, sa, sa, bounce!" quoth the guns; "Courage
my hearts!" quoth the captains; "Saint George!"
quoth the pikemen ; and withal, here they lay,
and there they lay : and yet for all this I am here,
wench.

WIFE. Be thankful for it, George ; for indeed 'tis
wonderful.]

SCENE II.—*A Street* (*and afterwards Mile End*).

Enter RALPH *and Company of Soldiers* (*among whom are*
WILLIAM HAMMERTON *and* GEORGE GREENGOOSE), *with
drums and colours.*

RALPH. March fair, my hearts ! Lieutenant, beat the
rear up.—Ancient, let your colours fly ; but have a great
care of the butchers' hooks at Whitechapel ; they have
been the death of many a fair ancient.—Open your files,
that I may take a view both of your persons and munition.
—Sergeant, call a muster.

SERGEANT. A stand !—William Hammerton, pewterer !

HAMMERTON. Here, captain !

RALPH. A corselet and a Spanish pike; 'tis well: can you shake it with a terror?

HAMMERTON. I hope so, captain.

RALPH. Charge upon me. [*He charges on* RALPH.] 'Tis with the weakest: put more strength, William Hammerton, more strength. As you were again!—Proceed, Sergeant.

SERGEANT. George Greengoose, poulterer!

GREENGOOSE. Here!

RALPH. Let me see your piece, neighbour Greengoose: when was she shot in?

GREENGOOSE. An't like you, master captain, I made a shot even now, partly to scour her, and partly for audacity.

RALPH. It should seem so certainly, for her breath is yet inflamed; besides, there is a main fault in the touchhole, it runs and stinketh; and I tell you moreover, and believe it, ten such touchholes would breed the pox in the army. Get you a feather, neighbour, get you a feather, sweet oil, and paper, and your piece may do well enough yet. Where's your powder?

GREENGOOSE. Here.

RALPH. What, in a paper! as I am a soldier and a gentleman, it craves a martial court! you ought to die for 't. Where's your horn? answer me to that.

GREENGOOSE. An't like you, sir, I was oblivious.

RALPH. It likes me not you should be so; 'tis a shame for you, and a scandal to all our neighbours, being a man of worth and estimation, to leave your horn behind you: I am afraid 'twill breed example. But let me tell you no more on 't.—Stand, till I view you all.—What's become o' the nose of your flask?

FIRST SOLDIER. Indeed, la, captain, 'twas blown away with powder.

RALPH. Put on a new one at the city's charge.—Where's the stone of this piece?

SECOND SOLDIER. The drummer took it out to light tobacco.

RALPH. 'Tis a fault, my friend ; put it in again.—You want a nose,—and you a stone.—Sergeant, take a note on
5 't, for I mean to stop it in the pay.—Remove, and march !
[*They march.*] Soft and fair, gentlemen, soft and fair !
double your files ! as you were ! faces about ! Now, you
with the sodden face, keep in there ! Look to your match,
sirrah, it will be in your fellow's flask anon. So ; make
10 a crescent now ; advance your pikes ; stand and give
ear !—Gentlemen, countrymen, friends, and my fellow-
soldiers, I have brought you this day, from the shops of
security and the counters of content, to measure out in these
furious fields honour by the ell, and prowess by the pound.
15 Let it not, oh, let it not, I say, be told hereafter, the noble
issue of this city fainted ; but bear yourselves in this fair
action like men, valiant men, and free men ! Fear not the
face of the enemy, nor the noise of the guns, for, believe
me, brethren, the rude rumbling of a brewer's car [1] is far
20 more terrible, of which you have a daily experience ;
neither let the stink of powder offend you, since a more
valiant stink is nightly with you.

To a resolvèd mind his home is everywhere :
I speak not this to take away
25 The hope of your return ; for you shall see
(I do not doubt it) and that very shortly
Your loving wives again and your sweet children,
Whose care doth bear you company in baskets.
Remember, then, whose cause you have in hand,
30 And, like a sort of true-born scavengers,
Scour me this famous realm of enemies.
I have no more to say but this :
Stand to your tacklings, lads, and show to the world
You can as well brandish a sword as shake an apron.
35 Saint George, and on, my hearts !

[1] *cart*—Weber.

ALL.   Saint George, Saint George ! [*Exeunt.*

[WIFE. 'Twas well done, Ralph ! I'll send thee a
cold capon a-field and a bottle of March beer ; and, it
may be, come myself to see thee.

CITIZEN. Nell, the boy hath deceived me much ; I   5
did not think it had been in him. He has performed
such a matter, wench, that, if I live, next year I'll have
him captain of the galley-foist, or I'll want my will.]

SCENE III.—*A Room in* MERRYTHOUGHT'S *House.*

Enter MERRYTHOUGHT.

MERRYTHOUGHT. Yet, I thank God, I break not a wrinkle
more than I had. Not a stoop, boys ? Care, live with 10
cats : I defy thee ! My heart is as sound as an oak ; and
though I want drink to wet my whistle, I can sing ; [*Sings.*]

Come no more there, boys, come no more there ;
For we shall never whilst we live come any more there.

Enter BOY, *and two* MEN *bearing a Coffin.*

BOY. God save you, sir !   15
MERRYTHOUGHT. It 's a brave boy. Canst thou sing ?
BOY. Yes, sir, I can sing ; but 'tis not so necessary at
this time.
MERRYTHOUGHT [*sings*].

          Sing we, and chant it ;
          Whilst love doth grant it.   20

BOY. Sir, sir, if you knew what I have brought you,
you would have little list to sing.
MERRYTHOUGHT [*sings*].

          Oh, the Mimon round,
          Full long I have thee sought,
          And now I have thee found,   25
          And what hast thou here brought ?

BOY. A coffin, sir, and your dead son Jasper in it.

[*Exit with* MEN.

MERRYTHOUGHT. Dead! [*Sings.*]

> Why, farewell he!
> Thou wast a bonny boy,
5 > And I did love thee.

Enter JASPER.

JASPER. Then, I pray you, sir, do so still.

MERRYTHOUGHT. Jasper's ghost! [*Sings.*]

> Thou art welcome from Stygian lake so soon;
> Declare to me what wondrous things in Pluto's court
> are done.

10 JASPER. By my troth, sir, I ne'er came there; 'tis too hot for me, sir.

MERRYTHOUGHT. A merry ghost, a very merry ghost! [*Sings.*]

> And where is your true love? Oh, where is yours?

JASPER. Marry, look you, sir!

[*Removes the cloth, and* LUCE *rises up out of the Coffin.*

15 MERRYTHOUGHT. Ah, ha! art thou good at that, i' faith?

[*Sings.*] With hey, trixy, terlery-whiskin,
> The world it runs on wheels.

MISTRESS MERRYTHOUGHT *and* MICHAEL *within.*

MISTRESS MERRYTHOUGHT [*within*]. What, Master Merry-
20 thought! will you not let 's in? what do you think shall become of us?

MERRYTHOUGHT [*sings*].

> What voice is that that calleth at our door?

MISTRESS MERRYTHOUGHT [*within*]. You know me well enough; I am sure I have not been such a stranger to you.

MERRYTHOUGHT [*sings*].

> And some they whistled, and some they sung,
>> Hey, down, down !
> And some did loudly say,
> Ever as the Lord Barnet's horn blew,
>> " Away, Musgrave, away ! "   5

MISTRESS MERRYTHOUGHT [*within*]. You will not have us starve here, will you, Master Merrythought ?

JASPER. Nay, good sir, be persuaded ; she is my mother :
If her offences have been great against you,
Let your own love remember she is yours,   10
And so forgive her.

LUCE.   Good Master Merrythought,
Let me entreat you ; I will not be denied.

MISTRESS MERRYTHOUGHT [*within*]. Why, Master Merry-thought, will you be a vexed thing still ?

MERRYTHOUGHT. Woman, I take you to my love again ;   15
but you shall sing before you enter ; therefore dispatch
your song and so come in.

MISTRESS MERRYTHOUGHT [*within*]. Well, you must have
your will, when all 's done.—Mick, what song canst thou
sing, boy ?   20

MICHAEL [*within*]. I can sing none, forsooth, but " A
Lady's Daughter, of Paris properly,"

[*Sings within*]. It was a lady's daughter, &c.

> MERRYTHOUGHT *opens the Door* ; *enter* MISTRESS
> MERRYTHOUGHT *and* MICHAEL.

MERRYTHOUGHT. Come, you're welcome home again.

[*Sings.*] If such danger be in playing,   25
> And jest must to earnest turn,
> You shall go no more a-maying——

VENTUREWELL [*within*]. Are you within, sir ? Master
Merrythought !

JASPER. It is my master's voice : good sir, go hold him
In talk, whilst we convey ourselves into
Some inward room.   [*Exit with* LUCE.

MERRYTHOUGHT. What are you ? are you merry ?
5 You must be very merry, if you enter.

VENTUREWELL [*within*]. I am, sir.

MERRYTHOUGHT. Sing, then.

VENTUREWELL [*within*]. Nay, good sir, open to me.

MERRYTHOUGHT.   Sing, I say,
Or, by the merry heart, you come not in !

10 VENTUREWELL [*within*]. Well, sir, I'll sing.

[*Sings.*] Fortune, my foe, &c.

MERRYTHOUGHT *opens the Door* : *Enter* VENTUREWELL.

MERRYTHOUGHT. You are welcome, sir, you are welcome :
you see your entertainment ; pray you, be merry.

VENTUREWELL. Oh, Master Merrythought, I am come
to ask you
15 Forgiveness for the wrongs I offered you,
And your most virtuous son ! they 're infinite ;
Yet my contrition shall be more than they :
I do confess my hardness broke his heart,
For which just Heaven hath given me punishment
20 More than my age can carry ; his wandering spirit,
Not yet at rest, pursues me everywhere,
Crying, " I'll haunt thee for thy cruelty."
My daughter, she is gone, I know not how,
Taken invisible, and whether living
25 Or in [the] grave, 'tis yet uncertain to me.
Oh, Master Merrythought, these are the weights
Will sink me to my grave ! forgive me, sir.

MERRYTHOUGHT. Why, sir, I do forgive you ; and be
merry :
And if the wag in 's lifetime played the knave,
30 Can you forgive him too ?

VENTUREWELL.   With all my heart, sir.

MERRYTHOUGHT. Speak it again, and heartily.

VENTUREWELL.   I do, sir ;
Now, by my soul, I do.

Re-enter LUCE *and* JASPER.

MERRYTHOUGHT [*sings*].

> With that came out his paramour ;
> She was as white as the lily-flower :
>   Hey, troul, troly, loly !
> With that came out her own dear knight ;   5
> He was as true as ever did fight, &c.

Sir, if you will forgive 'em, clap their hands together ;
there 's no more to be said i' the matter.

VENTUREWELL. I do, I do.   10

[CITIZEN. I do not like this. Peace, boys ! Hear
me, one of you : everybody's part is come to an end
but Ralph's, and he 's left out.

BOY. 'Tis 'long of yourself, sir ; we have nothing to
do with his part.   15

CITIZEN. Ralph, come away !—Make [an end] on
him, as you have done of the rest, boys ; come.

WIFE. Now, good husband, let him come out and die.

CITIZEN. He shall, Nell.—Ralph, come away quickly,
and die, boy !   20

BOY. 'Twill be very unfit he should die, sir, upon no
occasion—and in a comedy, too.

CITIZEN. Take you no care of that, sir boy ; is not
his part at an end, think you, when he 's dead ?—
Come away, Ralph !]   25

Enter RALPH, *with a forked Arrow through his Head.*

RALPH. When I was mortal, this my costive corps
Did lap up figs and raisins in the Strand ;
Where sitting, I espied a lovely dame,
Whose master wrought with lingel and with awl,

And underground he vampèd many a boot.
Straight did her love prick forth me, tender sprig,
To follow feats of arms in warlike wise
Through Waltham Desert ; where I did perform
5 Many achievements, and did lay on ground
Huge Barbaroso, that insulting giant,
And all his captives set at liberty.
Then honour pricked me from my native soil
Into Moldavia, where I gained the love
10 Of Pompiona,[1] his beloved daughter ;
But yet proved constant to the black-thumbed maid
Susan, and scornèd Pompiona's love ;
Yet liberal I was, and gave her pins,
And money for her father's officers.
15 I then returnèd home, and thrust myself
In action, and by all men chosen was
Lord of the May, where I did flourish it,
With scarfs and rings, and posy in my hand.
After this action I preferrèd was,
20 And chosen city-captain at Mile End,
With hat and feather, and with leading-staff,
And trained my men, and brought them all off clear,
Save one man that berayed him with the noise.
But all these things I Ralph did undertake
25 Only for my belovèd Susan's sake.
Then coming home, and sitting in my shop
With apron blue, Death came into my stall
To cheapen aquavitae ; but ere I
Could take the bottle down and fill a taste,
30 Death caught a pound of pepper in his hand,
And sprinkled all my face and body o'er,
And in an instant vanishèd away.

[CITIZEN. 'Tis a pretty fiction, i' faith.]

[1] Old Editions have Pompiana here but Pompiona in Act IV,
Sc. ii.

RALPH. Then took I up my bow and shaft in hand,
And walked into Moorfields to cool myself :
But there grim cruel Death met me again,
And shot this forkèd arrow through my head ;
And now I faint ; therefore be warned by me,   5
My fellows every one, of forkèd heads !
Farewell, all you good boys in merry London !
Ne'er shall we more upon Shrove Tuesday meet,
And pluck down houses of iniquity ;—
I die ! fly, fly, my soul, to Grocers' Hall !   10
Oh, oh, oh, &c.   [*Dies.*

[WIFE. Well said, Ralph ! do your obeisance to the
gentlemen, and go your ways : well said, Ralph !]
                  [RALPH *rises, makes obeisance, and exit.*

MERRYTHOUGHT.   Methinks all we, thus kindly and un-
expectedly reconciled, should not depart without a song. 15
VENTUREWELL. A good motion.
MERRYTHOUGHT. Strike up, then !

SONG

Better music ne'er was known
Than a quire of hearts in one.
Let each other, that hath been   20
Troubled with the gall or spleen,
Learn of us to keep his brow
Smooth and plain, as ours are now !
Sing ! though before the hour of dying,
He shall rise, and then be crying,   25
" Hey, ho, 'tis nought but mirth
That keeps the body from the earth ! "   [*Exeunt.*

CITIZEN. Come, Nell, shall we go ? the play 's done.
WIFE. Nay, by my faith, George, I have more manners
than so ; I'll speak to these gentlemen first. — I thank you 30
    19 I

all, gentlemen, for your patience and countenance to
Ralph, a poor fatherless child ; and if I might see you at
my house, it should go hard but I would have a pottle of
wine and a pipe of tobacco for you : for, truly, I hope you
5 do like the youth, but I would be glad to know the truth ;
I refer it to your own discretions, whether you will applaud
him or no ; for I will wink, and whilst you shall do what
you will.   I thank you with all my heart.   God give you
good night ! — Come, George.   [*Exeunt.*

IV
THE RESTORATION DRAMA

THE RESTORATION DRAMA

It is an interesting fact that, practically speaking, the great period of English drama falls within the first quarter of the seventeenth century. It is true that Shakespeare's predecessors towards the end of the sixteenth century represent the dawn which preceded this splendid day, and that there is an afterglow apparent in the work of dramatists such as Massinger and Ford, but even with them the first spots of the approaching decay are evident, and it is a fact that it is easier to state than to account for. Whether it was impossible to sustain the heights reached in this period, whether subsequent to this era only lesser men were available, whether the attempts at progress ended only in chaos and formlessness of versification and plot, or whether it is the change in times and difference of temper and philosophic outlook to which we must ascribe the falling off in the quality of the drama, does not alter the fact that the deterioration is palpable.

It is useless here to give a mere list of names of dramatists of the Carolingian period, while space precludes a detailed examination of them, and it is a fact that, with the one exception of Massinger in comedy — Sir Giles Overreach in *A New Way to Pay Old Debts* is a masterpiece — and Ford in tragedy, and perhaps Shirley, there are no outstanding figures in the drama and no plays on which posterity has set the seal of universal approval, until we come to the Restoration period. For nearly twenty years the theatres had been closed, but it would take much more than an outburst of Puritan denunciation to kill so integral a part of national life as the drama, and there is little doubt that all this while some sort of dramatic activity was in existence, partly in the presentation of " drolls " and farces, and occasionally in a performance of one of the " taboo " plays. In 1660 the drama rears its head openly again, in a different theatre and under different conditions. The " pageant " of the Miracle plays had given way to performances in galleried inn yards from which the theatre took shape, and when Shakespeare was in London the theatre was usually a wooden structure of round—" this wooden O" (*Henry V*, Prologue)—or octagonal shape open to the sky except for a covered gallery which encircled the theatre ; here were the more expensive seats. The groundlings stood, while the gallants had stools on the stage like the citizen and his wife in *The Knight of the Burning Pestle.* The stage, called an " apron " stage, jutted out into the standing throng ; at the back was a curtained recess used for any scene where an inner room was required, and above this and again roofed over was an upper balcony from which Jessica would escape to her Lorenzo or Juliet sigh out her soul to Romeo ; where Desdemona's father would appear or where heralds would blare forth a challenge from the battlements. There was little scenery or scenic effect — it is always interesting to notice how Elizabethan dramatists achieve their effects — and, as we know, female parts were played by boys.

Now with the return of Charles II in 1660, there were several striking changes. Actresses were imported from France and gradually established their place on the boards ; ballet was introduced and scenery was elaborated. The theatre was now much more the haunt and hobby of courtiers and aristocrats : the citizen and his wife would have been out of place here. It is obvious that a change of audience will bring a demand for a different type of play, as also will changed conditions call forth plays not only with a different structure, but with new or adapted methods of production. The theatre now is roofed and artificially lighted, so there is no call for the sometimes elaborate devices employed to put over an effect as noted above. One of the best examples of the old tradition may be found in *Julius Cæsar*, where the conspirators meet in Brutus' orchard and discuss the dawn, wrangling over the exact position of the approaching sunrise. With the gradual altering of theatrical conditions all this sort of thing becomes more and more unnecessary, until we come to the modern picture stage where the sun rises or sets, accompanied by a series of clicking switches from the electrician's box. With the modern possibilities of lighting and the multiple devices at the disposal of a clever producer almost any effect can be achieved — though we may be the poorer in imagination. It is the old convention, obviously lending itself to burlesque if unsurely handled, which Sheridan ridicules in *The Critic*. Puff opens his play with a clock striking, and although Shakespeare introduces a clock into *Julius Cæsar*, a very anachronistic chronometer, it saves, as Puff says, " a description of the rising sun, and a great deal about gilding the eastern hemisphere ".

Who then are the dramatists who write for this different theatre, this changed audience and these new actors and actresses ?

One of the most important, serving as he does as a link between the early Carolingian drama and the Restoration period, is Sir William D'Avenant (1606-68). He was the only man to whom licence was given to stage dramatic shows during the Commonwealth era, and he enjoyed the patronage of Charles II when the king returned, forming one of the companies of actors. He tried his hand at nearly all forms of drama : the tragicomedy, which helped to pave the way for the heroic tragedy essayed by Dryden ; the horror tragedy, where he follows the example of Ford and Webster in plays like *The Tragedy of Albovine* and *The Cruel Brother* — grim and gloomy dramas indeed ; the Masque and the Opera. It is perhaps significant that his first play, *The Siege of Rhodes*, was a heroic play in operatic form.

It is the heroic tragedy which at first, mainly at the hands of Dryden, is the most typical feature of this age. At its worst it lends itself patently to the burlesquing it received in Buckingham's *The Rehearsal* (1671) and Sheridan's *The Critic* ; at its best it is but a shadow, distorted as most shadows are, of Shakespeare's great tragedy, but this in itself is interesting as showing how potent still was Shakespeare's influence and how outstanding his genius. In a sense all the ingredients he used are present now, but none is capable of mixing them as he did. Dryden had a fine sense of the essentials of great drama, but by comparison, perhaps an unfair comparison, he is stilted and restrained, and does not in his plays attain the heights of emotion and passion. A comparison of *All for Love*, great play though it is, with *Antony and Cleopatra* makes this clear enough. Whether the cause lie in the failings of the man or the faults of the age in which he lived is open to question. He takes his place deservedly in the Hall of the Immortals, but his title to fame has not been won by his dramatic work, or at least by his work in Comedy, his contribution to Tragedy being much greater.

There is one innovation of this period which must be noted here, the attempt to introduce the rhymed couplet as the medium for tragedy. On his return Charles had a marked liking for things French, and it was doubtless due to his influence that the attempt was made to import this vehicle of expression from France to England. It was an attempt which never wholly succeeded, and though a good many plays were written in this style, Dryden, who had used this medium in his earlier plays, and other writers returned to blank verse with its greater flexibility and possibilities, and with this return came also reawakened interest in Shakespeare, not so much as a model perhaps but as a master, as exemplified in Dryden's comedies, and in Otway's *Venice Preserved* and *The Orphan*. It is necessary to turn from Dryden to see the beginnings of the true Restoration comedy which flourished at the hands of Wycherley, Congreve, and Vanbrugh. It was George Etheridge with his three plays written between 1664 and 1676 who prepared the way for Wycherley, whose plays appeared between 1672 and 1677. Each contains something of the merits, and more perhaps of the failings, of the brilliant comedy of manners that was to follow. Wit indeed is present, but without any real approach to the brilliant invention of the later group, and there is already something of that looseness of moral tone which is so typical of the Restoration period, and which naturally finds its way into the drama reflecting that period. Wycherley comes next in the story of Restoration drama with his four comedies. All reflect the gay and frivolous temper of the times and begin this period of the artificial comedy of manners at which Congreve excelled. The plays are coarse, but there is evident a strong vein of satire in Wycherley's work, particularly in *The Plain Dealer*. Neither the construction of the plays nor the character- isation is of outstanding merit, but he foreshadows that wit and brilliance of dialogue which, scintillating in his hands, blazed with Congreve. That of all things is typical : dialogue which flickers and flashes like light on the swords in a fencing match. It is Molière's big legacy to this era of English comedy.

Congreve is the master of this type and the outstanding figure of the group, also with four comedies, of which the later pair stand out pre-eminent — *Love for Love* (1695) and *The Way of the World* (1700). Here is a group of characters, affected and artificial, but, of their type, perfect, with Millamant and her bewitching coquetry and delicious whimsicality the crowning achievement in *The Way of the World*, though Foresight and Frail, Lady Wishfort and Mrs Marwood, Tattle and Fainall all are good. Mirabell's announcement of Millamant's approach prepares us most admirably for the entry of this perfect and lovable coquette, who is a close relation of Beatrice :

Here she comes, i' faith, full sail, with her fan spread, and her streamers out, and a shoal of fools for tenders.

It is even more in the style of his dialogue that Congreve excels, and it is interesting to quote what Hazlitt says: " The style of Congreve is inimitable, nay perfect. It is the highest model of comic dialogue. Every sentence is replete with sense and satire, conveyed in the most polished and pointed terms. Every page presents a shower of brilliant conceits, is a tissue of epigrams in prose, is a new triumph of wit, a new conquest over dullness ", etc. Meredith compares the wit of Congreve with that of Molière in his *Essay on Comedy* :

> "That of the first is a Toledo blade, sharp, and wonderfully supple for steel; cast for duelling, restless in the scabbard, being so pretty when out of it. To shine it must have an adversary. Molière's wit is like a running brook. . . . It does not run in search of obstructions, to be noisy over them. . . . Without effort, and with no dazzling flashes of achievement, it is full of healing, the wit of good breeding, the wit of wisdom ".

Imitators he has had : Sheridan aimed at the same target, but was not so consistently good a shot, and Wilde, Shaw, and Coward have all realised that one of the most vital factors of true comedy is witty, brilliant dialogue.

Vanbrugh and Farquhar are the remaining pair of this group of Restoration writers who preceded Sheridan. The term Restoration is rather loosely used to cover this period although Charles II had died. With Farquhar we reach the end of that particular stage in the development and history of the drama and are faced by a most interesting fact. From the beginning of the eighteenth century until the end of the nineteenth, there are, with the exception of Goldsmith and Sheridan, no outstanding writers for the theatre. There were a number of minor writers for the stage whose work had not sufficient dramatic value to survive, and there were also those, right on into the nineteenth century, who wrote plays, but rather for the study than the theatre. It does not mean that drama ceased — it flows always on, changing as it needs must according to the temper of the times — but that this is an arid period in which Sheridan and Goldsmith form a welcome oasis. After the death of Charles the artificiality, the wit, the elegance and immorality of the Court, which is so clearly reflected in the contemporary comedy of manners, persisted for a time, but inevitably reaction set in. In 1698 Jeremy Collier published his *Short View of the Profaneness and*

Immorality of the English Stage. He " distributes his swashing blows right and left among Wycherley, Congreve, and Van-brugh ", and he gained a large following. Two years later *The Way of the World* was produced ; and it failed on the stage. The result of all this was the growth of the Sentimental Comedy which Sheridan satirises, and though this was laudable enough in its aim to raise the moral tone, humour was ousted from its rightful place, and Sentimental Comedy became didactic and unnatural. Hazlitt says of Steele's plays that they were " not comedies but homilies ". In view of these remarks it is not very difficult to find the reason for the success of Goldsmith and Sheridan.

It is *She Stoops to Conquer* much more than *The Good-natured Man* (in the Preface to which he attacks the dull, unnatural Sentimental Comedy) which places Goldsmith high in any consideration of dramatic writers. Here is something very different from the Restoration comedy considered earlier. Simple and natural rather than artificial, though the situations may be occasionally unreal (yet reported to be based on an experience of his own), it is good-humoured, healthy comedy, with lovable human characters and dialogue which, though lacking the brilliance of Congreve, has a charming and enduring quality. Sheridan, the other notable writer of this period, as the author of our second play must have more detailed consideration.

V

INTRODUCTION TO "THE CRITIC"

THEATRE ROYAL, DRURY LANE, FROM GREAT RUSSELL STREET (1812)

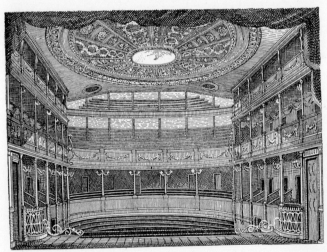

INTERNAL VIEW OF THE OLD THEATRE ROYAL, DRURY LANE (1792)

THE CRITIC

THE LIFE OF SHERIDAN

RICHARD BRINSLEY SHERIDAN was born in Dublin in 1751. His father, Thomas Sheridan, had won a great reputation on the stage, and was talked of as the rival of Garrick. He later became manager of the Theatre Royal, Dublin, and married Miss Frances Chamberlaine. She had literary ambitions, which in large measure were fulfilled by the publication of a novel, *Memoirs of Miss Sidney Bidulph* (1761). Two years later Garrick produced her play, *The Discovery*, at Drury Lane, with himself and Thomas Sheridan in the leading parts. *The Dupe*, her next play, was a failure, and *A Journey to Bath*, a subsequent venture, was not produced. But in this way " the theatre " was in Sheridan's blood. When the family settled in London, Richard ultimately went to Harrow for his schooling. His earliest literary efforts were in collaboration with an old school friend, Nathaniel Halhed. Halhed had written a farce, *Ixion*, which was revised and rechristened *Jupiter* by Sheridan. It is an early trying of his wings in the style of *The Rehearsal*, a style of burlesque which he was to bring to perfection in *The Critic*. The friends had great hopes of it, but these hopes never materialised.

The Sheridan family had now moved to Bath, where Richard met and fell in love with Elizabeth Linley. Member of a musical family, an accomplished singer herself, and a very beautiful girl, she had a host of admirers, among them being Major Mathews, a married man from whose persecution she fled to France under Sheridan's protection. Here, before she temporarily took refuge in a convent at Lille, they were married, being remarried formally in England in 1773,

Sheridan having previously fought two duels with the un-
scrupulous Mathews.

Sheridan now seriously set about writing for the theatre.
His first play, *The Rivals*, was produced at Covent Garden on
17th January 1775. It was at first a failure due in great
part to slipshod production. Mr Lee, the actor who played
Sir Lucius O'Trigger, was badly miscast and Mr Shuter was
very far from word-perfect and only vaguely familiar with his
lines. At the second attempt, however, Shuter had apparently
learnt his words, Lee was replaced by Clinch, and Sheridan had
pruned and revised the play, which now became an established
success in London and at Bath. In the same year (May)
St. Patrick's Day or The Scheming Lieutenant was produced,
and in November, Covent Garden Theatre put on *The Duenna*.
This was a great success, and Sheridan had now secured a firm
foothold on the ladder of fame.

In 1776 he took a further important step by succeeding
Garrick as manager of Drury Lane, in partnership with his
father-in-law and Dr Ford, and he opened his first season
at the theatre on 21st September 1776, and made his first contribution in February 1777 with *A Trip to Scarborough*, not an
original work but an expurgated adaptation of Vanbrugh's
The Relapse. This was, however, only preparatory to his
greatest success of all, *The School for Scandal*, which opened
on 8th May 1777. Brilliantly acted by the original cast and
universally well-received, it set the seal on Sheridan's prowess
as a playwright, and has retained its popularity as one of the
masterpieces of artificial comedy and a superb example of the
use of satire to attack a folly or abuse of the times which has
remained, and must always be, one of the most powerful weapons
in the armoury of comedy.

In this same year Sheridan, sponsored by Dr Johnson,
became a member of the notable " Literary Club ", of which
Burke, Fox, Garrick, and Sir Joshua Reynolds (whose portrait of
Sheridan's wife as St Cecilia is so famous) were fellow members.

In spite of this success as dramatist, his affairs as manager did not prosper, partly owing to his own slackness and partly owing to the incompetence of his father whom he had appointed stage manager.

In 1779, on 30th October, his career as a playwright may be said to end with the production of *The Critic*, and in the next year starts the second phase of his life, his political career. This third masterpiece, *The Critic*, though not often revived to-day except for occasional performances, shows yet another side of his powers, the handling of the burlesque, and remains almost unquestionably the finest example of the type.

His rise in Parliament was as rapid and effective as had been his dramatic career. It would be surprising that a man with Sheridan's wit, eloquence, and sense of the dramatic should not succeed as an orator, and though his earliest speeches are not universally praised by critics, and though Saintsbury uses of them the phrase " theatrical and rather brassy oratory ", he was gradually working towards the acknowledged triumph of the famous " Begum Speech " in his attack on Warren Hastings in 1787. This speech won the almost extravagant praise of his contemporaries. But while his political star was at its zenith his theatrical career suffered, partly because of continued bad management and inefficiency. In 1791 the theatre at Drury Lane had to be rebuilt at tremendous expense owing to its unsafe condition, and during this period of stress Sheridan suffered the great grief of losing his wife in 1792.

In 1794 the theatre was reopened with a performance of *Macbeth*, followed by two adaptations by Sheridan, *The Stranger* and *Pizarro*. In 1795 he married his second wife, Miss Elizabeth Ogle, the daughter of the Dean of Winchester. It was an ill-assorted marriage — she was only twenty — and her extravagance did nothing to help in the precarious position which Sheridan was rapidly approaching. The disaster of 1809, when Drury Lane was burned down, was the beginning of the end for him, and within a year or two his theatrical and political careers were closed. A committee was formed to

19 K

rebuild the theatre, but Sheridan was ousted from his position as manager, and though he received something for his share, his financial position was so acute that in 1812 he was unable to find the necessary funds for his representation of Stafford. He had for long enjoyed the friendship and confidence of the Prince of Wales, now Regent, but this availed him nothing, and in 1816, after a final struggle against debt and illness, he died. He was buried at Westminster Abbey in Poets' Corner, fittingly enough, since it is rather as a dramatist than a states-man that his memory has survived.

SHERIDAN'S CONTRIBUTION TO THE DRAMA, AND "THE CRITIC"

If Sheridan owes a debt to any of his predecessors in the drama, it is to the Restoration group that we must turn to find this influence. It is to be found perhaps first of all in the fact that two of his three masterpieces, *The Rivals*, *The School for Scandal*, and *The Critic*, are examples of the artificial comedy of manners which, started by Ben Jonson, passed through the hands of Congreve to its perfection in Sheridan. In wit and brilliance of dialogue he does not imitate, although he is certainly influenced by, this most striking feature of Congreve's work. Sheridan, however, achieves his end with-out the blemish of coarseness so characteristic of the Restora-tion dramatists, because so characteristic of the times. Lady Teazle would have deteriorated in the hands of Congreve. His characters are real though occasionally exaggerated. While not faultless, *The Rivals* and *The School for Scandal* are on the whole well developed, and plot-structure generally was not a strong feature of his Restoration predecessors.

Sheridan's portrait gallery contains some masterly creations : Mrs Malaprop, with her "nice derangement of epitaphs", is open to the charge of exaggeration, but she lives in the same street as Dogberry and Gobbo. Sir Anthony Absolute, the type of all irascible gout-ridden fathers ; Sir Lucius O'Trigger, that bloodthirsty Irishman ; Bob Acres, full of strange, but inevitably apt, oaths ; Joseph Surface, that smug hypocrite ; Lady Teazle, quite as delightful as Millamant, though not so lovable ; Puff, the complete panegyrist ; and Sir Fretful Plagiary, all are alive and live still, and that is one notable feature of Sheridan's drama.

In addition to his castigation of the scandal-mongering propensities of society in *The School for Scandal* — and as Dryden truly observes, one of the opportunities of comedy is, by means of satire, to laugh abuse out of countenance — Sheridan also attacks the Sentimental Comedy. Between the decline of Restoration Comedy and Sheridan's own rise into the world of the theatre this had become popular in such plays as Kelly's *False Delicacy* and Cumberland's *The West Indian,* and had been fostered also by the sentimental novels of the type on which Lydia Languish battens.

That the Julia-Faulkland scenes in *The Rivals* pander to the sentimentalists is true, but in *The School for Scandal* Sheridan breaks right away, and by the time he had finished with her in *The Critic,* he had succeeded in replacing the tears of " The Sentimental Muse " with a broad smile. It is this that is the keynote of *The Critic,* a burlesque farce, the subject of the burlesque being the extravagant type of romantic tragedy. The burlesque is at times exquisite, and *The Critic* remains the finest example of its type. That the play owes something to the *The Rehearsal* of Villiers, Duke of Buckingham, there is no doubt, but Sheridan had from the time of his early efforts in this line (the *Jupiter* which he adapted from Halhed's *Ixion*) toyed with the idea of doing a burlesque. That *The Rehearsal* contains the figure of Bayes (whether he represents Dryden, D'Avenant, or merely a poet laureate) may have suggested to Sheridan the opportunity of bringing Sir Fretful Plagiary, who is known to represent Cumberland, into his own play. There is one feature common to *The Knight of the Burning Pestle* and *The Critic* — the interruption of the play by those not acting in it — and in each case this device, an obvious and legitimate device, provides a great deal of the humour.

In his burlesque of the romantic tragedy Sheridan is less concerned with the parody of individual scenes or particular plays than a general parody of the worst absurdities of the type — the tediousness of opening scenes, the bombastic speeches, absurdity of situation, the " ridiculous recognition scene ", and portrayal of character. All these are the targets for Sheridan's fire. And in several passages in the play he has a final shot at the Sentimental Comedy.

VI

THE CRITIC

OR

A TRAGEDY REHEARSED

A DRAMATIC PIECE IN THREE ACTS

AS PERFORMED AT THE

THEATRE ROYAL IN DRURY LANE

DRAMATIS PERSONÆ

AS ORIGINALLY ACTED AT DRURY LANE THEATRE
30TH OCTOBER 1779

DANGLE	*Mr Dodd*
SNEER	*Mr Palmer*
SIR FRETFUL PLAGIARY	*Mr Parsons*
SIGNOR PASTICCIO RITORNELLO . . .	*Mr Delpini*
INTERPRETER	*Mr Baddeley*
UNDER PROMPTER	*Mr Phillimore*
PUFF	*Mr King*
MRS DANGLE	*Mrs Hopkins*
ITALIAN GIRLS	{ *Miss Field and the Miss Abrams*

CHARACTERS OF THE TRAGEDY

LORD BURLEIGH	*Mr Moody*
GOVERNOR OF TILBURY FORT . . .	*Mr Wrighten*
EARL OF LEICESTER	*Mr Farren*
SIR WALTER RALEIGH	*Mr Burton*
SIR CHRISTOPHER HATTON . . .	*Mr Waldron*
MASTER OF THE HORSE . . .	*Mr Kenny*
BEEFEATER	*Mr Wright*
JUSTICE	*Mr Packer*
SON	*Mr Lamash*
CONSTABLE	*Mr Fawcett*
THAMES	*Mr Gawdry*
DON FEROLO WHISKERANDOS . . .	*Mr Bannister, jun.*
FIRST NIECE	*Miss Collet*
SECOND NIECE	*Miss Kirby*
JUSTICE'S LADY	*Mrs Johnston*
CONFIDANTE	*Mrs Bradshaw*
TILBURINA	*Miss Pope*

Guards, Constables, Servants, Chorus, Rivers,
Attendants, &c., &c.

The text here is based on the first printed edition, but with the permission of Mr Philip Nutt, I have made certain additions from Fraser Rae's text of "Sheridan's Plays now printed as he wrote them" David Nutt, 1902), *indicated at the foot of the page by S.*

G. P. W. E.

TO MRS GREVILLE

Madam,

In requesting your permission to address the following pages to you, which as they aim themselves to be critical, require every protection and allowance that approving taste or friendly prejudice can give them, I yet ventured to mention no other motive than the gratification of private friendship and esteem. Had I suggested a hope that your implied approbation would give a sanction to their defects, your particular reserve, and dislike to the reputation of critical taste, as well as of poetical talent, would have made you refuse the protection of your name to such a purpose. However, I am not so ungrateful as now to attempt to combat this disposition in you. I shall not here presume to argue that the present state of poetry claims and expects every assistance that taste and example can afford it : nor endeavour to prove that a fastidious concealment of the most elegant productions of judgement and fancy is an ill return for the possession of those endowments. Continue to deceive yourself in the idea that you are known only to be eminently admired and regarded for the valuable qualities that attach private friendships, and the graceful talents that adorn conversation. Enough of what you have written, has stolen into full public notice to answer my purpose ; and you will, perhaps, be the only person, conversant in elegant literature, who shall read this address and not perceive that by publishing your particular approbation of the following drama, I have a more interested object than to boast the true respect and regard with which

I have the honour to be, Madam,

Your very sincere

And obedient humble servant,

R. B. SHERIDAN

PROLOGUE

By the Hon. Richard Fitzpatrick

The Sister Muses, whom these realms obey,
Who o'er the Drama hold divided sway,
Sometimes, by evil counsellors, 'tis said,
Like earth-born potentates have been misled:
In those gay days of wickedness and wit,   5
When Villiers criticiz'd what Dryden writ,
The Tragic Queen, to please a tasteless crowd
Had learn'd to bellow, rant, and roar so loud,
That frighten'd Nature, her best friend before,
The blust'ring beldam's company forswore.   10
Her Comic Sister, who had wit, 'tis true,
With all her merits, had her failings too;
And would sometimes in mirthful moments use
A style too flippant for a well-bred Muse.
Then female modesty abash'd began   15
To seek the friendly refuge of the fan,
Awhile behind that slight entrenchment stood,
'Till driv'n from thence, she left the stage for good.
In our more pious, and far chaster times,
These sure no longer are the Muse's crimes!   20
But some complain that, former faults to shun,
The reformation to extremes has run.
The frantic hero's wild delirium past,
Now insipidity succeeds bombast;
So slow Melpomene's cold numbers creep,   25
Here Dullness seems her drowsy court to keep,
And we are scarce awake, whilst you are fast asleep.
Thalia, once so ill-behav'd and rude,

Reform'd, is now become an arrant prude,
Retailing nightly to the yawning pit
The purest morals, undefil'd by wit!
Our Author offers in these motley scenes
5   A slight remonstrance to the Drama's queens:
Nor let the goddesses be over-nice;
Free-spoken subjects give the best advice.
Although not quite a novice in his trade,
His cause to-night requires no common aid.
10   To this, a friendly, just, and pow'rful court,
I come Ambassador to beg support.
Can he undaunted, brave the critic's rage?
In civil broils, with brother bards engage?
Hold forth their errors to the public eye,
15   Nay more, e'en newspapers themselves defy!
Say, must his single arm encounter all?
By numbers vanquish'd, e'en the brave may fall;
And though no leader should success distrust
Whose troops are willing, and whose cause is just;
20   To bid such hosts of angry foes defiance,
His chief dependence must be, YOUR ALLIANCE.

THE CRITIC

OR, A TRAGEDY REHEARSED

ACT I

SCENE I.—MR *and* MRS DANGLE *at breakfast, and reading newspapers.*

DANG. [*reading*]. "Brutus to Lord North." "Letter the second on the State of the Army"—Pshaw! "To the first L dash D of the A dash Y." — "Genuine Extract of a Letter from St Kitt's."—"Coxheath Intelligence."—"It is now confidently asserted that Sir 5 Charles Hardy."—Pshaw!—Nothing but about the fleet and the nation!—and I hate all politics but theatrical politics.—Where's the *Morning Chronicle*?

MRS DANG. Yes, that's your *Gazette*.

DANG. So, here we have it.—"*Theatrical intelligence* 10 *extraordinary.*—We hear there is a new tragedy in rehearsal at Drury Lane Theatre, called *The Spanish Armada*, said to be written by Mr Puff, a gentleman well known in the theatrical world; if we may allow ourselves to give credit to the report of the performers, 15 who, truth to say, are in general but indifferent judges, this piece abounds with the most striking and received beauties of modern composition."—So! I am very glad my friend Puff's tragedy is in such forwardness.—Mrs Dangle, my dear, you will be very glad to hear that 20 Puff's tragedy——

MRS DANG. Lord, Mr Dangle, why will you plague me about such nonsense? Now the plays are begun I shall have no peace. Isn't it sufficient to make yourself

ridiculous by your passion for the theatre, without continually teasing me to join you ? Why can't you ride
your hobby-horse without desiring to place me on a
pillion behind you, Mr Dangle ?

5   DANG. Nay, my dear, I was only going to read——

MRS DANG. No, no ; you will never read anything
that's worth listening to :—you hate to hear about
your country ; there are letters every day with Roman
signatures, demonstrating the certainty of an invasion,
10 and proving that the nation is utterly undone. But you
never will read anything to entertain one.

DANG. What has a woman to do with politics, Mrs
Dangle ?

MRS DANG. And what have you to do with the theatre,
15 Mr Dangle ? Why should you affect the character
of a critic ? I have no patience with you ! haven't
you made yourself the jest of all your acquaintance by
your interference in matters where you have no business ?
Are not you called a theatrical Quidnunc, and a mock
20 Maecenas to second-hand authors ?

DANG. True ; my power with the managers is pretty
notorious ; but is it no credit to have applications from
all quarters for my interest ? From lords to recommend
fiddlers, from ladies to get boxes, from authors to get
25 answers, and from actors to get engagements.

MRS DANG. Yes, truly ; you have contrived to get a
share in all the plague and trouble of theatrical property,
without the profit, or even the credit of the abuse that
attends it.

30   DANG. I am sure, Mrs Dangle, you are no loser by it,
however ; *you* have all the advantages of it :—mightn't
you, last winter, have had the reading of the new panto-
mime a fortnight previous to its performance ? And
doesn't Mr Fosbrook let you take places for a play before
35 it is advertised, and set you down for a box for every
new piece through the season ? And didn't my friend,

Mr Smatter, dedicate his last farce to you at my particular request, Mrs Dangle ?

MRS DANG. Yes ; but wasn't the farce damned, Mr Dangle ? And to be sure it is extremely pleasant to have one's house made the motley rendezvous of all the 5 lackeys of literature—the very high 'Change of trading authors and jobbing critics !—Yes, my drawing-room is an absolute register-office for candidate actors, and poets without character ; then to be continually alarmed with misses and ma'ams piping hysteric changes on 10 Juliets and Dorindas, Pollies and Ophelias ; and the very furniture trembling at the probationary starts and unprovoked rants of would-be Richards and Hamlets ! And what is worse than all, now that the manager has monopolized the Opera House, haven't we the 15 signors and signoras calling here, sliding their smooth semibreves, and gargling glib divisions in their out-landish throats—with foreign emissaries and French spies, for aught I know, disguised like fiddlers and figure-dancers ! 20

DANG. Mercy ! Mrs Dangle !

MRS DANG. And to employ yourself so idly at such an alarming crisis as this, too—when, if you had the least spirit, you would have been at the head of one of the Westminster associations—or trailing a volunteer pike 25 in the Artillery Ground ? But you—o' my conscience, I believe if the French were landed to-morrow your first inquiry would be, whether they had brought a theatrical troop with them.

DANG. Mrs Dangle, it does not signify—I say the stage 30 is " the mirror of Nature ", and the actors are " the abstract, and brief chronicles of the time " :—and pray, what can a man of sense study better ? Besides, you will not easily persuade me that there is no credit or im-portance in being at the head of a band of critics, who 35 take upon them to decide for the whole town, whose opinion and patronage all writers solicit, and whose recommendation no manager dares refuse!

MRS DANG. Ridiculous! Both managers and authors of the least merit laugh at your pretensions. The Public is their Critic—without whose fair approbation they know no play can rest on the stage, and with whose applause they welcome such attacks as yours, and laugh at the malice of them, where they can't at the wit.

DANG. Very well, madam—very well.

Enter SERVANT.

SERV. Mr Sneer, sir, to wait on you.

DANG. Oh, show Mr Sneer up. [*Exit* SERVANT.] Plague on't, now we must appear loving and affectionate, or Sneer will hitch us into a story.

MRS DANG. With all my heart; you can't be more ridiculous than you are.

DANG. You are enough to provoke——

Enter MR SNEER.

Ha! my dear Sneer, I am vastly glad to see you. My dear, here's Mr Sneer.

MRS DANG. Good morning to you, sir.

DANG. Mrs Dangle and I have been diverting ourselves with the papers. Pray, Sneer, won't you go to Drury Lane Theatre the first night of Puff's tragedy?

SNEER. Yes; but I suppose one shan't be able to get in, for on the first night of a new piece they always fill the house with orders to support it. But here, Dangle, I have brought you two pieces, one of which you must exert yourself to make the managers accept; I can tell you that, for 'tis written by a person of consequence.

DANG. So! now my plagues are beginning.

SNEER. Aye, I am glad of it, for now you'll be happy. Why, my dear Dangle, it is a pleasure to see how you enjoy your volunteer fatigue, and your solicited solicitations.

DANG. It's a great trouble—yet, egad, it's pleasant too. Why, sometimes of a morning, I have a dozen people call on me at breakfast time, whose faces I never 5 saw before, nor ever desire to see again.

SNEER. That must be very pleasant indeed !

DANG. And not a week but I receive fifty letters, and not a line in them about any business of my own.

SNEER. An amusing correspondence ! 10

DANG. [*reading*]. " Bursts into tears, and exit." What, is this a tragedy ?

SNEER. No, that's a genteel comedy, not a translation —only *taken from the French* ; it is written in a style which they have lately tried to run down ; the true 15 sentimental, and nothing ridiculous in it from the beginning to the end.

MRS DANG. Well, if they had kept to that, I should not have been such an enemy to the stage : there was some edification to be got from those pieces, Mr Sneer ! 20

SNEER. I am quite of your opinion, Mrs Dangle ; the theatre, in proper hands, might certainly be made the school of morality ; but now, I am sorry to say it, people seem to go there principally for their entertainment.

MRS DANG. It would have been more to the credit of 25 the managers to have kept it in the other line.

SNEER. Undoubtedly, madam, and hereafter perhaps to have had it recorded, that in the midst of a luxurious and dissipated age, they preserved *two* houses in the capital, where the conversation was always moral at least, 30 if not entertaining !

DANG. Now, egad, I think the worst alteration is in the nicety of the audience. No double entendre, no smart innuendo admitted ; even Vanbrugh and Congreve obliged to undergo a bungling reformation ! 35

SNEER. Yes, and our prudery in this respect is just on

a par with the artificial bashfulness of a courtesan, who increases the blush upon her cheek in an exact proportion to the diminution of her modesty.

DANG. Sneer can't even give the public a good word !—
5 But what have we here ?   This seems a very odd——

SNEER. Oh, that 's a comedy, on a very new plan ; replete with wit and mirth, yet of a most serious moral ! You see it is called *The Reformed Housebreaker* ; where by the mere force of humour, *housebreaking* is put into
10 so ridiculous a light, that if the piece has its proper run, I have no doubt but that bolts and bars will be entirely useless by the end of the season.

DANG. Egad, this is new indeed !

SNEER. Yes ; it is written by a particular friend of
15 mine, who has discovered that the follies and foibles of society are subjects unworthy the notice of the Comic Muse, who should be taught to stoop only at the greater vices and blacker crimes of humanity—gibbeting capital offences in five acts and pillorying petty larcenies in two.
20 In short, his idea is to dramatize the penal laws, and make the stage a court of ease to the Old Bailey.

DANG. It is truly moral.

Enter SERVANT.

SERV. Sir Fretful Plagiary, sir.

DANG. Beg him to walk up.— [*Exit* SERVANT.]   Now,
25 Mrs Dangle, Sir Fretful Plagiary is an author to your own taste.

MRS DANG. I confess he is a favourite of mine, because everybody else abuses him.

SNEER. Very much to the credit of your charity, madam,
30 if not of your judgement.

DANG. But, egad, he allows no merit to any author but himself, that 's the truth on't—though he 's my friend.

SNEER. Never.   He is as envious as an old maid verging on the desperation of six-and-thirty : and then the insidious humility with which he seduces you to give a free opinion on any of his works, can be exceeded only by the petulant arrogance with which he is sure to reject your observations.

DANG. Very true, egad—though he's my friend. 5

SNEER. Then his affected contempt of all newspaper strictures; though, at the same time, he is the sorest man alive, and shrinks like scorched parchment from the fiery ordeal of true criticism: yet is he so covetous of popularity, that he had rather be abused than not 10 mentioned at all.

DANG. There's no denying it—though he is my friend.

SNEER. You have read the tragedy he has just finished, haven't you?

DANG. Oh, yes; he sent it to me yesterday. 15

SNEER. Well, and you think it execrable, don't you?

DANG. Why, between ourselves, egad, I must own— though he's my friend—that it is one of the most—— He's here [*Aside*]—finished and most admirable per- form—— 20

SIR FRET. [*without*]. Mr Sneer with him, did you say?

Enter SIR FRETFUL.

DANG. Ah, my dear friend!—Egad, we were just speak- ing of your tragedy.   Admirable, Sir Fretful, admirable!

SNEER. You never did anything beyond it, Sir Fretful— never in your life. 25

SIR FRET. You make me extremely happy; for without a compliment, my dear Sneer, there isn't a man in the world whose judgement I value as I do yours—and Mr Dangle's.

MRS DANG. They are only laughing at you, Sir Fretful; 30 for it was but just now that——

DANG. Mrs Dangle!   Ah, Sir Fretful, you know Mrs Dangle.   My friend Sneer was rallying just now.   He knows how she admires you, and——

19 L

SIR FRET. O Lord, I am sure Mr Sneer has more taste and sincerity than to— [*Aside*] A damned double-faced fellow !

DANG. Yes, yes,—Sneer *will* jest—but a better-humoured——

SIR FRET. Oh, I know——

DANG. He has a ready turn for ridicule—his wit costs him nothing.

SIR FRET. No, egad,—or I should wonder how he came by it.   [*Aside.*

MRS DANG. Because his jest is always at the expense of his friend.   [*Aside.*

DANG. But, Sir Fretful, have you sent your play to the managers yet ?—or can I be of any service to you ?

SIR FRET. No, no, I thank you ; I believe the piece had sufficient recommendation with it.   I thank you, though —I sent it to the manager of Covent Garden Theatre this morning.

SNEER. I should have thought, now, that it might have been cast (as the actors call it) better at Drury Lane.

SIR FRET. O Lud ! no—never send a play there while I live—hark'ee !   [*Whispers* SNEER.

SNEER. *Writes himself !*—I know he does——

SIR FRET. I say nothing—I take away from no man's merit—I am hurt at no man's good fortune—I say nothing—But this I will say—through all my knowledge of life, I have observed—that there is not a passion so strongly rooted in the human heart as envy !

SNEER. I believe you have reason for what you say, indeed.

SIR FRET. Besides, I can tell you it is not always so safe to leave a play in the hands of those who write themselves.

SNEER. What, they may steal from them, hey, my dear Plagiary ?

SIR FRET. Steal!—to be sure they may; and, egad, serve your best thoughts as gipsies do stolen children, disfigure them to make 'em pass for their own.

SNEER. But your present work is a sacrifice to Melpomene, and *he*, you know, never—— 5

SIR FRET. That's no security. A dexterous plagiarist may do anything. Why, sir, for aught I know, he might take out some of the best things in my tragedy and put them into his own comedy.

SNEER. That might be done, I dare be sworn. 10

SIR FRET. And then, if such a person gives you the least hint or assistance, he is devilish apt to take the merit of the whole——

DANG. If it succeeds.

SIR FRET. Aye,—but with regard to this piece, I think 15 I can hit that gentleman, for I can safely swear he never read it.

SNEER. I'll tell you how you may hurt him more.

SIR FRET. How?

SNEER. Swear he wrote it. 20

SIR FRET. Plague on't now, Sneer, I shall take it ill. I believe you want to take away my character as an author!

SNEER. Then I am sure you ought to be very much obliged to me. 25

SIR FRET. Hey!—Sir!——

DANG. Oh, you know, he never means what he says.

SIR FRET. Sincerely then—you do like the piece?

SNEER. Wonderfully.

SIR FRET. But come now, there must be something 30 that you think might be mended, hey?—Mr Dangle, has nothing struck you?

DANG. Why, faith, it is but an ungracious thing for the most part to——

SIR FRET. With most authors it is just so, indeed; 35 they are in general strangely tenacious! But, for my part, I am never so well pleased as when a judicious critic points out any defect to me ; for what is the purpose of showing a work to a friend, if you don't mean to profit by his opinion ?

5 SNEER. Very true. Why, then, though I seriously admire the piece upon the whole, yet there is one small objection ; which, if you'll give me leave, I'll mention.

SIR FRET. Sir, you can't oblige me more.

SNEER. I think it wants incident.

10 SIR FRET. Good God !—you surprise me !—wants incident !

SNEER. Yes ; I own I think the incidents are too few.

SIR FRET. Good God ! Believe me, Mr Sneer, there is no person for whose judgement I have a more implicit
15 deference. But I protest to you I am only apprehensive that the incidents are too crowded.—My dear Dangle, how does it strike you ?

DANG. Really, I can't agree with my friend Sneer. I think the plot quite sufficient ; and the four first acts
20 by many degrees the best I ever read or saw in my life. If I might venture to suggest anything, it is that the interest rather falls off in the fifth act.

SIR FRET. Rises, I believe you mean, sir.

DANG. No, I don't, upon my word.

25 SIR FRET. Yes, yes, you do, upon my soul—it certainly don't fall off, I assure you. No, no, it don't fall off !

DANG. Now, Mrs Dangle, didn't you say it struck you in the same light ?

MRS DANG. No, indeed, I did not—I did not see a fault
30 in any part of the play from the beginning to the end.

SIR FRET. Upon my soul, the women are the best judges after all !

MRS DANG. Or if I made any objection, I am sure it was to nothing in the piece ! but that I was afraid it was, on
35 the whole, a little too long.

SIR FRET. Pray, madam, do you speak as to duration of

time ; or do you mean that the story is tediously spun out ?

MRS DANG. O Lud ! no. I speak only with reference to the usual length of acting plays.

SIR FRET. Then I am very happy—very happy indeed— because the play is a short play, a remarkably short play. I should not venture to differ with a lady on a point of taste ; but, on these occasions, the watch, you know, is the critic.

MRS DANG. Then, I suppose, it must have been Mr Dangle's drawling manner of reading it to me.

SIR FRET. Oh, if Mr Dangle read it, that 's quite another affair ! But I assure you, Mrs Dangle, the first evening you can spare me three hours and a half, I'll undertake to read you the whole from beginning to end, with the prologue and epilogue, and allow time for the music between the acts.

MRS DANG. I hope to see it on the stage next.

DANG. Well, Sir Fretful, I wish you may be able to get rid as easily of the newspaper criticisms as you do of ours.

SIR FRET. The *newspapers* ! Sir, they are the most villainous—licentious—abominable—infernal—Not that I ever read them—no—I make it a rule never to look into a newspaper.

DANG. You are quite right, for it certainly must hurt an author of delicate feelings to see the liberties they take.

SIR FRET. No !—quite the contrary ; their abuse is, in fact, the best panegyric—I like it of all things. An author's reputation is only in danger from their support.

SNEER. Why, that 's true—and that attack now on you the other day——

SIR FRET. What ? where ?

DANG. Aye, you mean in a paper of Thursday ; it was completely ill-natured, to be sure.

SIR FRET. Oh, so much the better. Ha ! ha ! ha ! I wouldn't have it otherwise.

DANG. Certainly it is only to be laughed at ; for——

SIR FRET. You don't happen to recollect what the fellow said, do you ?

SNEER. Pray, Dangle — Sir Fretful seems a little anxious——

SIR FRET. O Lud, no !—anxious,—not I,—not the least.—I—But one may as well hear, you know.

DANG. Sneer, do *you* recollect ? [*Aside*] Make out something.

SNEER [*aside to* DANGLE]. I will.—Yes, yes, I remember perfectly.

SIR FRET. Well, and pray now—not that it signifies— what might the gentleman say ?

SNEER. Why, he roundly asserts that you have not the slightest invention or original genius whatever ; though you are the greatest traducer of all other authors living.

SIR FRET. Ha! ha! ha!—very good!

SNEER. That as to Comedy, you have not one idea of your own, he believes, even in your common-place book, where stray jokes and pilfered witticisms are kept with as much method as the ledger of the Lost-and-Stolen Office.

SIR FRET. Ha ! ha ! ha !—very pleasant !

SNEER. Nay, that you are so unlucky as not to have the skill even to *steal* with taste : but that you glean from the refuse of obscure volumes, where more judicious plagiarists have been before you ; so that the body of your work is a composition of dregs and sediments—like a bad tavern's worst wine.

SIR FRET. Ha! ha!

SNEER. In your more serious efforts, he says, your bombast would be less intolerable, if the thoughts were ever suited to the expression ; but the homeliness of the sentiment stares through the fantastic encumbrance of its fine language, like a clown in one of the new uniforms !

SIR FRET. Ha! ha!

SNEER. That your occasional tropes and flowers suit the

general coarseness of your style, as tambour sprigs would a ground of linsey-woolsey ; while your imitations of Shake-speare resemble the mimicry of Falstaff's page, and are about as near the standard of the original.

SIR FRET. Ha!   5

SNEER. In short, that even the finest passages you steal are of no service to you ; for the poverty of your own language prevents their assimilating ; so that they lie on the surface like lumps of marl on a barren moor, en-cumbering what it is not in their power to fertilize !   10

SIR FRET. [*after great agitation*]. Now another person would be vexed at this.

SNEER. Oh ! but I wouldn't have told you, only to divert you.

SIR FRET. I know it—I *am* diverted—ha ! ha ! ha !— 15
not the least invention ! Ha ! ha ! ha ! very good !— very good !

SNEER. Yes—no genius ! Ha ! ha ! ha !

DANG. A severe rogue ! ha ! ha ! ha ! But you are quite right, Sir Fretful, never to read such nonsense.   20

SIR FRET. To be sure—for if there is anything to one's praise, it is a foolish vanity to be gratified at it, and if it is abuse—why one is always sure to hear of it from one damned good-natured friend or other !

Enter SERVANT.

SERV. Sir, there is an Italian gentleman with a French 25
interpreter, and three young ladies, and a dozen musicians, who say they are sent by Lady Rondeau and Mrs Fugue.

DANG. Gadso ! they come by appointment. Dear Mrs Dangle, do let them know I'll see them directly.

MRS DANG. You know, Mr Dangle, I shan't understand 30
a word they say.

DANG. But you hear there's an interpreter.

MRS DANG. Well, I'll try to endure their complaisance till you come.   [*Exit.*

SERV. And Mr Puff, sir, has sent word that the last rehearsal is to be this morning, and that he'll call on you presently.

DANG. That's true—I shall certainly be at home. [*Exit*
5 SERVANT.]   Now, Sir Fretful, if you have a mind to have justice done you in the way of answer—egad, Mr Puff's your man.

SIR FRET. Psha! sir, why should I wish to have it answered, when I tell you I am pleased at it?

10 DANG. True, I had forgot that.   But I hope you are not fretted at what Mr Sneer——

SIR FRET. Zounds! no, Mr Dangle, don't I tell you these things never fret me in the least.

DANG. Nay, I only thought——

15 SIR FRET. And let me tell you, Mr Dangle, 'tis damned affronting in you to suppose that I am hurt, when I tell you I am not.

SNEER. But why so warm, Sir Fretful?

SIR FRET. Gad's life!   Mr Sneer, you are as absurd as
20 Dangle; how often must I repeat it to you, that nothing can vex me but your supposing it possible for me to mind the damned nonsense you have been repeating to me!— and let me tell you, if you continue to believe this, you must mean to insult me, gentlemen—and then your disre-
25 spect will affect me no more than the newspaper criticisms— and I shall treat it—with exactly the same calm indifference and philosophic contempt—and so, your servant.   [*Exit.*

SNEER. Ha! ha! ha!   Poor Sir Fretful!   Now will he go and vent his philosophy in anonymous abuse of all
30 modern critics and authors.   But, Dangle, you must get your friend Puff to take me to the rehearsal of his tragedy.

DANG. I'll answer for't, he'll thank you for desiring it. But come and help me to judge of this musical family;
35 they are recommended by people of consequence, I assure you.

SNEER. I am at your disposal the whole morning—but I thought you had been a decided critic in music, as well as in literature.

DANG. So I am—but I have a bad ear. I'faith, Sneer, though, I am afraid we were a little too severe on Sir 5 Fretful—though he is my friend.

SNEER. Why, 'tis certain, that unnecessarily to mortify the vanity of any writer, is a cruelty which mere dullness never can deserve ; but where a base and personal malignity usurps the place of literary emulation, the 10 aggressor deserves neither quarter nor pity.

DANG. That 's true, egad !—though he 's my friend !

SCENE II.—*A Drawing-room, Harpsichord, &c.* ITALIAN FAMILY, FRENCH INTERPRETER, MRS DANGLE, *and* SERVANTS *discovered.*

INTERP. Je dis, madame, j'ai l'honneur *to introduce* et de vous demander votre protection pour le Signor Pasticcio Ritornello et pour sa charmante famille. 15

SIGNOR PAST. Ah ! vossignoria, noi vi preghiamo di favorirci colla vostra protezione.

FIRST DAUGH. Vossignoria, fateci questa grazia.

SEC. DAUGH. Sì, signora.

INTERP. Madame—*me interpret.* C'est-à-dire—*in English* 20 —qu'ils vous prient de leur faire l'honneur——

MRS DANG. I say again, gentlemen, I don't understand a word you say.

SIGNOR PAST. Questo signore spiegherà.

INTERP. Oui—*me interpret.* Nous avons les lettres de 25 recommandation pour Monsieur Dangle de——

MRS DANG. Upon my word, sir, I don't understand you.

SIGNOR PAST. La Contessa Rondeau è nostra padrona.

THIRD DAUGH. Sì, padre, et Miladi Fugue. 30

INTERP. Oh !—*me interpret.* Madame, ils disent—*in*

English—qu'ils ont l'honneur d'être protégés de ces dames. *You understand?*

MRS DANG. No, sir—no understand!

Enter DANGLE *and* SNEER.

INTERP. Ah, voici Monsieur Dangle!

5   ALL ITALIANS. Ah! Signor Dangle!

MRS DANG. Mr Dangle, here are two very civil gentle-men trying to make themselves understood, and I don't know which is the interpreter.

DANG. Eh bien!

[INTERPRETER *and* SIGNOR PASTICCIO *speak together.*

10   INTERP. Monsieur Dangle—le grand bruit de vos talens pour la critique, et de votre intérêt avec messieurs les directeurs à tous les théâtres—

SIGNOR PAST. Vossignoria siete si famoso per la vostra conoscenza, e vostro interesse coi direttori da——

15   DANG. Egad, I think the interpreter is the hardest to be understood of the two!

SNEER. Why, I thought, Dangle, you had been an admirable linguist!

DANG. So I am, if they would not talk so damned 20 fast.

SNEER. Well, I'll explain that—the less time we lose in hearing them the better—for that, I suppose, is what they are brought here for.

[SNEER *speaks to* SIGNOR PASTICCIO. *They sing trios, &c.,* DANGLE *beating out of time.* SERVANT *enters and whispers* DANGLE.

DANG. Show him up. [*Exit* SERVANT.] Bravo! admir-25 able! bravissimo! admirabilissimo! Ah, Sneer! where will you find voices such as these in England?

SNEER. Not easily.

DANG. But Puff is coming. Signor and little signoras—obligatissimo!—Sposa Signora Danglena—Mrs Dangle,

shall I beg you to offer them some refreshments, and take
their address in the next room.

[*Exit* MRS DANGLE *with the* ITALIANS *and* INTER-
PRETER *ceremoniously.*

Re-enter SERVANT.

SERV. Mr Puff, sir !
DANG. My dear Puff !

Enter PUFF.

PUFF. My dear Dangle, how is 't with you ?   5
DANG. Mr Sneer, give me leave to introduce Mr Puff
to you.
PUFF. Mr Sneer, is this ?   Sir, he is a gentleman whom
I have long panted for the honour of knowing—a gentleman whose critical talents and transcendent judgement—— 10
SNEER. Dear sir——
DANG. Nay, don't be modest, Sneer, my friend Puff
only talks to you in the style of his profession.
SNEER. His profession !
PUFF. Yes, sir ; I make no secret of the trade I follow 15
—among friends and brother authors, Dangle knows I
love to be frank on the subject, and to advertise myself
viva voce. I am, sir, a practitioner in panegyric, or to
speak more plainly—a professor of the art of puffing, at
your service—or anybody else's.   20
SNEER. Sir, you are very obliging !—I believe, Mr
Puff, I have often admired your talents in the daily
prints.
PUFF. Yes, sir, I flatter myself I do as much business
in that way as any six of the fraternity in town.   Devilish 25
hard work all the summer, friend Dangle ! never worked
harder ! But, hark'ee—the winter managers were a little
sore, I believe.
DANG. No—I believe they took it all in good part.
PUFF. Ah ! then that must have been affectation in 30

them ; for, egad, there were some of the attacks which
there was no laughing at !

SNEER. Aye, the humorous ones. But I should think,
Mr Puff, that authors would in general be able to do this
5 sort of work for themselves.

PUFF. Why, yes—but in a clumsy way. Besides, we
look on that as an encroachment, and so take the opposite
side. I dare say now you conceive half the very civil
paragraphs and advertisements you see, to be written
10 by the parties concerned, or their friends ? No such
thing. Nine out of ten, manufactured by me in the way
of business.

SNEER. Indeed !

PUFF. Even the auctioneers now—the auctioneers, I
15 say, though the rogues have lately got some credit for
their language—not an article of the merit theirs !—take
'em out of their pulpits, and they are as dull as cata-
logues !——No, sir ; 'twas I first enriched their style—
'twas I first taught them to crowd their advertisements
20 with panegyrical superlatives, each epithet rising above
the other—like the bidders in their own auction-rooms !
From *me* they learned to inlay their phraseology with
variegated chips of exotic metaphor : by *me* too their
inventive faculties were called forth. Yes, sir, by *me*
25 they were instructed to clothe ideal walls with gratuitous
fruits—to insinuate obsequious rivulets into visionary
groves—to teach courteous shrubs to nod their approbation of the grateful soil ! or on emergencies to raise up-
start oaks, where there never had been an acorn ; to
30 create a delightful vicinage without the assistance of a
neighbour ; or fix the temple of Hygeia in the fens of
Lincolnshire !

DANG. I am sure you have done them infinite service ;
for now, when a gentleman's ruined, he parts with his
35 house with some credit.

SNEER. Service ! egad if they had any gratitude, they

would erect a statue to him; they would figure him as
a presiding Mercury, the god of traffic and fiction, with
a hammer in his hand instead of a caduceus. But pray,
Mr Puff, what first put you on exercising your talents in
this way?   5

PUFF. Egad, sir—sheer necessity—the proper parent
of an art so nearly allied to invention: you must know,
Mr Sneer, that from the first time I tried my hand at an
advertisement my success was such, that for some time
after I led a most extraordinary life indeed!   10

SNEER. How, pray?

PUFF. Sir, I supported myself two years entirely by my
misfortunes.

SNEER. By your misfortunes?

PUFF. Yes, sir, assisted by long sickness, and other   15
occasional disorders; and a very comfortable living I
had of it.

SNEER. From sickness and misfortunes! You practised
as a doctor and an attorney at once?

PUFF. No, egad; both maladies and miseries were   20
my own.

SNEER. Hey!—what the plague!

DANG. 'Tis true, i'faith.

PUFF. Hark'ee! By advertisements—" To the charitable and humane!" and " To those whom Providence   25
hath blessed with affluence!"

SNEER. Oh, I understand you.

PUFF. And, in truth, I deserved what I got; for I
suppose never man went through such a series of calamities in the same space of time! Sir, I was five times   30
made a bankrupt, and reduced from a state of affluence
by a train of unavoidable misfortunes! Then, sir, though
a very industrious tradesman, I was twice burnt out, and
lost my little all, both times! I lived upon those fires
a month. I soon after was confined by a most excruciat- 35
ing disorder, and lost the use of my limbs! That told.

very well ; for I had the case strongly attested, and went about to collect the subscriptions myself.

DANG. Egad, I believe that was when you first called on me——

5 PUFF. In November last ? Oh, no !—I was at that time a close prisoner in the Marshalsea, for a debt benevolently contracted to serve a friend ! I was afterwards twice tapped for a dropsy, which declined into a very profitable consumption ! I was then reduced to—oh, no, 10 then, I became a widow with six helpless children—after having had eleven husbands pressed, and being left every time eight months gone with child, and without money to get me into a hospital !

SNEER. And you bore all with patience, I make no 15 doubt ?

PUFF. Why, yes, though I made some occasional attempts at *felo de se* ; but as I did not find those *rash actions* answer, I left off killing myself very soon. Well, sir, at last, what with bankruptcies, fires, gouts, dropsies, 20 imprisonments, and other valuable calamities, having got together a pretty handsome sum, I determined to quit a business which had always gone rather against my conscience, and in a more liberal way still to indulge my talents for fiction and embellishment, through my favourite 25 channels of diurnal communication—and so, sir, you have my history.

SNEER. Most obligingly communicative indeed ; and your confession, if published, might certainly serve the cause of true charity, by rescuing the most useful channels 30 of appeal to benevolence from the cant of imposition. But surely, Mr Puff, there is no great *mystery* in your present profession ?

PUFF. Mystery, sir ! I will take upon me to say the matter was never scientifically treated, nor reduced to 35 rule before.

SNEER. Reduced to rule ?

PUFF. O Lud, sir, you are very ignorant, I am afraid. Yes, sir, puffing is of various sorts : the principal are, the puff direct—the puff preliminary—the puff collateral —the puff collusive, and the puff oblique, or puff by implication. These all assume, as circumstances require, the various forms of Letter to the Editor—Occasional Anecdote—Impartial Critique—Observation from Correspondent, or Advertisement from the Party.

SNEER. The puff direct, I can conceive——

PUFF. Oh, yes, that's simple enough ; for instance, a new comedy or farce is to be produced at one of the theatres (though, by the by, they don't bring out half what they ought to do) : the author, suppose Mr Smatter, or Mr Dapper—or any particular friend of mine. Very well ; the day before it is to be performed, I write an account of the manner in which it was received : I have the plot from the author, and only add—" Characters strongly drawn—highly coloured—hand of a master— fund of genuine humour—mine of invention—neat dialogue—Attic salt ! " Then for the performance—" Mr Dodd was astonishingly great in the character of Sir Harry ! That universal and judicious actor, Mr Palmer, perhaps never appeared to more advantage than in the Colonel ; but it is not in the power of language to do justice to Mr King ! Indeed, he more than merited those repeated bursts of applause which he drew from a most brilliant and judicious audience ! " As to the scenery— " The miraculous powers of De Loutherbourg's pencil are universally acknowledged ! In short, we are at a loss which to admire most—the unrivalled genius of the author, the great attention and liberality of the managers, the wonderful abilities of the painter, or the incredible exertions of all the performers ! "

SNEER. That's pretty well indeed, sir.

PUFF. Oh, cool—quite cool—to what I sometimes do.

SNEER. And do you think there are any who are influenced by this.

PUFF. O Lud! yes, sir; the number of those who undergo the fatigue of judging for themselves is very small indeed!

SNEER. Well, sir—the puff preliminary?

PUFF. Oh, that, sir, does well in the form of a *caution*. In a matter of gallantry now—Sir Flimsy Gossamer wishes to be well with Lady Fanny Fete. He applies to me—I open trenches for him with a paragraph in the *Morning Post*:—"It is recommended to the beautiful and accomplished Lady F four stars F dash E to be on her guard against that dangerous character, Sir F dash G; who, however pleasing and insinuating his manners may be, is certainly not remarkable for the *constancy of his attachments!*"—in italics. Here, you see, Sir Flimsy Gossamer is introduced to the particular notice of Lady Fanny—who, perhaps, never thought of him before; she finds herself publicly cautioned to avoid him, which naturally makes her desirous of seeing him; the observation of their acquaintance causes a pretty kind of mutual embarrassment, this produces a sort of sympathy of interest—which, if Sir Flimsy is unable to improve effectually, he at least gains the credit of having their names mentioned together, by a particular set, and in a particular way—which nine times out of ten is the full accomplishment of modern gallantry.

DANG. Egad, Sneer, you will be quite an adept in the business.

PUFF. Now, sir, the puff collateral is much used as an appendage to advertisements, and may take the form of anecdote.—"Yesterday, as the celebrated George Bon-Mot was sauntering down St James's Street, he met the lively Lady Mary Myrtle, coming out of the Park—'Good God, Lady Mary, I'm surprised to meet you in a white jacket, for I expected never to have seen you but in a

full-trimmed uniform and a light-horseman's cap!'
'Heavens, George, where could you have learned that?'
'Why,' replied the wit, 'I just saw a print of you, in
a new publication called the *Camp Magazine*, which, by
the by, is a devilish clever thing, and is sold at No. 3,   5
on the right hand of the way, two doors from the printing-
office, the corner of Ivy Lane, Paternoster Row, price
only one shilling!'"

SNEER. Very ingenious indeed!

PUFF. But the puff collusive is the newest of any; for 10
it acts in the disguise of determined hostility. It is much
used by bold booksellers and enterprising poets.—" An
indignant correspondent observes, that the new poem
called *Beelzebub's Cotillion, or Proserpine's Fête Champêtre*,
is one of the most unjustifiable performances he ever 15
read! The severity with which certain characters are
handled is quite shocking! And as there are many
descriptions in it too warmly coloured for female delicacy,
the shameful avidity with which this piece is bought by
all people of fashion is a reproach on the taste of the 20
times, and a disgrace to the delicacy of the age!"—Here,
you see, the two strongest inducements are held forth:
first, that nobody ought to read it; and secondly, that
everybody buys it; on the strength of which the pub-
lisher boldly prints the tenth edition, before he had sold 25
ten of the first; and then establishes it by threatening
himself with the pillory, or absolutely indicting himself
for *scan. mag.*!

DANG. Ha! ha! ha!—'gad, I know it is so.

PUFF. As to the puff oblique, or puff by implication, 30
it is too various and extensive to be illustrated by an
instance; it attracts in titles and presumes in patents;
it lurks in the *limitation* of a subscription, and invites in
the assurance of crowd and incommodation at public
places; it delights to draw forth concealed merit, with 35
a most disinterested assiduity; and sometimes wears a

countenance of smiling censure and tender reproach. It has a wonderful memory for parliamentary debates, and will often give the whole speech of a favoured member with the most flattering accuracy. But, above all, it is a great dealer in reports and suppositions. It has the earliest intelligence of intended preferments that will reflect *honour* on the *patrons*; and embryo promotions of modest gentlemen—who know nothing of the matter themselves. It can hint a ribbon for implied services, in the air of a common report; and with the carelessness of a casual paragraph, suggest officers into commands, to which they have no pretension but their wishes. This, sir, is the last principal class in the art of puffing—an art which I hope you will now agree with me is of the highest dignity—yielding a tablature of benevolence and public spirit; befriending equally trade, gallantry, criticism, and politics: the applause of genius! the register of charity! the triumph of heroism! the self-defence of contractors! the fame of orators!—and the gazette of ministers!

SNEER. Sir, I am completely a convert both to the importance and ingenuity of your profession; and now, sir, there is but one thing which can possibly increase my respect for you, and that is, your permitting me to be present this morning at the rehearsal of your new trage——

PUFF. Hush, for Heaven's sake. *My* tragedy! Egad, Dangle, I take this very ill—you know how apprehensive I am of being known to be the author.

DANG. I'faith, I would not have told, but it's in the papers, and your name at length—in the *Morning Chronicle*.

PUFF. Ah! those damned editors never can keep a secret! Well, Mr Sneer, no doubt you will do me great honour—I shall be infinitely happy—highly flattered——

DANG. I believe it must be near the time—shall we go together?

PUFF. No ; it will not be yet this hour, for they are always late at that theatre : besides, I must meet you there, for I have some little matters here to send to the papers, and a few paragraphs to scribble before I go. [*Looking at memorandums.*] Here is " A conscientious baker, on the subject of the army bread " ; and " A detester of visible brick-work, in favour of the new-invented stucco " ; both in the style of Junius, and promised for to-morrow. The Thames navigation too is at a stand. Miso-mud or Anti-shoal must go to work again directly. Here too are some political memor-andums, I see ; aye—To take Paul Jones, and get the Indiamen out of the Shannon—reinforce Byron—compel the Dutch to—so !—I must do that in the evening papers, or reserve it for the *Morning Herald* ; for I know that I have undertaken to-morrow, besides to establish the unanimity of the fleet in the *Public Advertiser*, and to shoot Charles Fox in the *Morning Post*. So, egad, I ha'n't a moment to lose !

DANG. Well !—we'll meet in the Green Room.

[*Exeunt severally.*

ACT II

SCENE I.—*The Theatre.*

Enter DANGLE, PUFF, *and* SNEER, *as before the Curtain.*

PUFF. No, no, sir ; what Shakespeare says of actors may be better applied to the purpose of plays ; *they* ought to be " the abstract and brief chronicles of the times ". Therefore when history, and particularly the history of our own country, furnishes anything like a case in point, to the time in which an author writes, if he knows his own interest he'll take advantage of it ; so, sir, I call my tragedy *The Spanish Armada* ; and have laid the scene before Tilbury Fort.

SNEER. A most happy thought, certainly !

DANG. Egad, it was—I told you so. But pray, now, I don't understand how you have contrived to introduce any love into it.

PUFF. Love ! Oh, nothing so easy : for it is a received point among poets, that where history gives you a good hereoic outline for a play, you may fill up with a little love at your own discretion : in doing which, nine times out of ten, you only make up a deficiency in the private history of the times. Now I rather think I have done this with some success.

SNEER. No scandal about Queen Elizabeth, I hope ?

PUFF. O Lud ! no, no. I only suppose the Governor of Tilbury Fort's daughter to be in love with the son of the Spanish admiral.

SNEER. Oh, is that all !

DANG. Excellent, i'faith ! I see it at once. But won't this appear rather improbable ?

PUFF. To be sure it will—but what the plague ! a play is not to show occurrences that happen every day, but things just so strange, that though they never *did*, they might happen.

SNEER. Certainly nothing is unnatural, that is not physically impossible.

PUFF. Very true, and for that matter Don Ferolo Whiskerandos—for that 's the lover's name—might have been over here in the train of the Spanish ambassador ; or Tilburina, for that is the lady's name, might have been in love with him, from having heard his character, or seen his picture ; or from knowing that he was the last man in the world she ought to be in love with— or for any other good female reason. However, sir, the fact is, that though she is but a knight's daughter, egad ! she is in love like any princess !

DANG. Poor young lady ! I feel for her already ! for I can conceive how great the conflict must be between her passion and her duty ! her love for her country, and her love for Don Ferolo Whiskerandos !

PUFF. Oh, amazing !—her poor susceptible heart is swayed to and fro by contending passions like——

Enter UNDER PROMPTER.

UND. PROMP. Sir, the scene is set, and everything is ready to begin, if you please.

PUFF. 'Egad ; then we'll lose no time.

UND. PROMP. Though I believe, sir, you will find it very short, for all the performers have profited by the kind permission you granted them.

PUFF. Hey ! what !

UND. PROMP. You know, sir, you gave them leave to cut out or omit whatever they found heavy or un-necessary to the plot, and I must own they have taken very liberal advantage of your indulgence.

PUFF. Well, well. They are in general very good judges ; and I know I am luxuriant.—Now, Mr Hopkins, as soon as you please.

UND. PROMP. [*to the music*]. Gentlemen, will you play a few bars of something just to——

PUFF. Aye, that 's right—for as we have the scenes and dresses, egad, we'll go to't, as if it was the first night's performance ; but you need not mind stopping between the Acts. [*Exit* UNDER PROMPTER. *Orchestra play. Then the bell rings.*] Soh ! stand clear, gentlemen. Now you know there will be a cry of Down !—down !—hats off ! —silence ! Then up curtain—and let us see what our painters have done for us.

Scene II.—*Before Tilbury Fort.*

Two SENTINELS *asleep.*

DANG. Tilbury Fort !—very fine indeed !

PUFF. Now, what do you think I open with ?

SNEER. Faith, I can't guess.

PUFF. A clock. Hark ! [*Clock strikes.*] I open with
5 a clock striking, to beget an awful attention in the
audience—it also marks the time, which is four o'clock
in the morning, and saves a description of the rising sun,
and a great deal about gilding the eastern hemisphere.

DANG. But pray, are the sentinels to be asleep ?

10 PUFF. Fast as watchmen.

SNEER. Isn't that odd, though, at such an alarming crisis?

PUFF. To be sure it is, but smaller things must give
way to a striking scene at the opening ; that 's a rule.
And the case is, that two great men are coming to this
15 very spot to begin the piece ; now, it is not to be supposed
they would open their lips, if these fellows were watching
them, so, egad, I must either have sent them off their
posts, or set them asleep.

SNEER. Oh, that accounts for it—but tell us, who are
20 these coming ?

PUFF. These are they—Sir Walter Raleigh and Sir
Christopher Hatton. You'll know Sir Christopher by
his turning out his toes—famous, you know, for his
dancing. I like to preserve all the little traits of character.
25 —Now attend.

[*Enter* SIR WALTER RALEIGH *and* SIR CHRISTOPHER
HATTON.

SIR CHRIST. True, gallant Raleigh !]

DANG. What ! they had been talking before ?

PUFF. Oh, yes ; all the way as they came along.—

I beg pardon, gentlemen [*to the actors*], but these are particular friends of mine, whose remarks may be of great service to us.—Don't mind interrupting them whenever anything strikes you.   [*To* SNEER *and* DANG.

[SIR CHRIST. True, gallant Raleigh !   5
But oh, thou champion of thy country's fame,
There *is* a question which I yet must ask ;
A question which I never asked before—
What mean these mighty armaments ?
This general muster ? and this throng of chiefs ?]   10

SNEER. Pray, Mr Puff, how came Sir Christopher Hatton never to ask that question before ?
PUFF. What, before the play began ? how the plague could he ?
DANG. That's true, i'faith !   15
PUFF. But you will hear what he thinks of the matter.

[SIR CHRIST. Alas, my noble friend, when I behold
Yon tented plains in martial symmetry
Arrayed—when I count o'er yon glittering lines
Of crested warriors, where the proud steeds neigh,   20
And valour-breathing trumpet's shrill appeal
Responsive vibrates on my listening ear ;
When virgin majesty herself I view,
Like her protecting Pallas veiled in steel,
With graceful confidence exhort to arms !   25
When briefly all I hear or see bears stamp
Of martial vigilance and stern defence,
I cannot but surmise—Forgive, my friend,
If the conjecture's rash—I cannot but
Surmise——the State some danger apprehends !]   30

SNEER. A very cautious conjecture that.
PUFF. Yes, that's his character ; not to give an opinion, but on secure grounds.—Now then.

[SIR WALT. Oh, most accomplished Christopher——]

PUFF. He calls him by his Christian name, to show that they are on the most familiar terms.

[SIR WALT. Oh, most accomplished Christopher, I find
Thy stanch sagacity still tracks the future,
5   In the fresh print of the o'ertaken past.]

PUFF. Figurative!

[SIR WALT. Thy fears are just.
  SIR CHRIST. But where? whence? when? and what
The danger is—methinks I fain would learn.
10   SIR WALT. You know, my friend, scarce two revolving suns
And three revolving moons have closed their course,
Since haughty Philip, in despite of peace,
With hostile hand hath struck at England's trade.
  SIR CHRIST. I know it well.
15   SIR WALT. Philip, you know, is proud Iberia's king!
  SIR CHRIST. He is.
  SIR WALT. His subjects in base bigotry
And Catholic oppression held,—while we,
You know, the Protestant persuasion hold.
20   SIR CHRIST. We do.
  SIR WALT. You know, beside, his boasted armament,
The famed Armada, by the Pope baptized,
With purpose to invade these realms——
  SIR CHRIST.   Is sailed,
Our last advices so report.
25   SIR WALT. While the Iberian admiral's chief hope,
His darling son——
  SIR CHRIST.   Ferolo Whiskerandos hight——
  SIR WALT. The same—by chance a prisoner hath been ta'en,
And in this fort of Tilbury——
  SIR CHRIST.   Is now
Confined,—'tis true, and oft from yon tall turret's top

I've marked the youthful Spaniard's haughty mien—
Unconquered, though in chains.

SIR WALT.   You also know——]

DANG. Mr Puff, as he *knows* all this, why does Sir
Walter go on telling him ?

PUFF. But the audience are not supposed to know any- 5
thing of the matter, are they ?

SNEER. True, but I think you manage ill : for there
certainly appears no reason why Sir Walter should be so
communicative.

PUFF. 'Fore Gad, now, that's one of the most ungrate- 10
ful observations I ever heard—for the less inducement he
has to tell all this the more, I think, you ought to be
obliged to him ; for I am sure you'd know nothing of the
matter without it.

DANG. That's very true, upon my word.   15

PUFF. But you will find he was *not* going on.

[SIR CHRIST. Enough, enough,—'tis plain—and I no
     more
Am in amazement lost !——]

PUFF. Here now, you see, Sir Christopher did not in fact
ask any one question for his own information.   20

SNEER. No, indeed : his has been a most disinterested
curiosity !

DANG. Really, I find we are very much obliged to them
both.

PUFF. To be sure you are. Now then for the Com- 25
mander-in-Chief, the Earl of Leicester ; who, you know,
was no favourite but of the Queen's—We left off—" in
amazement lost ! "——

[SIR CHRIST. Am in amazement lost.——
But see, where noble Leicester comes ! supreme   30
In honours and command.

SIR WALT.   And yet methinks,

At such a time, so perilous, so feared,
That staff might well become an abler grasp.
    SIR CHRIST. And so, by Heaven! think I; but soft,
he's here!]

5   PUFF. Aye, they envy him.
    SNEER. But who are these with him?
    PUFF. Oh! very valiant knights; one is the Governor
of the Fort, the other the Master of the Horse.—And now,
I think, you shall hear some better language: I was
10 obliged to be plain and intelligible in the first scene,
because there was so much matter of fact in it; but now,
i'faith, you have trope, figure, and metaphor as plenty
as noun-substantives.

[*Enter* EARL OF LEICESTER, *the* GOVERNOR, MASTER OF
    THE HORSE, *and others.*

    LEIC. How's this, my friends! is't thus your new-
        fledged zeal
15   And plumèd valour moulds in roosted sloth?
    Why dimly glimmers that heroic flame,
    Whose reddening blaze, by patriot spirit fed,
    Should be the beacon of a kindling realm?
    Can the quick current of a patriot heart
20   Thus stagnate in a cold and weedy converse,
    Or freeze in tideless inactivity?
    No! rather let the fountain of your valour
    Spring through each stream of enterprise,
    Each petty channel of conducive daring,
25   Till the full torrent of your foaming wrath
    O'erwhelm the flats of sunk hostility!]

    PUFF. There it is—followed up!

    [SIR WALT. No more! the freshening breath of thy
        rebuke
    Hath filled the swelling canvas of our souls!

And thus, though fate should cut the cable of
                             [*All take hands.*
Our topmost hopes, in friendship's closing line
We'll grapple with despair, and if we fall,
We'll fall in Glory's wake !

    LEIC. There spoke Old England's genius !   5
Then, are we all resolved ?

    ALL. We are—all resolved !

    LEIC. To conquer—or be free ?

    ALL. To conquer, or be free !

    LEIC. All ?   10

    ALL. All !]

DANG. *Nem. con.* egad !

PUFF. Oh, yes, where they *do* agree on the stage, their unanimity is wonderful !

    [LEIC. Then let 's embrace—and now—— [*Kneels.*]
                                        15

SNEER. What the plague, is he going to pray ?

PUFF. Yes, hush !—in great emergencies there is nothing like a prayer !

    [LEIC. O mighty Mars !]

DANG. But why should he pray to *Mars* ?

PUFF. Hush !   20

    [LEIC.   If in thy homage bred,
Each point of discipline I've still observed ;
Nor but by due promotion, and the right
Of service, to the rank of Major-General
Have risen ; assist thy votary now !   25

    GOV. Yet do not rise,—hear me !

    MAST. And me !

    KNIGHT. And me !

    SIR WALT. And me !

    SIR CHRIST. And me !]   30

PUFF. Now, pray all together.

[ALL. Behold thy votaries submissive beg,
That thou wilt deign to grant them all they ask ;
Assist them to accomplish all their ends,
And sanctify whatever means they use
5 To gain them !] •

SNEER. A very orthodox quintetto !

PUFF. Vastly well, gentlemen.—Is that well managed or not ?   Have you such a prayer as that on the stage ?

SNEER. Not exactly.

10 LEIC. [*to* PUFF]. But, sir, you haven't settled how we are to get off here.

PUFF. You could'nt go off kneeling, could you ?

SIR WALT. [*to* PUFF]. Oh, no, sir ! impossible !

PUFF. It would have a good effect, i'faith, if you could !
15 exeunt praying ! [1] Yes, and would vary the established mode of springing off with a glance at the Pit.

SNEER. Oh, never mind ; so as you get them off, I'll answer for it the audience won't care how.

PUFF. Well, then, repeat the last line standing, and go
20 off the old way.

[ALL. And sanctify whatever means they use
To gain them.   [*Exeunt.*]

DANG. Bravo ! a fine exit.

SNEER. Well really, Mr Puff——

25 PUFF. Stay a moment.—

[*The* SENTINELS *get up.*

FIRST SENT. All this shall to Lord Burleigh's ear.

SEC. SENT. 'Tis meet it should.   [*Exeunt* SENTINELS.]

DANG. Hey ! why, I thought those fellows had been asleep ?

30 PUFF. Only a pretence, there's the art of it ; they were spies of Lord Burleigh's.

[1] could exeunt praying ! *some eds.*

SNEER. But isn't it odd, they were never taken notice of, not even by the Commander-in-Chief ?

PUFF. O Lud, sir, if people who want to listen, or over-hear, were not always connived at in a tragedy, there would be no carrying on any plot in the world. 5

DANG. That's certain !

PUFF. But take care, my dear Dangle, the morning gun is going to fire. [*Cannon fires.*

DANG. Well, that will have a fine effect.

PUFF. I think so, and helps to realize the scene. [*Cannon* 10 *twice.*][1] What the plague !—*three* morning guns !—there never is but one !—aye, this is always the way at the theatre—give these fellows a good thing, and they never know when to have done with it. You have no more cannon to fire ? 15

PROMPT. [*from within*]. No, sir.

PUFF. Now, then, for soft music.

SNEER. Pray, what's that for ?

PUFF. It shows that Tilburina is coming ; nothing intro-duces you a heroine like soft music.—Here she comes. 20

DANG. And her confidant, I suppose ?

PUFF. To be sure : here they are—inconsolable to the minuet in Ariadne ! [*Soft music.*

[*Enter* TILBURINA *and* CONFIDANT.

TILB. Now has the whispering breath of gentle morn
Bid Nature's voice and Nature's beauty rise ; 25
While orient Phœbus with unborrowed hues
Clothes the waked loveliness which all night slept
In heavenly drapery ! Darkness is fled.
Now flowers unfold their beauties to the sun,
And blushing, kiss the beam he sends to wake them. 30
The striped carnation and the guarded rose,
The vulgar wallflower and smart gillyflower,

---

[1] S. gives this speech as "I think so, and helps to realize the scene. There are more cannon to fire ".

The polyanthus mean—the dapper daisy,
Sweet-william and sweet marjoram, and all
The tribe of single and of double pinks !
Now, too, the feathered warblers tune their notes
5   Around, and charm the listening grove—The lark !
The linnet ! chaffinch ! bullfinch ! goldfinch ! green-
          finch !
But oh, to me no joy can they afford !
Nor rose, nor wallflower, nor smart gillyflower,
Nor polyanthus mean, nor dapper daisy,
10   Nor William sweet, nor marjoram—nor lark,
Linnet, nor all the finches of the grove !]

PUFF. Your white handkerchief, madam.
TILB. I thought, sir, I wasn't to use that till " heart-
rending woe."
15   PUFF. Oh, yes, madam—at " the finches of the grove,"
if you please.

          [TILB.   Nor lark,
Linnet, nor all the finches of the grove !   [*Weeps.*]

PUFF. Vastly well, madam !
20   DANG. Vastly well, indeed !

          [TILB. For, oh, too sure, heart-rending woe is now
The lot of wretched Tilburina !]

DANG. Oh !—'tis too much.
SNEER. Oh !—it is, indeed.

25   [CON. Be comforted, sweet lady—for who knows
But Heaven has yet some milk-white day in store.
          TILB. Alas, my gentle Nora,
Thy tender youth as yet hath never mourned
Love's fatal dart.   Else wouldst thou know that when
30   The soul is sunk in comfortless despair,
It cannot taste of merriment.]

DANG. That 's certain.

[CON. But see where your stern father comes ;
It is not meet that he should find you thus.]

PUFF. Hey, what the plague ! what a cut is here !—
why, what 's become of the description of her first meeting
with Don Whiskerandos ? his gallant behaviour in the 5
sea fight, and the simile of the canary bird ?
TILB. Indeed, sir, you'll find they will not be missed.
PUFF. Very well.—Very well !
TILB. [*to* CONFIDANT]. The cue, ma'am, if you please.

[CON. It is not meet that he should find you thus. 10
TILB. Thou counsel'st right, but 'tis no easy task
For barefaced grief to wear a mask of joy.

Enter GOVERNOR.

GOV. How 's this—in tears ?—O Tilburina, shame !
Is this a time for maudling tenderness,
And Cupid's baby woes ?—hast thou not heard 15
That haughty Spain's Pope-consecrated fleet
Advances to our shores, while England's fate,
Like a clipped guinea, trembles in the scale !
TILB. Then is the crisis of *my* fate at hand !
I see the fleet's approach—I see——] 20

PUFF. Now pray, gentlemen, mind. This is one of the
most useful figures we Tragedy writers have, by which a
hero or heroine, in consideration of their being often
obliged to overlook things that *are* on the stage, is allowed
to hear and see a number of things that are not. 25
SNEER. Yes—a kind of poetical second-sight !
PUFF. Yes.—Now then, madam.

[TILB.   I see their decks
Are cleared !— I see the signal made !
The line is formed !—a cable's length asunder ! 30
I see the frigates stationed in the rear ;
And now I hear the thunder of the guns !

I hear the victor's shouts—I also hear
The vanquished groan!—and now 'tis smoke—and now
I see the loose sails shiver in the wind!
I see—I see—what soon you'll see——
5   GOV. Hold, daughter! peace! this love hath
            turned thy brain:
The Spanish fleet thou *canst* not see—because
——It is not yet in sight!]

DANG. Egad, though, the Governor seems to make no
allowance for this poetical figure you talk of.
10   PUFF. No, a plain matter-of-fact man—that's his
character.

[TILB. But will you then refuse his offer?
GOV. I must—I will—I can—I ought—I do.
TILB. Think what a noble price.
15   GOV. No more—you urge in vain—
TILB. His liberty is all he asks.]

SNEER. All *who* asks, Mr Puff? Who is——
PUFF. Egad, sir, I can't tell. Here has been such
cutting and slashing I don't know where they have got
20 to myself.
TILB. Indeed, sir, you will find it will connect very
well.

[——And your reward secure.]

PUFF. Oh, if they hadn't been so devilish free with
25 their cutting here, you would have found that Don
Wiskerandos has been tampering for his liberty, and
has persuaded Tilburina to make this proposal to her
father. And now, pray observe the conciseness with
which the argument is conducted—egad, the *pro* and *con*
30 goes as smart as hits in a fencing match. It is indeed a
sort of small-sword logic, which we have borrowed from
the French.

[TILB. A retreat in Spain!
GOV. Outlawry here!
TILB. Your daughter's prayer!
GOV. Your father's oath!
TILB. My lover! 5
GOV. My country!
TILB. Tilburina!
GOV. England!
TILB. A title!
GOV. Honour! 10
TILB. A pension!
GOV. Conscience!
TILB. A thousand pounds!
GOV. Hah! thou hast touched me nearly!]

PUFF. There, you see—she threw in *Tilburina*. Quick, 15
parry carte with *England*! Hah! thrust in tierce *a
title*!—parried by *honour*. Hah! *a pension* over the
arm! put by by *conscience*. Then flankonade with *a
thousand pounds*—and a palpable hit, egad!

[TILB.   Canst thou 20
Reject the suppliant, and the daughter too?
GOV. No more; I would not hear thee plead in vain,
The father softens—but the governor
Is fixed!   [*Exit.*]

DANG. Aye, that antithesis of persons is a most estab- 25
lished figure.

[TILB. 'Tis well—hence then fond hopes, fond passion
    hence;
Duty, behold I am all over thine——
WHISK. [*without*]. Where is my love—my——
TILB. Ha! 30
WHISK. [*entering*]. My beauteous enemy——]

PUFF. Oh, dear, ma'am, you must start a great deal
more than that; consider you had just determined in
19 N

favour of duty, when in a moment the sound of his voice revives your passion—overthrows your resolution—destroys your obedience. If you don't express all that in your start you do nothing at all.

5   TILB. Well, we'll try again !

DANG. Speaking from within has always a fine effect.

SNEER. Very.

[TILB. Behold I am all over thine.

WHISK. Where is my love ? my——

10   TILB. Ha !

WHISK. My beauteous enemy !
My conquering Tilburina ! How ! is't thus
We meet ? why are thy looks averse ? what means
That falling tear—that frown of boding woe ? [1]

15   Hah ! now indeed I am a prisoner !
Yes, now I feel the galling weight of these
Disgraceful chains—which, cruel Tilburina !
Thy doting captive gloried in before.—
But thou art false, and Whiskerandos is undone !

20   TILB. Oh, no ; how little dost thou know thy
         Tilburina !

WHISK. Art thou then true ?   Begone cares, doubts,
         and fears,
I make you all a present to the winds ;
And if the winds reject you—try the waves.]

PUFF. The wind, you know, is the established receiver

25 of all stolen sighs, and cast-off griefs and apprehensions.

[TILB. Yet must we part ?—stern duty seals our
         doom :
Though here I call yon conscious clouds to witness,
Could I pursue the bias of my soul,
All friends, all rights of parents I'd disclaim,

---

[1] S. omits from here to "The less is said the better", which perhaps gives more point to Puff's "Hey day ! here's a cut !" and his remark about "mutual protestations".

And thou, my Whiskerandos, shouldst be father
And mother, brother, cousin, uncle, aunt,
And friend to me!

WHISK. O matchless excellence!—and must we part?
Well, if we must—we must—and in that case   5
The less is said the better.]

PUFF. Hey day! here's a cut! What, are all the
mutual protestations out?

TILB. Now pray, sir, don't interrupt us just here, you
ruin our feelings.   10

PUFF. *Your* feelings!—but zounds, *my* feelings,
ma'am!

SNEER. No; pray don't interrupt them.

[WHISK. One last embrace——
TILB. Now—farewell, for ever.   15
WHISK. For ever!
TILB. Aye, for ever.   [*Going.*]

PUFF. 'Sdeath and fury! Gad's life! sir! madam, if
you go out without the parting look, you might as well
dance out. Here, here!   20

CON. But pray, sir, how am *I* to get off here?

PUFF. *You,* pshaw! what the devil signifies how *you*
get off! edge away at the top, or where you will. [*Pushes
the* CONFIDANT *off.*] Now, ma'am, you see——

TILB. We understand you, sir.   25

[——Aye, for ever.
BOTH. Oh!—
[*Turning back and exeunt. Scene closes.*]

DANG. Oh, charming!

PUFF. Hey!—'tis pretty well, I believe: you see I
don't attempt to strike out anything new, but I take it   30
I improve on the established modes.

SNEER. You do, indeed. But pray, is not Queen
Elizabeth to appear?

PUFF. No, not once—but she is to be talked of for ever; so that, egad, you'll think a hundred times that she is on the point of coming in.

SNEER. Hang it, I think it's a pity to keep *her* in the green room all the night.

PUFF. Oh, no, that always has a fine effect—it keeps up expectation.

DANG. But are we not to have a battle?

PUFF. Yes, yes, you will have a battle at last, but, egad, it's not to be by land, but by sea—and that is the only quite new thing in the piece.

DANG. What, Drake at the Armada, hey?

PUFF. Yes, i'faith—fireships and all: then we shall end with the procession. Hey! that will do, I think?

SNEER. No doubt on't.

PUFF. Come, we must not lose time—so now for the *underplot*.

SNEER. What the plague, have you another plot?

PUFF. O Lud, yes—ever while you live have two plots to your tragedy. The grand point in managing them is only to let your underplot have as little connexion with your main plot as possible. I flatter myself nothing can be more distinct than mine, for as in my chief plot the characters are all great people, I have laid my underplot in low life; and as the former is to end in deep distress, I make the other end as happy as a farce.—Now, Mr Hopkins, as soon as you please.

Enter UNDER PROMPTER.

UND. PROMP. Sir, the carpenter says it is impossible you can go to the park scene yet.

PUFF. The park scene! No—I mean the description scene here, in the wood.

UND. PROMP. Sir, the performers have cut it out.

PUFF. Cut it out!

UND. PROMP. Yes, sir.

PUFF. What! the whole account of Queen Elizabeth?

UND. PROMP. Yes, sir.

PUFF. And the description of her horse and side-saddle?

UND. PROMP. Yes, sir.

PUFF. So, so, this is very fine indeed! Mr Hopkins, how the plague could you suffer this?

HOPKINS [*from within*]. Sir, indeed the pruning-knife——

PUFF. The pruning-knife—zounds, the axe! why, here has been such lopping and topping, I shan't have the bare trunk of my play left presently. Very well, sir—the performers must do as they please, but upon my soul, I'll print it, every word.

SNEER. That I would, indeed.

PUFF. Very well, sir—then we must go on. Zounds! I would not have parted with the description of the horse! Well, sir, go on.—Sir, it was one of the finest and most laboured things.—Very well, sir, let them go on.—There you had him and his accoutrements from the bit to the crupper.—Very well, sir, we must go to the park scene.

UND. PROMP. Sir, there is the point, the carpenters say that unless there is some business put in here before the drop, they shan't have time to clear away the fort, or sink Gravesend and the river.

PUFF. So! this is a pretty dilemma, truly! [1] Do call the Head Carpenter to me.

UND. PROMP. Mr Butler. [*Enter* CARPENTER *dress'd.*] Here he is, Sir.

PUFF. Hey—this is the Head Carpenter!

UND. PROMP. Yes—Sir—He was to have walked as one of the Generals at the Review.—For the truth is your Tragedy employs everybody in the company.

PUFF. Then pray, Mr General-Carpenter what is all this?

[1] "Do call the Head Carpenter." From here to the end of the Scene inserted from S.

CARP. Why Sir, you only consider what my men have to do—they have to remove Tilbury Fort with the Cannon and to sink Gravesend and the River and I only desire three minutes to do it in.

5 PUFF. Hah! and they've cut the Scene.

CARP. Besides if I could manage in less I question if the Lamplighter could clear away the Sun in the time.

PUFF. Do call one of them here.

CARP. Master Lamplighter! [*Without*] Mr Langley!
10 Here [*enter* LAMPLIGHTER *as a River God and a Page holding up his train*].

PUFF. Sir—your most obedient servant—Who the Devil's this!

UND. PROMP. The master Lamplighter, Sir. He does
15 one of the River Gods in the Procession.

PUFF. O, a River God is he—well Sir you won't have time I understand——

L. Three minutes at least Sir—unless you have a mind to burn the Fort.

20 PUFF. Hah! and they've cut out the Scene!

CARP. Lord Sir, there only wants a little business to be put in here—just as long as while we have been speaking will do it——

PUFF. What then are you all ready now? [*From*
25 *behind*] Yes all clear.

PUFF. O then I shall easily manage it——

UND. PROMP. Clear the Stage.

PUFF. And do General keep a sharp look out and beg the River God not to spare his Oyl in the last scene—
30 it must be brilliant. Gentlemen I beg a thousand pardons.

SNEER. Oh, dear sir, these little things will happen.[1]

PUFF. To cut out this scene!—but I'll print it—egad, I'll print it, every word!   [*Exeunt.*

---

[1] S. ends with this speech of Sneer's.

ACT III

SCENE I.—*Before the Curtain.*

Enter PUFF, SNEER, *and* DANGLE.

PUFF. Well, we are ready—now then for the justices.

> [*Curtain rises;* JUSTICES, CONSTABLES, *&c.,*
> *discovered.*]

SNEER. This, I suppose, is a sort of senate scene.

PUFF. To be sure—there has not been one yet.

DANG. It is the underplot, isn't it?

PUFF. Yes. What, gentlemen, do you mean to go at 5
once to the discovery scene?

JUST. If you please, sir.

PUFF. Oh, very well—hark'ee, I don't choose to say
anything more, but i'faith, they have mangled my play
in a most shocking manner! 10

DANG. It's a great pity!

PUFF. Now then, Mr Justice, if you please.

> [JUST. Are all the volunteers without?
> CONST.   They are,
> Some ten in fetters, and some twenty drunk.
>   JUST. Attends the youth, whose most opprobrious
>   fame 15
> And clear convicted crimes have stamped him soldier?
>   CONST. He waits your pleasure; eager to repay
> The blest reprieve that sends him to the fields
> Of glory, there to raise his branded hand
> In honour's cause.
>   JUST.   'Tis well—'tis Justice arms him! 20
> Oh! may he now defend his country's laws
> With half the spirit he has broke them all!
> If 'tis your worship's pleasure, bid him enter.
>   CONST. I fly—the herald of your will.
> [*Exit* CONSTABLE.]

PUFF. Quick, sir !

SNEER. But, Mr Puff, I think not only the Justice but the clown seems to talk in as high a style as the first hero among them.

5   PUFF. Heaven forbid they should not in a free country ! Sir, I am not for making slavish distinctions, and giving all the fine language to the upper sort of people.

DANG. That's very noble in you indeed.

[*Enter* JUSTICE'S LADY.]

PUFF. Now pray mark this scene.

10   [LADY. Forgive this interruption, good my love ;
But as I just now passed a prisoner youth,
Whom rude hands hither lead, strange bodings seized
My fluttering heart, and to myself I said,
An if our Tom had lived, he'd surely been
15   This stripling's height !

        JUST. Ha ! sure some powerful sympathy directs
Us both——

Enter SON *and* CONSTABLE.

    JUST. What is thy name ?

    SON. My name's Tom Jenkins [1]—*alias*, have I none—
20   Though orphaned and without a friend !

    JUST. Thy parents ?

    SON. My father dwelt in Rochester, and was,
As I have heard, a fishmonger—no more.]

PUFF. What, sir, do you leave out the account of your
25 birth, parentage, and education ?

    SON. They have settled it so, sir, here.

PUFF. Oh ! oh !

    [LADY. How loudly nature whispers at my heart !
Had he no other name ?

---

[1] S. has John Wilkins.

SON.   I've seen a bill
Of his, signed *Tomkins*, creditor.

JUST. [1] Ha! by Heavens! Our boy is now before
    us!

LADY. Has he his ears?

SON. Lady—for three long winters have I mourned
    their loss.   5

LADY. It is! It is!

JUST. This does indeed confirm each circumstance
The gipsy told!—Prepare!

SON. I do.

JUST. No orphan, nor without a friend, art thou—   10
I am thy father, *here's* thy mother, *there*
Thy uncle—this thy first cousin, and those
Are all your near relations!

MOTHER. O ecstasy of bliss!

SON. O most unlooked-for happiness!   15

JUST. O wonderful event!
           [*They faint alternately in each others arms.*]

PUFF. There, you see relationship, like murder, will out.

[JUST. Now let's revive—else were this joy too
    much!
But come—and we'll unfold the rest within,
And thou, my boy, must needs want rest and food.   20
Hence may each orphan hope, as chance directs,
To find a father—where he least expects!   [*Exeunt.*]

PUFF. What do you think of that?

DANG. One of the finest discovery-scenes I ever saw!
Why, this underplot would have made a tragedy itself.   25

SNEER. Aye, or a comedy either.

PUFF. And keeps quite clear, you see, of the other.

Enter SCENEMEN, *taking away the seats.*

PUFF. The scene remains, does it?

[1] "Ha! by Heavens!"—from here to "It is! It is!" inserted from S.

SCENEMAN. Yes, sir.

PUFF. You are to leave one chair, you know. But it is always awkward in a tragedy to have you fellows coming in in your playhouse liveries to remove things. I 5 wish that could be managed better.—So now for my mysterious yeoman.

[*Enter a* BEEFEATER.

BEEF. Perdition catch my soul, but I do love thee.]

SNEER. Haven't I heard that line before ?

PUFF. No, I fancy not. Where, pray ?

10 DANG. Yes, I think there is something like it in *Othello*.

PUFF. Gad ! now you put me in mind on't, I believe there is ; but that 's of no consequence—all that can be said is, that two people happened to hit on the same thought—and Shakespeare made use of it first, 15 that 's all.

SNEER. Very true.

PUFF. Now, sir, your soliloquy—but speak more to the pit, if you please—the soliloquy always to the pit—that 's a rule.

20   [BEEF. Though hopeless love finds comfort in
            despair,
      It never can endure a rival's bliss !
      But soft—I am observed.   [*Exit* BEEFEATER.]

DANG. That 's a very short soliloquy.

PUFF. Yes, but it would have been a great deal longer if 25 he had not been observed.

SNEER. A most sentimental Beefeater that, Mr Puff.

PUFF. Hark'ee, I would not have you be too sure that he *is* a Beefeater.

SNEER. What, a hero in disguise ?

30 PUFF. No matter ! I only give you a hint. But now for my principal character. Here he comes—Lord Burleigh

in person! Pray, gentlemen, step this way—softly—I only hope the Lord High Treasurer is perfect—if he is but perfect!

[*Enter* LORD BURLEIGH, *goes slowly to a chair and sits.*]

SNEER. Mr Puff!

PUFF. Hush! vastly well, sir! vastly well! a most 5 interesting gravity!

DANG. What, isn't he to speak at all?

PUFF. Egad, I thought you'd ask me that—yes, it is a very likely thing that a minister in his situation, with the whole affairs of the nation on his head, should have time 10 to talk!—but hush! or you'll put him out.

SNEER. Put him out! how the plague can that be, if he's not going to say anything?

PUFF. There's a reason! why his part is to *think*, and how the plague do you imagine he can *think* if you keep 15 talking?

DANG. That's very true, upon my word!

[LORD BURLEIGH *comes forward, shakes his head, and exit.*]

SNEER. He is very perfect, indeed. Now pray, what did he mean by that?

PUFF. You don't take it? 20

SNEER. No I don't, upon my soul.

PUFF. Why, by that shake of the head, he gave you to understand that even tho' they had more justice in their cause and wisdom in their measures, yet, if there was not a greater spirit shown on the part of the people, the 25 country would at last fall a sacrifice to the hostile ambition of the Spanish monarchy.

SNEER. The devil!—did he mean all that by shaking his head?

PUFF. Every word of it—if he shook his head as I taught 30 him.

DANG. Ah! there certainly is a vast deal to be done on the stage by dumb show, and expression of face, and a judicious author knows how much he may trust to it.

SNEER. Oh, here are some of our old acquaintance.

[*Enter* SIR CHRISTOPHER HATTON *and*
SIR WALTER RALEIGH.

5   SIR CHRIST. *My* niece, and *your* niece too!
By Heaven, there's witchcraft in't—he could not else
Have gained their hearts.—But see where they
        approach,
Some horrid purpose lowering on their brows!
SIR WALT. Let us withdraw and mark them.

[*They withdraw.*]

10   SNEER. What is all this?
PUFF. Ah! here has been more pruning!—but the fact is, these two young ladies are also in love with Don Whiskerandos. Now, gentlemen, this scene goes entirely for what we call *situation* and *stage effect*, by which the
15 greatest applause may be obtained, without the assistance of language, sentiment, or character: pray mark!

[*Enter the two* NIECES.

FIRST NIECE. Ellena here!
She is his scorn as much as I—that is
Some comfort still!]

20   PUFF. Oh, dear madam, you are not to say that to her face!—*aside*, ma'am, *aside*. The whole scene is to be *aside*.

[FIRST NIECE. She is his scorn as much as I—that is
Some comfort still!   [*Aside.*
25   SEC. NIECE. I know he prizes not Pollina's love,
But Tilburina lords it o'er his heart.   [*Aside.*
FIRST NIECE. But see the proud destroyer of my
        peace.

Revenge is all the good I've left.   [*Aside.*
   SEC. NIECE. He comes, the false disturber of my
      quiet.
Now, vengeance, do thy worst.—   [*Aside.*

                Enter WHISKERANDOS.

   WHISK. O hateful liberty—if thus in vain
I seek my Tilburina !   5
   BOTH NIECES. And ever shalt !

   SIR CHRISTOPHER *and* SIR WALTER *come forward.*

   BOTH. Hold ! we will avenge you.
   WHISK. Hold *you*——or see your nieces bleed !
      [*The two nieces draw their two daggers to strike*
         WHISKERANDOS *; the two uncles at the*
         instant, with their two swords drawn, catch
         their two nieces' arms, and turn the points
         of their swords to WHISKERANDOS, *who*
         immediately draws two daggers, and holds
         them to the two nieces' bosoms.]

   PUFF. There's situation for you ! there's an heroic
group ! You see the ladies can't stab Whiskerandos— 10
he durst not strike them for fear of their uncles—the
uncles durst not kill him because of their nieces. I have
them all at a dead lock !—for every one of them is
afraid to let go first.
   SNEER. Why, then, they must stand there for ever !   15
   PUFF. So they would, if I hadn't a very fine contrivance for't. Now mind——

      [*Enter* BEEFEATER *with his Halberd.*

   BEEF. In the Queen's name I charge you all to drop
Your swords and daggers !
            [*They drop their swords and daggers.*]

   SNEER. That is a contrivance, indeed.   20
   PUFF. Aye—in the Queen's name.

[SIR CHRIST. Come, niece!

SIR WALTER. Come, niece! [*Exeunt with the two nieces.*

WHISK. What's he, who bids us thus renounce our
guard?

BEEF. Thou must do more—renounce thy love!

5 WHISK. Thou liest—base Beefeater!

BEEF.   Ha! Hell! the lie!

By Heaven, thou'st roused the lion in my heart!

Off, yeomen's habit!—base disguise! off! off!

[*Discovers himself, by throwing off his upper dress,
and appearing in a very fine waistcoat.*

Am I a Beefeater now?

Or beams my crest as terrible as when

10 In Biscay's Bay I took thy captive sloop?]

PUFF. There, egad! he comes out to be the very
captain of the privateer who had taken Whiskerandos
prisoner, and was himself an old lover of Tilburina's.

DANG. Admirably managed, indeed!

15 PUFF. Now, stand out of their way.

[WHISK. I thank thee, Fortune! thou hast thus
bestowed

A weapon to chastise this insolent.

                             [*Takes up one of the swords.*

BEEF. I take thy challenge, Spaniard, and I thank

Thee, Fortune, too!—   [*Takes up the other sword.*]

20 DANG. That's excellently contrived!—it seems as if
the two uncles had left their swords on purpose for them.

PUFF. No, egad, they could not help leaving them.

[WHISK. Vengeance and Tilburina!

BEEF.   Exactly so.

[*They fight, and after the usual number of wounds
given,* WHISKERANDOS *falls.*

WHISK. Oh, cursed parry!—that last thrust in tierce

25 Was fatal!—Captain, thou hast fenced well!

And Whiskerandos quits this bustling scene

For all eter——

    BEEF. ——nity—he would have added, but stern death

Cut short his being, and the noun at once !]

PUFF. Oh, my dear sir, you are too slow ; now mind me. Sir, shall I trouble you to die again ?   5

    [WHISK. And Whiskerandos quits this bustling scene

For all eter——

    BEEF. ——nity—he would have added——]

PUFF. No, sir—that 's not it—once more, of you please.

WHISK. I wish, sir, you would practise this without me—I can't stay dying here all night.   10

PUFF. Very well, we'll go over it by and by. [*Exit* WHISKERANDOS.] I must humour these gentlemen !

    [BEEF. Farewell, brave Spaniard ! and when next——]

PUFF. Dear sir, you needn't speak that speech as the body has walked off.   15

BEEF. That 's true sir—then I'll join the fleet.

PUFF. If you please. [*Exit* BEEFEATER.] Now, who comes on ?

    [*Enter* GOVERNOR, *with his hair properly disordered.*

    GOV. A hemisphere of evil planets reign !   20

And every planet sheds contagious frenzy !

My Spanish prisoner is slain ! my daughter,

Meeting the dead corse borne along, has gone

Distract !   [*A loud flourish of trumpets.*

    But hark ! I am summoned to the fort ;

Perhaps the fleets have met ! amazing crisis !   25

O Tilburina ! from thy aged father's beard

Thou'st plucked the few brown hairs which time had left !   [*Exit* GOVERNOR.

SNEER. Poor gentleman!

PUFF. Yes—and no one to blame, but his daughter!

DANG. And the planets——

PUFF. True.   Now enter Tilburina!

5   SNEER. Egad, the business comes on quick here.

PUFF. Yes, sir—now she comes in stark mad in white satin.

SNEER. Why in white satin!

PUFF. O Lud, sir, when a heroine goes mad she always
10 goes into white satin—don't she, Dangle?

DANG. Always—it's a rule.

PUFF. Yes—here it is. [*Looking at the book.*]   " Enter
Tilburina stark mad in white satin, and her confidant
stark mad in white linen."

[*Enter* TILBURINA *and* CONFIDANT *mad, according to
custom.*]

15 SNEER. But what the deuce! is the confidant to be
mad too?

PUFF. To be sure she is : the confidant is always to
do whatever her mistress does ; weep when she weeps,
smile when she smiles, go mad when she goes mad.   Now,
20 madam—but keep your madness in the background, if
you please.

[TILB. The wind whistles—the moon rises—see,
They have killed my squirrel in his cage!
Is this a grasshopper!—Ha! no, it is my
25   Whiskerandos—you shall not keep him—
I know you have him in your pocket—
An oyster may be crossed in love!—Who says
A whale's a bird?—Ha! did you call, my love?
—He's here!   He's there!—He's everywhere!
30   Ah me!   He's nowhere!   [*Exit* TILBURINA.]

PUFF. There, do you ever desire to see anybody madder
than that?

SNEER. Never, while I live!

PUFF. You observed how she mangled the metre?

DANG. Yes, egad, it was the first thing made me suspect she was out of her senses.

SNEER. And pray, what becomes of her? 5

PUFF. She is gone to throw herself into the sea, to be sure—and that brings us at once to the scene of action, and so to my catastrophe—my sea-fight, I mean.

SNEER. What, you bring that in at last?

PUFF. Yes, yes—you know my play is *called* the *Spanish* 10 *Armada*; otherwise, egad, I have no occasion for the battle at all. Now, then, for my magnificence!—my battle!—my noise!—and my procession! You are all ready?

PROMP. [*within*]. Yes, sir. 15

PUFF. Is the Thames dressed?

Enter THAMES *with two* ATTENDANTS.

THAMES. Here I am, sir.

PUFF. Very well, indeed. See, gentlemen, there's a river for you! This is blending a little of the masque with my tragedy, a new fancy, you know, and very useful 20 in my case: for as there *must be a procession*, I suppose Thames and all his tributary rivers to compliment Britannia with a fête in honour of the victory.

SNEER. But pray, who are these gentlemen in green with him? 25

PUFF. Those?—those are his banks.

SNEER. His banks?

PUFF. Yes, one crowned with alders and the other with a villa!—you take the allusions? But hey! what the plague! you have got both your banks on one side. Here, 30 sir, come round. Ever while you live, Thames, go between your banks. [*Bell rings.*] There, soh! now for't! Stand aside, my dear friends!—away, Thames!

[*Exit* THAMES *between his banks.*

[*Flourish of drums—trumpets—cannon, &c., &c.
Scene changes to the sea—the fleets engage—the
music plays "Britons, strike home".—Spanish
fleet destroyed by fireships, &c.—English fleet
advances—music plays "Rule Britannia". The
procession of all the English rivers and their
tributaries with their emblems, &c., begins with
Handel's water music, ends with a chorus, to the
march in "Judas Maccabaeus". During this
scene,* PUFF *directs and applauds everything—
then*]

PUFF. Well, pretty well—but not quite perfect. So,
ladies and gentlemen, if you please, we'll rehearse this
piece again to-morrow.

CURTAIN DROPS

VII

NINETEENTH CENTURY DRAMA

NINETEENTH CENTURY DRAMA

THE story of the drama for nearly a hundred years after the production of *The Critic* is an interesting and rather paradoxical one. There was at the same time an increase in the popularity of the drama among less educated people and a marked decrease in the quality offered to fulfil this demand. It may be that in attempting to widen its scope it lost something of its literary quality, and at the same time gained nothing in dramatic values. Social conditions doubtless had something to do with it, as they always must, the drama reflecting the social conditions of its period. The drama was now to have a wider appeal and an appeal to a different type of audience. In Elizabethan times Shakespeare could write plays with a universal and lasting appeal, but during this hundred years there were written practically no plays which have survived on their own merits. There was no lack of excellent actors, there were plenty of writers, there was the demand, and there was a supply of a sort, which included farce, burlesque, melodrama, and opera ; but it was ephemeral stuff, on the whole of poor quality, out of touch with life and human nature. This surely is an essential for the writer of both tragedy and comedy : to preserve a contact with life and reality and to translate these into terms of his own interpretative imagination. The conditions of the theatre at the time contributed in some measure to the difficulties. As was the case when Shakespeare first came to London, until the middle of the nineteenth century, there were still only three " licensed " houses — Drury Lane, Covent Garden, and, a little later, the Haymarket — which could produce Shakespeare and the " legitimate " drama. Obviously these were not enough and other theatres sprang up, but in order to outwit the Lord Chamberlain they were some-times put to strange shifts to disguise their performances as something other than they were by the introduction of music, dancing, and even performing animals, which interpolations are obviously not conducive to good drama! However, this did in fact mean that they had the advantage of greater freedom over the three controlled houses, and it led finally to the Act of 1843, whereby the ban was lifted and every properly con-ducted theatre was enabled to obtain a licence. Now was the chance for dramatists to avail themselves of this emancipation and raise the level of the drama again. However, many years passed before dramatists really succeeded in breaking away from the farces, melodramas, and hotch-potches of " borrow-ings " from all sorts of sources, both at home and abroad, and restored the drama to its rightful contact with life, wiping the fog from the mirror that its reflection might no longer be a grotesque distortion of nature.

The first English dramatist to stand out as a pioneer in this task of getting back on to the stage plays which should be English without any borrowed trimmings, which should have some relation to the life of his times and should reflect in some way social conditions, was Robertson. His comedies, written in the third quarter of the nineteenth century, fulfil all these requirements, and all have as a marked characteristic satire, not mordant and particular but ranging widely to include in its laughter many follies and foibles of different strata of con-temporary society. We have seen that this has been nearly always a characteristic of good comedy, but it was not always so in tragedy. It was the Norwegian, Henrik Ibsen, whose influence on English drama has been so great, who was the pioneer in this field. And it was he who realised and made his followers realise, although at first they misunderstood his aims, that contemporary life with its human problems *could* be made the subject of tragedy provided the figures were great enough. Tragedy is concerned with the conflict of good and evil, and in the romantic tragedy the characters were in themselves the great ones of the earth apart from this conflict, but in the domestic tragedy and in modern drama it is realised, as Ibsen realised, that in human nature and the faithful depicting of it lies the food for great drama, irrespective of the status of the protagonists.

In comedy then it is Robertson who, with his satirical plays depicting contemporary society — *Society, Caste* are titles of two of his plays — goes back to the comedy of manners and forward away from artificial comedy to a realistic comedy of life, and makes in that way an important contribution to the drama at this period. Robertson had also another characteristic which has been shown to be essential to good comedy, the ability to write witty dialogue, though in his plays it inclines perhaps to a too obvious " thrust and parry" repartee. In spite of all this his influence was not a lasting one, or rather dramatists who followed him were affected not by him but by another foreign influence coming from France, in the adaptation of plays by Sardou, of which *Diplomacy* is a notable example. Robertson's lessons were forgotten or never learned, and we swing away from his laudable attempt to get naturalism into the drama to something more artificial again. Above all, the main criterion at this period was that a play should be " well-made ", again on the model of the French Sardou, so that in that sense there was no loss in the swing of the pendulum. With Henry Arthur Jones and Pinero it swings once more to the realisation that contemporary life provides the material for the dramatist, and it is his translation of the problems, follies, and foibles of men and women into terms of his own vision that makes the dramatic work of art in tragedy and comedy.

Henry Arthur Jones made a very big step forward in his plays by his serious consideration of life for portrayal on the stage, even in his comedies. Comedy can be serious, but too great an earnestness of purpose will obtrude itself in a didactic tone, and that is a danger in comedy. It is the more serious side of drama that Jones and Sir Arthur Pinero contribute, although both wrote a great many plays with comic interest.

The work of these two marks a definite stage in progress from the mediocrity of the preceding age, but there is still a good deal of artificiality and staginess in their work. Pinero particularly is very much concerned with the French idea that the perfectly constructed play — *la pièce bien faite* — is of paramount importance. But they both move very definitely in the right direction in raising the level of the drama, giving it true importance as a work of art and not a thing designed primarily for trivial or passing amusement, and making it more closely related to life and an interpretation of life. Pinero's dialogue is noteworthy for the brilliance of wit and repartee which is an essential weapon in the armoury of the writer of good comedy; but here again what is in fact a virtue carries with it a menace — that of artificiality.

These two were pioneers and did a tremendous amount in paving the way for our modern drama, but following them comes the man whose contribution to this modern drama has been enormous — George Bernard Shaw. It is manifestly impossible to consider his work here. He has been writing plays for forty years, and in fact where he starts we may well end, at the close of the nineteenth century. The tendencies and exponents of modern drama demand a volume to themselves; these interchapters have merely tried to show the main stages of development of the drama, linking the three plays presented in this volume.

VIII

INTRODUCTION TO
THE IMPORTANCE OF BEING EARNEST

" What is the matter, Uncle Jack?   You look as if you had toothache "

(*From a contemporary photograph*)

THE IMPORTANCE OF BEING EARNEST

AT the close of the nineteenth century — *The Importance of Being Earnest* was produced three years after Shaw's first play, *Widowers' Houses* — we come to the last author represented here.

Oscar Wilde was born in Dublin on 15th October 1856, the son of Sir William Wilde, an eminent surgeon, and a mother who wrote "graceful" verse under the *nom de plume* of "Speranza". He had a brilliant academic career at Trinity College, Dublin, and Magdalen College, Oxford, where he won the Newdigate prize in 1878 with his poem *Ravenna*. He was the leader of the æsthetic cult affecting to follow the newly propounded doctrine of " Art for Art's sake ", a cult ridiculed by W. S. Gilbert in *Patience*. He wrote a good deal of poetry and prose which appealed to the few rather than the many, and in 1882 he went on a lecture tour to America, where he wrote a drama, *Vera*.

It was with his plays that he captured a wider public in England. His poems had shown signs of his most marked characteristic — a coruscating brilliance of wit, which reached its zenith in his plays. We have seen what an essential feature of the comic writer's equipment is this power, and it is particularly valuable where it is used to coat the pill of didactism. Not that this is the case with Wilde. His are " trivial comedies for serious people ". But with all his triviality there is often underneath, and sometimes not very far below the surface, a seriousness which belies the trifler. All his plays were successful on the stage mainly owing to this quality of the dialogue, which he handles with marked skill and ingenuity. Every sentence bristles with epigrams and every other line is written with paradoxical brilliance, sometimes as if he is deliberately setting

out to say exactly the opposite of what he might be expected
to say, a sort of " verbal wit-trap " which reaches its height in
The Importance of Being Earnest. Although this feature is
rather adversely commented on in a contemporary account of
the first performance, the critic goes on to say : " However,
the liveliness of the dialogue saved the piece, even rendered it
very successful ". Wilde wrote to George Alexander while the
play was being written : " The real claim of the play, if it is
to have a claim, must be in the dialogue. The plot is slight
but I think adequate. . . . Well, I think an amusing thing
with lots of fun and wit might be made ". Wilde's continual
interruptions during rehearsals were so disconcerting that no
scene could be taken right through. As the date of production
drew nearer Alexander said to him : " We know now everything
you want, and if you'll leave us alone . . . we shall try our best
to give it to you. But if you don't we shall never be ready.
So I'll send you a box for the first night and see you again
after the performance ". Apparently Wilde was a little taken
aback ; but then with tremendous solemnity he replied : " My
dear Aleck, I have still one more thing to say to you and to
Aynesworth. So if you will both of you come and have
supper with me to-night at the Albemarle Club I shall not
trouble you again ". When the two actors arrived with some
trepidation at the club Wilde met them in full evening dress.
He laid one friendly hand on Alexander's shoulder, the other
upon Aynesworth's. " My dear Aleck ", he said, " and my
dear Tony, I have only one thing to say to you. You are
neither of you my favourite actor. We will now go in to
supper ". After that he left the company to its own devices ! [1]

In his earlier plays — *A Woman of No Importance* (1893),
The Ideal Husband (1895), and *Lady Windermere's Fan* (1892)
— he is trying his hand at the more serious problem-play with
a strong dash of sentimentalism and an artificial staginess
common to the drama before Jones and Pinero, and in this
sense he looks back rather than marches forward.

[1] " George Alexander and the St James Theatre ", by A. E. W. Mason.

There is no problem, however, in *The Importance of Being Earnest*, unless it be the problem of Mr Worthing's ancestral handbag ! The whole tone of the play is farcical from cucumber sandwiches to muffins, and the ending is as much burlesque as the recognition scene in Puff's drama in *The Critic*. Wilde himself described the play in these words : " The first Act is ingenious, the second beautiful and the third abominably clever". The whole thing is "abominably clever" and dexterously worked out. The play scintillates, and often he indulges in sheer verbal absurdity as, for example, in the passage between Algernon and Cecily about missing a business appointment. Here again in this very virtue lies the danger of artificiality, and even in the society Wilde is portraying — he never strays far from Mayfair, the problems of the middle and working classes come later to inspire dramatists — it is difficult to believe that his characters really spoke like that, some of them might some of the time but not all of them all the time ! Wilde is, however, following the convention of the artificial comedy of contemporary manners, as did Wycherley and Congreve, and, to quote Puff, " Heaven forbid they should not in a free country " talk as they do ! In any case this is not realism, and art must always temper realism in the drama.

An interesting feature of the opening stages of the first Act is Wilde's use of " expectation in preference to surprise as a dramatic motive ", a phrase which Coleridge used of Shakespeare's comedies. It is always a telling device for achieving dramatic irony whereby the audience is in possession of a secret not shared by some of the actors. Sheridan in *The Rivals* quickly lets us know that Ensign Beverley and Captain Jack Absolute are one and the same person. Here Wilde soon introduces us to the knowledge of Jack Worthing's mythical brother, Ernest, and Algernon's account of his " incomparable " invalid friend. Algernon's obvious noting of Jack's country address serves to show us whither his " Bunburying " is to lead him.

The characters, though not by any means all entirely convincing, are on the whole well drawn. Lady Bracknell is an excellent portrait of the society " gorgon " ; Lane the perfect butler in the stage convention. Algy and Jack are alike but neatly differentiated, and Gwendolen and Cecily are interesting " modern " young women.

But it is the dialogue in this brilliant satire of the aristocracy which gave the play its first popularity, and has ensured for it some continuance of public favour, as its comparatively recent production at a London theatre and its more recent broadcasting serve to show. It is admittedly trivial. Mr St John Ervine has recently advanced a theory that great drama as a form of art can only emerge when a people is great, and that if the drama is trivial the fault lies in ourselves because we are trivial. It is an interesting theory, and is obviously true in the case of Shakespeare and the Elizabethan age, which was so gloriously robust in every way. It is of course particularly true of tragedy. Comedy can legitimately concern itself with the more trivial idiosyncrasies and follies of mankind and society, as so many of the great comic writers have proved.

However, despite the tremendous popularity of first the silent picture and then the talking films, the drama to-day is healthy, and the fact that it is particularly flourishing in the hands of the people in various amateur societies and in schools is in itself a really hopeful sign. Every kind of entertainment has its vogue to-day, but the dramatists whose work has lived through the ages and who will always prove to be the immortals are those who go to life for their plays, even if in comedy it is only a current folly they are mocking. It is significant perhaps that at its greatest period — the Shakespearean era — our drama was a poetic drama, and though it is not apparently suited to modern comedy, it may well be that we shall again achieve dramatic greatness when the drama returns, as with some dramatists it has shown signs of doing, to the poetic drama, not necessarily in form but in spirit.

IX

THE IMPORTANCE OF BEING EARNEST

A TRIVIAL COMEDY FOR SERIOUS PEOPLE

BY

OSCAR WILDE

THE PERSONS OF THE PLAY

JOHN WORTHING, J.P.
ALGERNON MONCRIEFF
REV. CANON CHASUBLE, D.D.
MERRIMAN, *Butler*
LANE, *Manservant*

LADY BRACKNELL
HON. GWENDOLEN FAIRFAX
CECILY CARDEW
MISS PRISM, *Governess*

THE SCENES OF THE PLAY

LONDON: ST JAMES'S THEATRE

Lessee and Manager : Mr George Alexander
14th February 1895

JOHN WORTHING, J.P. . . .	*Mr George Alexander*
ALGERNON MONCRIEFF . . .	*Mr Allen Aynesworth*
REV. CANON CHASUBLE, D.D. . .	*Mr H. H. Vincent*
MERRIMAN, *Butler* . . .	*Mr Frank Dyall*
LANE, *Manservant* . . .	*Mr F. Kinsey Peile*
LADY BRACKNELL . . .	*Miss Rose Leclercq*
HON. GWENDOLEN FAIRFAX .	*Miss Irene Vanbrugh*
CECILY CARDEW . . .	*Miss Evelyn Millard*
MISS PRISM, *Governess* . .	*Mrs George Canninge*

THE IMPORTANCE OF BEING EARNEST

FIRST ACT

SCENE.—*Morning-room in Algernon's flat in Half-Moon Street. The room is luxuriously and artistically furnished. The sound of a piano is heard in the adjoining room.*

LANE *is arranging afternoon tea on the table, and after the music has ceased,* ALGERNON *enters.*

ALGERNON. Did you hear what I was playing, Lane ?

LANE. I didn't think it polite to listen, sir.

ALGERNON. I'm sorry for that, for your sake. I don't play accurately—any one can play accurately—but I play with wonderful expression. As far as the piano is concerned, sentiment is my forte. I keep science for Life. 5

LANE. Yes, sir.

ALGERNON. And, speaking of the science of Life, have you got the cucumber sandwiches cut for Lady Bracknell ?

LANE. Yes, sir. [*Hands them on a salver.*] 10

ALGERNON [*inspects them, takes two, and sits down on the sofa*]. Oh ! . . . by the way, Lane, I see from your book that on Thursday night, when Lord Shoreman and Mr Worthing were dining with me, eight bottles of champagne are entered as having been consumed. 15

LANE. Yes, sir ; eight bottles and a pint.

ALGERNON. Why is it that at a bachelor's establishment the servants invariably drink the champagne ? I ask merely for information.

LANE. I attribute it to the superior quality of the wine, 20 sir. I have often observed that in married households the champagne is rarely of a first-rate brand.

ALGERNON. Good heavens ! Is marriage so demoralising as that ?

5 LANE. I believe it *is* a very pleasant state, sir. I have had very little experience of it myself up to the present. I have only been married once. That was in consequence of a misunderstanding between myself and a young person.

ALGERNON [*languidly*]. I don't know that I am much
10 interested in your family life, Lane.

LANE. No, sir ; it is not a very interesting subject. I never think of it myself.

ALGERNON. Very natural, I am sure. That will do, Lane, thank you.

15 LANE. Thank you, sir.   [LANE *goes out*.

ALGERNON. Lane's views on marriage seem somewhat lax. Really, if the lower orders don't set us a good example, what on earth is the use of them ? They seem, as a class, to have absolutely no sense of moral responsibility.

Enter LANE.

LANE. Mr Ernest Worthing.

Enter JACK. LANE *goes out*.

20 ALGERNON. How are you, my dear Ernest ? What brings you up to town ?

JACK. Oh, pleasure, pleasure ! What else should bring one anywhere ? Eating as usual, I see, Algy !

ALGERNON [*stiffly*]. I believe it is customary in good
25 society to take some slight refreshment at five o'clock. Where have you been since last Thursday ?

JACK [*sitting down on the sofa*]. In the country.

ALGERNON. What on earth do you do there ?

JACK [*pulling off his gloves*]. When one is in town one
30 amuses oneself. When one is in the country one amuses other people. It is excessively boring.

ALGERNON. And who are the people you amuse ?

JACK [*airily*]. Oh, neighbours, neighbours.

ALGERNON. Got nice neighbours in your part of Shropshire ?

JACK. Perfectly horrid ! Never speak to one of them. 5

ALGERNON. How immensely you must amuse them ! [*Goes over and takes sandwich.*] By the way, Shropshire is your county, is it not ?

JACK. Eh ? Shropshire ? Yes, of course. Hallo ! Why all these cups ? Why cucumber sandwiches ? Why such 10 reckless extravagance in one so young ? Who is coming to tea ?

ALGERNON. Oh ! merely Aunt Augusta and Gwendolen.

JACK. How perfectly delightful !

ALGERNON. Yes, that is all very well ; but I am afraid 15 Aunt Augusta won't quite approve of your being here.

JACK. May I ask why ?

ALGERNON. My dear fellow, the way you flirt with Gwendolen is perfectly disgraceful. It is almost as bad as the way Gwendolen flirts with you. 20

JACK. I am in love with Gwendolen. I have come up to town expressly to propose to her.

ALGERNON. I thought you had come up for pleasure ? . . . I call that business.

JACK. How utterly unromantic you are ! 25

ALGERNON. I really don't see anything romantic in proposing. It is very romantic to be in love. But there is nothing romantic about a definite proposal. Why, one may be accepted. One usually is, I believe. Then the excitement is all over. The very essence of romance is uncertainty. 30 If ever I get married, I 'll certainly try to forget the fact.

JACK. I have no doubt about that, dear Algy. The Divorce Court was specially invented for people whose memories are so curiously constituted.

ALGERNON. Oh ! there is no use speculating on that sub- 35 ject. Divorces are made in Heaven—— [JACK *puts out*

his hand to take a sandwich. ALGERNON *at once interferes.*]
Please don't touch the cucumber sandwiches. They are
ordered specially for Aunt Augusta. [*Takes one and eats it.*]

JACK. Well, you have been eating them all the time.

5   ALGERNON. That is quite a different matter. She is
my aunt. [*Takes plate from below*] Have some bread
and butter. The bread and butter is for Gwendolen.
Gwendolen is devoted to bread and butter.

JACK [*advancing to table and helping himself*]. And very
10 good bread and butter it is too.

ALGERNON. Well, my dear fellow, you need not eat as
if you were going to eat it all. You behave as if you were
married to her already. You are not married to her
already, and I don't think you ever will be.

15   JACK. Why on earth do you say that?

ALGERNON. Well, in the first place girls never marry the
men they flirt with. Girls don't think it right.

JACK. Oh, that is nonsense!

ALGERNON. It isn't. It is a great truth. It accounts
20 for the extraordinary number of bachelors that one sees
all over the place. In the second place, I don't give my
consent.

JACK. Your consent!

ALGERNON. My dear fellow, Gwendolen is my first
25 cousin. And before I allow you to marry her, you will
have to clear up the whole question of Cecily. [*Rings bell.*]

JACK. Cecily! What on earth do you mean? What
do you mean, Algy, by Cecily! I don't know any one of
the name of Cecily.

Enter LANE.

30   ALGERNON. Bring me that cigarette case Mr Worthing
left in the smoking-room the last time he dined here.

LANE. Yes, sir.   [LANE *goes out.*

JACK. Do you mean to say you have had my cigarette
case all this time? I wish to goodness you had let me

know. I have been writing frantic letters to Scotland Yard about it. I was very nearly offering a large reward.

ALGERNON. Well, I wish you would offer one. I happen to be more than usually hard up.

JACK. There is no good offering a large reward now that the thing is found.

Enter LANE *with the cigarette case on a salver.*
ALGERNON *takes it at once.* LANE *goes out.*

ALGERNON. I think that is rather mean of you, Ernest, I must say. [*Opens case and examines it.*] However, it makes no matter, for, now that I look at the inscription inside, I find that the thing isn't yours after all.

JACK. Of course it's mine. [*Moving to him.*] You have seen me with it a hundred times, and you have no right whatsoever to read what is written inside. It is a very ungentlemanly thing to read a private cigarette case.

ALGERNON. Oh! it is absurd to have a hard and fast rule about what one should read and what one shouldn't. More than half of modern culture depends on what one shouldn't read.

JACK. I am quite aware of the fact, and I don't propose to discuss modern culture. It isn't the sort of thing one should talk of in private. I simply want my cigarette case back.

ALGERNON. Yes ; but this isn't your cigarette case. This cigarette case is a present from some one of the name of Cicely, and you said you didn't know any one of that name.

JACK. Well, if you want to know, Cecily happens to be my aunt.

ALGERNON. Your aunt !

JACK. Yes. Charming old lady she is, too. Lives at Tunbridge Wells. Just give it back to me, Algy.

ALGERNON [*retreating to back of sofa*]. But why does she call herself little Cecily if she is your aunt and lives at

Tunbridge Wells ?   [*Reading*] " From little Cecily with her fondest love."

JACK [*moving to sofa and kneeling upon it*]. My dear fellow, what on earth is there in that ?   Some aunts are
5 tall, some aunts are not tall.   That is a matter that surely an aunt may be allowed to decide for herself.   You seem to think that every aunt should be exactly like your aunt ! That is absurd.   For Heaven's sake give me back my cigarette case.   [*Follows* ALGERNON *round the room.*]

10   ALGERNON.   Yes.   But why does your aunt call you her uncle ?   " From little Cecily, with her fondest love to her dear Uncle Jack."   There is no objection, I admit, to an aunt being a small aunt, but why an aunt, no matter what her size may be, should call her own nephew her
15 uncle, I can't quite make out.   Besides, your name isn't Jack at all ; it is Ernest.

JACK.   It isn't Ernest ; it 's Jack.

ALGERNON.   You have always told me it was Ernest.   I have introduced you to every one as Ernest.   You answer
20 to the name of Ernest.   You look as if your name was Ernest.   You are the most earnest-looking person I ever saw in my life.   It is perfectly absurd your saying that your name isn't Ernest.   It 's on your cards.   Here is one of them.   [*Taking it from case*] " Mr Ernest Worthing,
25 B. 4, The Albany."   I 'll keep this as a proof that your name is Ernest if ever you attempt to deny it to me, or to Gwendolen, or to any one else.   [*Puts the card in his pocket.*]

JACK.   Well, my name is Ernest in town and Jack in
30 the country, and the cigarette case was given to me in the country.

ALGERNON.   Yes, but that does not account for the fact that your small Aunt Cecily, who lives at Tunbridge Wells, calls you her dear uncle.   Come, old boy, you had
35 much better have the thing out at once.

JACK.   My dear Algy, you talk exactly as if you were

a dentist. It is very vulgar to talk like a dentist when one isn't a dentist. It produces a false impression.

ALGERNON. Well, that is exactly what dentists always do. Now, go on! Tell me the whole thing. I may mention that I have always suspected you of being a confirmed and secret Bunburyist; and I am quite sure of it now.

JACK. Bunburyist? What on earth do you mean by a Bunburyist?

ALGERNON. I'll reveal to you the meaning of that incomparable expression as soon as you are kind enough to inform me why you are Ernest in town and Jack in the country.

JACK. Well, produce my cigarette case first.

ALGERNON. Here it is. [*Hands cigarette case.*] Now produce your explanation, and pray make it improbable. [*Sits on sofa.*]

JACK. My dear fellow, there is nothing improbable about my explanation at all. In fact it's perfectly ordinary. Old Mr Thomas Cardew, who adopted me when I was a little boy, made me in his will guardian to his grand-daughter, Miss Cecily Cardew. Cecily, who addresses me as her uncle from motives of respect that you could not possibly appreciate, lives at my place in the country under the charge of her admirable governess, Miss Prism.

ALGERNON. Where is that place in the country, by the way?

JACK. That is nothing to you, dear boy. You are not going to be invited. . . . I may tell you candidly that the place is not in Shropshire.

ALGERNON. I suspected that, my dear fellow! I have Bunburyed all over Shropshire on two separate occasions. Now, go on. Why are you Ernest in town and Jack in the country?

JACK. My dear Algy, I don't know whether you will be

able to understand my real motives. You are hardly serious enough. When one is placed in the position of guardian, one has to adopt a very high moral tone on all subjects. It 's one's duty to do so. And as a high moral tone can hardly be said to conduce very much to either one's health or one's happiness, in order to get up to town I have always pretended to have a younger brother of the name of Ernest, who lives in the Albany, and gets into the most dreadful scrapes. That, my dear Algy, is the whole truth pure and simple.

ALGERNON. The truth is rarely pure and never simple. Modern life would be very tedious if it were either, and modern literature a complete impossibility !

JACK. That wouldn't be at all a bad thing.

ALGERNON. Literary criticism is not your forte, my dear fellow. Don't try it. You should leave that to people who haven't been at a University. They do it so well in the daily papers. What you really are is a Bunburyist. I was quite right in saying you were a Bunburyist. You are one of the most advanced Bunburyists I know.

JACK. What on earth do you mean ?

ALGERNON. You have invented a very useful younger brother called Ernest, in order that you may be able to come up to town as often as you like. I have invented an invaluable permanent invalid called Bunbury, in order that I may be able to go down into the country whenever I choose. Bunbury is perfectly invaluable. If it wasn't for Bunbury's extraordinary bad health, for instance, I wouldn't be able to dine with you at Willis's to-night, for I have been really engaged to Aunt Augusta for more than a week.

JACK. I haven't asked you to dine with me anywhere to-night.

ALGERNON. I know. You are absurdly careless about sending out invitations. It is very foolish of you. Nothing annoys people so much as not receiving invitations.

JACK. You had much better dine with your Aunt Augusta.

ALGERNON. I haven't the smallest intention of doing anything of the kind. To begin with, I dined there on Monday, and once a week is quite enough to dine with one's own relations. In the second place, whenever I do dine there I am always treated as a member of the family, and sent down with either no woman at all, or two. In the third place, I know perfectly well whom she will place me next to, to-night. She will place me next Mary Farquhar, who always flirts with her own husband across the dinner-table. That is not very pleasant. Indeed, it is not even decent . . . and that sort of thing is enormously on the increase. The amount of women in London who flirt with their own husbands is perfectly scandalous. It looks so bad. It is simply washing one's clean linen in public. Besides, now that I know you to be a confirmed Bunburyist I naturally want to talk to you about Bunburying. I want to tell you the rules.

JACK. I'm not a Bunburyist at all. If Gwendolen accepts me, I am going to kill my brother, indeed I think I'll kill him in any case. Cecily is a little too much interested in him. It is rather a bore. So I am going to get rid of Ernest. And I strongly advise you to do the same with Mr . . . with your invalid friend who has the absurd name.

ALGERNON. Nothing will induce me to part with Bunbury, and if you ever get married, which seems to me extremely problematic, you will be very glad to know Bunbury. A man who marries without knowing Bunbury has a very tedious time of it.

JACK. That is nonsense. If I marry a charming girl like Gwendolen, and she is the only girl I ever saw in my life that I would marry, I certainly won't want to know Bunbury.

ALGERNON. Then your wife will. You don't seem to

realise, that in married life three is company and two is none.

JACK [*sententiously*]. That, my dear young friend, is the theory that the corrupt French Drama has been pro-
5 pounding for the last fifty years.

ALGERNON. Yes ; and that the happy English home has proved in half the time.

JACK. For heaven's sake, don't try to be cynical. It 's perfectly easy to be cynical.

10 ALGERNON. My dear fellow, it isn't easy to be anything nowadays. There 's such a lot of beastly competition about. [*The sound of an electric bell is heard.*] Ah ! that must be Aunt Augusta. Only relatives, or creditors, ever ring in that Wagnerian manner. Now, if I get her out of
15 the way for ten minutes, so that you can have an oppor- tunity for proposing to Gwendolen, may I dine with you to-night at Willis's ?

JACK. I suppose so, if you want to.

ALGERNON. Yes, but you must be serious about it. I
20 hate people who are not serious about meals. It is so shallow of them.

Enter LANE.

LANE. Lady Bracknell and Miss Fairfax.

ALGERNON *goes forward to meet them. Enter*
LADY BRACKNELL *and* GWENDOLEN.

LADY BRACKNELL. Good afternoon, dear Algernon, I hope you are behaving very well.

25 ALGERNON. I'm feeling very well, Aunt Augusta.

LADY BRACKNELL. That 's not quite the same thing. In fact the two things rarely go together. [*Sees* JACK *and bows to him with icy coldness.*]

ALGERNON [*to* GWENDOLEN]. Dear me, you are smart !

30 GWENDOLEN. I am always smart ! Am I not, Mr Worthing ?

JACK. You 're quite perfect, Miss Fairfax.

GWENDOLEN. Oh ! I hope I am not that. It would leave no room for developments, and I intend to develop in many directions. [GWENDOLEN *and* JACK *sit down together in the corner.*]

LADY BRACKNELL. I 'm sorry if we are a little late, Algernon, but I was obliged to call on dear Lady Harbury. I hadn't been there since her poor husband's death. I never saw a woman so altered ; she looks quite twenty years younger. And now I 'll have a cup of tea, and one of those nice cucumber sandwiches you promised me.

ALGERNON. Certainly, Aunt Augusta. [*Goes over to tea-table.*]

LADY BRACKNELL. Won't you come and sit here, Gwendolen ?

GWENDOLEN. Thanks, mamma, I 'm quite comfortable where I am.

ALGERNON [*picking up empty plate in horror*]. Good heavens ! Lane ! Why are there no cucumber sand-wiches ? I ordered them specially.

LANE [*gravely*]. There were no cucumbers in the market this morning, sir. I went down twice.

ALGERNON. No cucumbers !

LANE. No, sir. Not even for ready money.

ALGERNON. That will do, Lane, thank you.

LANE. Thank you, sir. [*Goes out.*

ALGERNON. I am greatly distressed, Aunt Augusta, about there being no cucumbers, not even for ready money.

LADY BRACKNELL. It really makes no matter, Algernon. I had some crumpets with Lady Harbury, who seems to me to be living entirely for pleasure now.

ALGERNON. I hear her hair has turned quite gold from grief.

LADY BRACKNELL. It certainly has changed its colour. From what cause I, of course, cannot say. [ALGERNON *crosses and hands tea.*] Thank you. I 've quite a treat for you to-night, Algernon. I am going to send you down with Mary Farquhar. She is such a nice woman, and so attentive to her husband. It 's delightful to watch them.

ALGERNON. I am afraid, Aunt Augusta, I shall have to
5 give up the pleasure of dining with you to-night after all.

LADY BRACKNELL [*frowning*]. I hope not, Algernon. It would put my table completely out. Your uncle would have to dine upstairs. Fortunately he is accustomed to that.

10 ALGERNON. It is a great bore, and, I need hardly say, a terrible disappointment to me, but the fact is I have just had a telegram to say that my poor friend Bunbury is very ill again. [*Exchanges glances with* JACK.] They seem to think I should be with him.

15 LADY BRACKNELL. It is very strange. This Mr Bunbury seems to suffer from curiously bad health.

ALGERNON. Yes ; poor Bunbury is a dreadful invalid.

LADY BRACKNELL. Well, I must say, Algernon, that I think it is high time that Mr Bunbury made up his mind
20 whether he was going to live or to die. This shilly-shally-ing with the question is absurd. Nor do I in any way approve of the modern sympathy with invalids. I con-sider it morbid. Illness of any kind is hardly a thing to be encouraged in others. Health is the primary duty of
25 life. I am always telling that to your poor uncle, but he never seems to take much notice . . . as far as any im-provement in his ailment goes. I should be much obliged if you would ask Mr Bunbury, from me, to be kind enough not to have a relapse on Saturday, for I rely on you to
30 arrange my music for me. It is my last reception, and one wants something that will encourage conversation, particularly at the end of the season when every one has practically said whatever they had to say, which, in most cases, was probably not much.

35 ALGERNON. I 'll speak to Bunbury, Aunt Augusta, if he is still conscious, and I think I can promise you he 'll be

all right by Saturday. Of course the music is a great difficulty. You see, if one plays good music, people don't listen, and if one plays bad music people don't talk. But I 'll run over the programme I 've drawn out, if you will kindly come into the next room for a moment. 5

LADY BRACKNELL. Thank you, Algernon. It is very thoughtful of you. [*Rising, and following* ALGERNON.] I 'm sure the programme will be delightful, after a few expurgations. French songs I cannot possibly allow. People always seem to think that they are improper, and 10 either look shocked, which is vulgar, or laugh, which is worse. But German sounds a thoroughly respectable language, and indeed, I believe is so. Gwendolen, you will accompany me.

GWENDOLEN. Certainly, mamma. 15

[LADY BRACKNELL *and* ALGERNON *go into the music-room*, GWENDOLEN *remains behind*.

JACK. Charming day it has been, Miss Fairfax.

GWENDOLEN. Pray don't talk to me about the weather, Mr Worthing. Whenever people talk to me about the weather, I always feel quite certain that they mean something else. And that makes me so nervous. 20

JACK. I do mean something else.

GWENDOLEN. I thought so. In fact, I am never wrong.

JACK. And I would like to be allowed to take advantage of Lady Bracknell's temporary absence . . .

GWENDOLEN. I would certainly advise you to do so. 25 Mamma has a way of coming back suddenly into a room that I have often had to speak to her about.

JACK [*nervously*]. Miss Fairfax, ever since I met you I have admired you more than any girl . . . I have ever met since . . . I met you. 30

GWENDOLEN. Yes, I am quite well aware of the fact. And I often wish that in public, at any rate, you had been more demonstrative. For me you have always had an irresistible fascination. Even before I met you I was far

from indifferent to you. [JACK *looks at her in amazement.*]
We live, as I hope you know, Mr Worthing, in an age of
ideals. The fact is constantly mentioned in the more
expensive monthly magazines, and has reached the pro-
5 vincial pulpits, I am told ; and my ideal has always been
to love some one of the name of Ernest. There is something in that name that inspires absolute confidence.
The moment Algernon first mentioned to me that he
had a friend called Ernest, I knew I was destined to love
10 you.

JACK. You really love me, Gwendolen ?

GWENDOLEN. Passionately !

JACK. Darling ! You don't know how happy you 've
made me.

15 GWENDOLEN. My own Ernest !

JACK. But you don't really mean to say that you
couldn't love me if my name wasn't Ernest ?

GWENDOLEN. But your name is Ernest.

JACK. Yes, I know it is. But supposing it was some-
20 thing else ? Do you mean to say you couldn't love me
then ?

GWENDOLEN [*glibly*]. Ah ! that is clearly a metaphysical
speculation, and like most metaphysical speculations has
very little reference at all to the actual facts of real life,
25 as we know them.

JACK. Personally, darling, to speak quite candidly, I
don't much care about the name of Ernest. . . . I don't
think the name suits me at all.

GWENDOLEN. It suits you perfectly. It is a divine
30 name. It has a music of its own. It produces vibrations.

JACK. Well, really, Gwendolen, I must say that I think
there are lots of other much nicer names. I think Jack,
for instance, a charming name.

GWENDOLEN. Jack ? . . . No, there is very little music
35 in the name Jack, if any at all, indeed. It does not thrill.
It produces absolutely no vibrations. . . . I have known

several Jacks, and they all, without exception, were more than usually plain. Besides, Jack is a notorious domesticity for John ! And I pity any woman who is married to a man called John. She would probably never be allowed to know the entrancing pleasure of a single moment's solitude. The only really safe name is Ernest.

JACK. Gwendolen, I must get christened at once—I mean we must get married at once. There is no time to be lost.

GWENDOLEN. Married, Mr Worthing ?

JACK [*astounded*]. Well . . . surely. You know that I love you, and you led me to believe, Miss Fairfax, that you were not absolutely indifferent to me.

GWENDOLEN. I adore you. But you haven't proposed to me yet. Nothing has been said at all about marriage. The subject has not even been touched on.

JACK. Well . . . may I propose to you now ?

GWENDOLEN. I think it would be an admirable opportunity. And to spare you any possible disappointment, Mr Worthing, I think it only fair to tell you quite frankly beforehand that I am fully determined to accept you.

JACK. Gwendolen !

GWENDOLEN. Yes, Mr Worthing, what have you got to say to me ?

JACK. You know what I have got to say to you.

GWENDOLEN. Yes, but you don't say it.

JACK. Gwendolen, will you marry me ? [*Goes on his knees.*]

GWENDOLEN. Of course I will, darling. How long you have been about it ! I am afraid you have had very little experience in how to propose.

JACK. My own one, I have never loved any one in the world but you.

GWENDOLEN. Yes, but men often propose for practice. I know my brother Gerald does. All my girl-friends tell me so. What wonderfully blue eyes you have, Ernest !

19 Q

They are quite, quite, blue. I hope you will always look at me just like that, especially when there are other people present.

Enter LADY BRACKNELL.

LADY BRACKNELL. Mr Worthing! Rise, sir, from this
5 semi-recumbent posture. It is most indecorous.

GWENDOLEN. Mamma! [*He tries to rise; she restrains him.*] I must beg you to retire. This is no place for you. Besides, Mr Worthing has not quite finished yet.

LADY BRACKNELL. Finished what, may I ask?

10 GWENDOLEN. I am engaged to Mr Worthing, mamma. [*They rise together.*]

LADY BRACKNELL. Pardon me, you are not engaged to any one. When you do become engaged to some one, I, or your father, should his health permit him, will inform
15 you of the fact. An engagement should come on a young girl as a surprise, pleasant or unpleasant, as the case may be. It is hardly a matter that she could be allowed to arrange for herself. . . . And now I have a few questions to put to you, Mr Worthing. While I am making these
20 inquiries, you, Gwendolen, will wait for me below in the carriage.

GWENDOLEN [*reproachfully*]. Mamma!

LADY BRACKNELL. In the carriage, Gwendolen! [GWEN-DOLEN *goes to the door. She and* JACK *blow kisses to each
25 other behind* LADY BRACKNELL'S *back.* LADY BRACKNELL *looks vaguely about as if she could not understand what the noise was. Finally turns round.*] Gwendolen, the carriage!

GWENDOLEN. Yes, mamma. [*Goes out, looking back at* JACK.]

30 LADY BRACKNELL [*sitting down*]. You can take a seat, Mr Worthing.

[*Looks in her pocket for note-book and pencil.*

JACK. Thank you, Lady Bracknell, I prefer standing.

LADY BRACKNELL [*pencil and note-book in hand*]. I feel

bound to tell you that you are not down on my list of eligible young men, although I have the same list as the dear Duchess of Bolton has. We work together, in fact. However, I am quite ready to enter your name, should your answers be what a really affectionate mother re- 5 quires. Do you smoke ?

JACK. Well, yes, I must admit I smoke.

LADY BRACKNELL. I am glad to hear it. A man should always have an occupation of some kind. There are far too many idle men in London as it is. How old are you ? 10

JACK. Twenty-nine.

LADY BRACKNELL. A very good age to be married at. I have always been of opinion that a man who desires to get married should know either everything or nothing. Which do you know ? 15

JACK [*after some hesitation*]. I know nothing, Lady Bracknell.

LADY BRACKNELL. I am pleased to hear it. I do not approve of anything that tampers with natural ignorance. Ignorance is like a delicate exotic fruit ; touch it and the 20 bloom is gone. The whole theory of modern education is radically unsound. Fortunately in England, at any rate, education produces no effect whatsoever. If it did, it would prove a serious danger to the upper classes, and probably lead to acts of violence in Grosvenor Square. 25 What is your income ?

JACK. Between seven and eight thousand a year.

LADY BRACKNELL [*makes a note in her book*]. In land, or in investments ?

JACK. In investments, chiefly. 30

LADY BRACKNELL. That is satisfactory. What between the duties expected of one during one's lifetime, and the duties exacted from one after one's death, land has ceased to be either a profit or a pleasure. It gives one position, and prevents one from keeping it up. That 's all that 35 can be said about land.

JACK. I have a country house with some land, of course, attached to it, about fifteen hundred acres, I believe ; but I don't depend on that for my real income. In fact, as far as I can make out, the poachers are the
5 only people who make anything out of it.

LADY BRACKNELL. A country house ! How many bed-rooms ? Well, that point can be cleared up afterwards. You have a town house, I hope ? A girl with a simple, unspoiled nature, like Gwendolen, could hardly be expected
10 to reside in the country.

JACK. Well, I own a house in Belgrave Square, but it is let by the year to Lady Bloxham. Of course, I can get it back whenever I like, at six months' notice.

LADY BRACKNELL. Lady Bloxham ? I don't know her.

15 JACK. Oh, she goes about very little. She is a lady considerably advanced in years.

LADY BRACKNELL. Ah, nowadays that is no guarantee of respectability of character. What number in Belgrave Square ?

20 JACK. 149.

LADY BRACKNELL [*shaking her head*]. The unfashionable side. I thought there was something. However, that could easily be altered.

JACK. Do you mean the fashion, or the side ?

25 LADY BRACKNELL [*sternly*]. Both, if necessary, I pre-sume. What are your politics ?

JACK. Well, I am afraid I really have none. I am a Liberal Unionist.

LADY BRACKNELL. Oh, they count as Tories. They
30 dine with us. Or come in the evening, at any rate. Now to minor matters. Are your parents living ?

JACK. I have lost both my parents.

LADY BRACKNELL. To lose one parent, Mr Worthing, may be regarded as a misfortune ; to lose both looks like
35 carelessness. Who was your father ? He was evidently a man of some wealth. Was he born in what the Radical

papers call the purple of commerce, or did he rise from the ranks of the aristocracy?

JACK. I am afraid I really don't know. The fact is, Lady Bracknell, I said I had lost my parents. It would be nearer the truth to say that my parents seem to have lost me. . . . I don't actually know who I am by birth. I was . . . well, I was found.

LADY BRACKNELL. Found!

JACK. The late Mr Thomas Cardew, an old gentleman of a very charitable and kindly disposition, found me, and gave me the name of Worthing, because he happened to have a first-class ticket for Worthing in his pocket at the time. Worthing is a place in Sussex. It is a seaside resort.

LADY BRACKNELL. Where did the charitable gentleman who had a first-class ticket for this seaside resort find you?

JACK [*gravely*]. In a hand-bag.

LADY BRACKNELL. A hand-bag?

JACK [*very seriously*]. Yes, Lady Bracknell. I was in a hand-bag—a somewhat large, black leather hand-bag, with handles to it—an ordinary hand-bag in fact.

LADY BRACKNELL. In what locality did this Mr James, or Thomas, Cardew come across this ordinary hand-bag?

JACK. In the cloak-room at Victoria Station. It was given to him in mistake for his own.

LADY BRACKNELL. The cloak-room at Victoria Station?

JACK. Yes. The Brighton line.

LADY BRACKNELL. The line is immaterial. Mr Worthing, I confess I feel somewhat bewildered by what you have just told me. To be born, or at any rate bred, in a hand-bag, whether it had handles or not, seems to me to display a contempt for the ordinary decencies of family life that reminds one of the worst excesses of the French Revolution. And I presume you know what that unfortunate movement led to? As for the particular locality in which the hand-bag was found, a cloak-room at a railway station might serve to conceal a social in-discretion—has probably, indeed, been used for that purpose before now—but it could hardly be regarded as an assured basis for a recognised position in good society.

5 JACK. May I ask you then what you would advise me to do ? I need hardly say I would do anything in the world to ensure Gwendolen's happiness.

LADY BRACKNELL. I would strongly advise you, Mr Worthing, to try and acquire some relations as soon as 10 possible, and to make a definite effort to produce at any rate one parent, of either sex, before the season is quite over.

JACK. Well, I don't see how I could possibly manage to do that. I can produce the hand-bag at any moment. 15 It is in my dressing-room at home. I really think that should satisfy you, Lady Bracknell.

LADY BRACKNELL. Me, sir ! What has it to do with me ? You can hardly imagine that I and Lord Bracknell would dream of allowing our only daughter—a girl 20 brought up with the utmost care—to marry into a cloak-room, and form an alliance with a parcel. Good morning, Mr Worthing !

[LADY BRACKNELL *sweeps out in majestic in-dignation.*]

JACK. Good morning ! [ALGERNON, *from the other room, strikes up the Wedding March.* JACK *looks perfectly furious,* 25 *and goes to the door.*] For goodness' sake don't play that ghastly tune, Algy ! How idiotic you are !

[*The music stops and* ALGERNON *enters cheerily.*

ALGERNON. Didn't it go off all right, old boy ? You don't mean to say Gwendolen refused you ? I know it is a way she has. She is always refusing people. I think 30 it is most ill-natured of her.

JACK. Oh, Gwendolen is as right as a trivet. As far as she is concerned, we are engaged. Her mother is perfectly unbearable. Never met such a Gorgon. . . . I don't really know what a Gorgon is like, but I am quite sure that Lady Bracknell is one. In any case, she is a monster, without being a myth, which is rather unfair. . . . I beg your pardon, Algy, I suppose I shouldn't talk about your own aunt in that way before you. 5

ALGERNON. My dear boy, I love hearing my relations abused. It is the only thing that makes me put up with them at all. Relations are simply a tedious pack of people, who haven't got the remotest knowledge of how to live, nor the smallest instinct about when to die. 10

JACK. Oh, that is nonsense !

ALGERNON. It isn't !

JACK. Well, I won't argue about the matter. You always want to argue about things.

ALGERNON. That is exactly what things were originally 15 made for.

JACK. Upon my word, if I thought that, I 'd shoot myself. . . . [A pause.] You don't think there is any chance of Gwendolen becoming like her mother in about a hundred and fifty years, do you Algy ? 20

ALGERNON. All women become like their mothers. That is their tragedy. No man does. That 's his.

JACK. Is that clever ?

ALGERNON. It is perfectly phrased ! and quite as true as any observation in civilised life should be. 25

JACK. I am sick to death of cleverness. Everybody is clever nowadays. You can't go anywhere without meeting clever people. The thing has become an absolute public nuisance. I wish to goodness we had a few fools left.

ALGERNON. We have. 30

JACK. I should extremely like to meet them. What do they talk about ?

ALGERNON. The fools ? Oh ! about the clever people, of course.

JACK. What fools. 35

ALGERNON. By the way, did you tell Gwendolen the

truth about your being Ernest in town, and Jack in the country ?

JACK [*in a very patronising manner*]. My dear fellow, the truth isn't quite the sort of thing one tells to a nice, sweet, refined girl. What extraordinary ideas you have about the way to behave to a woman !

ALGERNON. The only way to behave to a woman is to make love to her, if she is pretty, and to some one else, if she is plain.

JACK. Oh, that is nonsense.

ALGERNON. What about your brother ? What about the profligate Ernest ?

JACK. Oh, before the end of the week I shall have got rid of him. I 'll say he died in Paris of apoplexy. Lots of people die of apoplexy, quite suddenly, don't they ?

ALGERNON. Yes, but it 's hereditary, my dear fellow. It 's a sort of thing that runs in families. You had much better say a severe chill.

JACK. You are sure a severe chill isn't hereditary, or anything of that kind ?

ALGERNON. Of course it isn't !

JACK. Very well, then. My poor brother Ernest is carried off suddenly, in Paris, by a severe chill. That gets rid of him.

ALGERNON. But I thought you said that . . . Miss Cardew was a little too much interested in your poor brother Ernest ? Won't she feel his loss a good deal ?

JACK. Oh, that is all right. Cecily is not a silly romantic girl, I am glad to say. She has got a capital appetite, goes long walks, and pays no attention at all to her lessons.

ALGERNON. I would rather like to see Cecily.

JACK. I will take very good care you never do. She is excessively pretty, and she is only just eighteen.

ALGERNON. Have you told Gwendolen yet that you have an excessively pretty ward who is only just eighteen ?

JACK. Oh! one doesn't blurt these things out to people. Cecily and Gwendolen are perfectly certain to be extremely great friends. I'll bet you anything you like that half an hour after they have met, they will be calling each other sister. 5

ALGERNON. Women only do that when they have called each other a lot of other things first. Now, my dear boy, if we want to get a good table at Willis's, we really must go and dress. Do you know it is nearly seven?

JACK [*irritably*]. Oh! it always is nearly seven. 10

ALGERNON. Well, I'm hungry.

JACK. I never knew you when you weren't. . . .

ALGERNON. What shall we do after dinner? Go to a theatre?

JACK. Oh no! I loathe listening. 15

ALGERNON. Well, let us go to the Club?

JACK. Oh, no! I hate talking.

ALGERNON. Well, we might trot round to the Empire at ten?

JACK. Oh, no! I can't bear looking at things. It is 20 so silly.

ALGERNON. Well, what shall we do?

JACK. Nothing!

ALGERNON. It is awfully hard work doing nothing. However, I don't mind hard work where there is no 25 definite object of any kind.

Enter LANE.

LANE. Miss Fairfax.

Enter GWENDOLEN. LANE *goes out.*

ALGERNON. Gwendolen, upon my word!

GWENDOLEN. Algy, kindly turn your back. I have something very particular to say to Mr Worthing. 30

ALGERNON. Really, Gwendolen, I don't think I can allow this at all.

GWENDOLEN. Algy, you always adopt a strictly immoral attitude towards life. You are not quite old enough to do that.   [ALGERNON *retires to the fireplace.*

JACK. My own darling!

5   GWENDOLEN. Ernest, we may never be married. From the expression on mamma's face I fear we never shall. Few parents nowadays pay any regard to what their children say to them. The old-fashioned respect for the young is fast dying out. Whatever influence I ever had 10 over mamma, I lost at the age of three. But although she may prevent us from becoming man and wife, and I may marry some one else, and marry often, nothing that she can possibly do can alter my eternal devotion to you.

JACK. Dear Gwendolen!

15   GWENDOLEN. The story of your romantic origin, as related to me by mamma, with unpleasing comments, has naturally stirred the deeper fibres of my nature. Your Christian name has an irresistible fascination. The simplicity of your character makes you exquisitely incom-20 prehensible to me. Your town address at the Albany I have. What is your address in the country?

JACK. The Manor House, Woolton, Hertfordshire.

[ALGERNON, *who has been carefully listening, smiles to himself, and writes the address on his shirt-cuff. Then picks up the Railway Guide.*

GWENDOLEN. There is a good postal service, I suppose? It may be necessary to do something desperate. That of 25 course will require serious consideration. I will communicate with you daily.

JACK. My own one!

GWENDOLEN. How long do you remain in town?

JACK. Till Monday.

30   GWENDOLEN. Good! Algy, you may turn round now.

ALGERNON. Thanks, I've turned round already.

GWENDOLEN. You may also ring the bell.

JACK. You will let me see you to your carriage, my own darling ?

GWENDOLEN. Certainly.

JACK [*to* LANE, *who now enters*]. I will see Miss Fairfax out. 5

LANE. Yes, sir. [JACK *and* GWENDOLEN *go off.*
[LANE *presents several letters on a salver to* ALGERNON. *It is to be surmised that they are bills, as* ALGERNON, *after looking at the envelopes, tears them up.*

ALGERNON. A glass of sherry, Lane.

LANE. Yes, sir.

ALGERNON. To-morrow, Lane, I 'm going Bunburying.

LANE. Yes, sir. 10

ALGERNON. I shall probably not be back till Monday. You can put up my dress clothes, my smoking jacket, and all the Bunbury suits . . .

LANE. Yes, sir. [*Handing sherry.*]

ALGERNON. I hope to-morrow will be a fine day, Lane. 15

LANE. It never is, sir.

ALGERNON. Lane, you 're a perfect pessimist.

LANE. I do my best to give satisfaction, sir.

Enter JACK. LANE *goes off.*

JACK. There 's a sensible, intellectual girl ! the only girl I ever cared for in my life. [ALGERNON *is laugh-* 20 *ing immoderately.*] What on earth are you so amused at ?

ALGERNON. Oh, I 'm a little anxious about poor Bunbury, that is all.

JACK. If you don't take care, your friend Bunbury will 25 get you into a serious scrape some day.

ALGERNON. I love scrapes. They are the only things that are never serious.

JACK. Oh, that 's nonsense, Algy. You never talk anything but nonsense. 30

ALGERNON. Nobody ever does.

> [JACK *looks indignantly at him, and leaves the room.*
> ALGERNON *lights a cigarette, reads his shirt-cuff, and smiles.*

ACT DROP.

SECOND ACT

SCENE.—*Garden at the Manor House. A flight of grey stone steps leads up to the house. The garden, an old-fashioned one, full of roses. Time of year, July. Basket chairs, and a table covered with books, are set under a large yew-tree.*

MISS PRISM *discovered seated at the table.* CECILY *is at the back watering flowers.*

MISS PRISM [*calling*]. Cecily, Cecily! Surely such a utilitarian occupation as the watering of flowers is rather Moulton's duty than yours? Especially at a moment
5 when intellectual pleasures await you. Your German grammar is on the table. Pray open it at page fifteen. We will repeat yesterday s lesson.

CECILY [*coming over very slowly*]. But I don t like German. It isn't at all a becoming language. I know
10 perfectly well that I look quite plain after my German lesson.

MISS PRISM. Child, you know how anxious your guardian is that you should improve yourself in every way. He laid particular stress on your German, as he was leaving
15 for town yesterday. Indeed, he always lays stress on your German when he is leaving for town.

CECILY. Dear Uncle Jack is so very serious! Sometimes he is so serious that I think he cannot be quite well.

MISS PRISM [*drawing herself up*]. Your guardian enjoys the best of health, and his gravity of demeanour is especially to be commended in one so comparatively young as he is. I know no one who has a higher sense of duty and responsibility.   5

CECILY. I suppose that is why he often looks a little bored when we three are together.

MISS PRISM. Cecily! I am surprised at you. Mr Worthing has many troubles in his life. Idle merriment and triviality would be out of place in his conversation. 10 You must remember his constant anxiety about that unfortunate young man his brother.

CECILY. I wish Uncle Jack would allow that unfortunate young man, his brother, to come down here sometimes. We might have a good influence over him, Miss Prism. I 15 am sure you certainly would. You know German, and geology, and things of that kind influence a man very much. [CECILY *begins to write in her diary*.]

MISS PRISM [*shaking her head*]. I do not think that even I could produce any effect on a character that according 20 to his own brother's admission is irretrievably weak and vacillating. Indeed I am not sure that I would desire to reclaim him. I am not in favour of this modern mania for turning bad people into good people at a moment's notice. As a man sows so let him reap. You must put away your 25 diary, Cecily. I really don't see why you should keep a diary at all.

CECILY. I keep a diary in order to enter the wonderful secrets of my life. If I didn't write them down, I should probably forget all about them.   30

MISS PRISM. Memory, my dear Cecily, is the diary that we all carry about with us.

CECILY. Yes, but it usually chronicles the things that have never happened, and couldn't possibly have happened. I believe that Memory is responsible for nearly all the 35 three-volume novels that Mudie sends us.

MISS PRISM. Do not speak slightingly of the three-volume novel, Cecily. I wrote one myself in earlier days.

CECILY. Did you really, Miss Prism? How wonderfully clever you are! I hope it did not end happily? 5 I don't like novels that end happily. They depress me so much.

MISS PRISM. The good ended happily, and the bad unhappily. That is what Fiction means.

CECILY. I suppose so. But it seems very unfair. And 10 was your novel ever published?

MISS PRISM. Alas! no. The manuscript unfortunately was abandoned. [CECILY *starts.*] I use the word in the sense of lost or mislaid. To your work, child, these speculations are profitless.

15 CECILY [*smiling*]. But I see dear Dr Chasuble coming up through the garden.

MISS PRISM [*rising and advancing*]. Dr Chasuble! This is indeed a pleasure.

Enter CANON CHASUBLE.

CHASUBLE. And how are we this morning? Miss Prism, 20 you are, I trust, well?

CECILY. Miss Prism has just been complaining of a slight headache. I think it would do her so much good to have a short stroll with you in the Park, Dr Chasuble.

MISS PRISM. Cecily, I have not mentioned anything 25 about a headache.

CECILY. No, dear Miss Prism, I know that, but I felt instinctively that you had a headache. Indeed I was thinking about that, and not about my German lesson, when the Rector came in.

30 CHASUBLE. I hope, Cecily, you are not inattentive.

CECILY. Oh, I am afraid I am.

CHASUBLE. That is strange. Were I fortunate enough to be Miss Prism's pupil, I would hang upon her lips. [MISS PRISM *glares.*] I spoke metaphorically.—My meta-

phor was drawn from bees. Ahem! Mr Worthing, I
suppose, has not returned from town yet?

MISS PRISM. We do not expect him till Monday afternoon.

CHASUBLE. Ah yes, he usually likes to spend his Sunday
in London. He is not one of those whose sole aim is
enjoyment, as, by all accounts, that unfortunate young
man his brother seems to be. But I must not disturb
Egeria and her pupil any longer.

MISS PRISM. Egeria? My name is Lætitia, Doctor.

CHASUBLE [*bowing*]. A classical allusion merely, drawn
from the Pagan authors. I shall see you both no doubt
at Evensong?

MISS PRISM. I think, dear Doctor, I will have a stroll
with you. I find I have a headache after all, and a walk
might do it good.

CHASUBLE. With pleasure, Miss Prism, with pleasure.
We might go as far as the schools and back.

MISS PRISM. That would be delightful. Cecily, you will
read your Political Economy in my absence. The chapter
on the Fall of the Rupee you may omit. It is somewhat too sensational. Even these metallic problems have
their melodramatic side.

[*Goes down the garden with* DR CHASUBLE.

CECILY [*picks up books and throws them back on table*].
Horrid Political Economy. Horrid Geography! Horrid,
horrid German!

Enter MERRIMAN *with a card on a salver.*

MERRIMAN. Mr Ernest Worthing has just driven over
from the station. He has brought his luggage with him.

CECILY [*takes the card and reads it*]. "Mr Ernest
Worthing, B. 4, The Albany, W." Uncle Jack's brother!
Did you tell him Mr Worthing was in town?

MERRIMAN. Yes, Miss. He seemed very much dis-
appointed. I mentioned that you and Miss Prism were

CECILY. You are looking a little worse.

ALGERNON. That is because I am hungry.

CECILY. How thoughtless of me. I should have remembered that when one is going to lead an entirely new
5 life, one requires regular and wholesome meals. Won't you come in?

ALGERNON. Thank you. Might I have a buttonhole first? I never have any appetite unless I have a buttonhole first.

10 CECILY. A Maréchal Niel? [*Picks up scissors.*]

ALGERNON. No, I'd sooner have a pink rose.

CECILY. Why? [*Cuts a flower.*]

ALGERNON. Because you are like a pink rose, Cousin Cecily.

15 CECILY. I don't think it can be right for you to talk to me like that. Miss Prism never says such things to me.

ALGERNON. Then Miss Prism is a short-sighted old lady.
[CECILY *puts the rose in his buttonhole.*] You are the prettiest girl I ever saw.

20 CECILY. Miss Prism says that all good looks are a snare.

ALGERNON. They are a snare that every sensible man would like to be caught in.

CECILY. Oh, I don't think I would care to catch a sensible man. I shouldn't know what to talk to him
25 about.

[*They pass into the house.* MISS PRISM *and* DR CHASUBLE *return.*

MISS PRISM. You are too much alone, dear Dr Chasuble. You should get married. A misanthrope I can understand—a womanthrope, never!

CHASUBLE [*with a scholar's shudder*]. Believe me, I do
30 not deserve so neologistic a phrase. The precept as well as the practice of the Primitive Church was distinctly against matrimony.

MISS PRISM [*sententiously*]. That is obviously the reason why the Primitive Church has not lasted up to the present day. And you do not seem to realise, dear Doctor, that by persistently remaining single, a man converts himself into a permanent public temptation. Men should be more careful; this very celibacy leads weaker vessels astray.

CHASUBLE. But is a man not equally attractive when married? 5

MISS PRISM. No married man is ever attractive except to his wife.

CHASUBLE. And often, I 've been told, not even to her.

MISS PRISM. That depends on the intellectual sympathies 10 of the woman. Maturity can always be depended on. Ripeness can be trusted. Young women are green. [DR CHASUBLE *starts.*] I spoke horticulturally. My metaphor was drawn from fruits. But where is Cecily?

CHASUBLE. Perhaps she followed us to the schools. 15

Enter JACK *slowly from the back of the garden. He is dressed in the deepest mourning, with crape hatband and black gloves.*

MISS PRISM. Mr Worthing!

CHASUBLE. Mr Worthing?

MISS PRISM. This is indeed a surprise. We did not look for you till Monday afternoon.

JACK. [*shakes* MISS PRISM'S *hand in a tragic manner*]. I 20 have returned sooner than I expected. Dr Chasuble, I hope you are well?

CHASUBLE. Dear Mr Worthing, I trust this garb of woe does not betoken some terrible calamity?

JACK. My brother. 25

MISS PRISM. More shameful debts and extravagance?

CHASUBLE. Still leading his life of pleasure?

JACK [*shaking his head*]. Dead!

CHASUBLE. Your brother Ernest dead?

JACK. Quite dead. 30

MISS PRISM. What a lesson for him! I trust he will profit by it.

CHASUBLE. Mr Worthing, I offer you my sincere condolence. You have at least the consolation of knowing that you were always the most generous and forgiving of brothers.

5 JACK. Poor Ernest! He had many faults, but it is a sad, sad blow.

CHASUBLE. Very sad indeed. Were you with him at the end?

JACK. No. He died abroad; in Paris, in fact. I
10 had a telegram last night from the manager of the Grand Hotel.

CHASUBLE. Was the cause of death mentioned?

JACK. A severe chill, it seems.

MISS PRISM. As a man sows, so shall he reap.

15 CHASUBLE [*raising his hand*]. Charity, dear Miss Prism, charity! None of us are perfect. I myself am peculiarly susceptible to draughts. Will the interment take place here?

JACK. No. He seems to have expressed a desire to be
20 buried in Paris.

CHASUBLE In Paris! [*Shakes his head.*] I fear that hardly points to any very serious state of mind at the last. You would no doubt wish me to make some slight allusion to this tragic domestic affliction next Sunday.
25 [JACK *presses his hand convulsively.*] My sermon on the meaning of the manna in the wilderness can be adapted to almost any occasion, joyful, or, as in the present case, distressing. [*All sigh.*] I have preached it at harvest celebrations, christenings, confirmations, on days of
30 humiliation and festal days. The last time I delivered it was in the Cathedral, as a charity sermon on behalf of the Society for the Prevention of Discontent among the Upper Orders. The Bishop, who was present, was much struck by some of the analogies I drew.

35 JACK. Ah! that reminds me, you mentioned christenings I think, Dr Chasuble? I suppose you know how to

christen all right ? [DR CHASUBLE *looks astounded.*] I
mean, of course, you are continually christening, aren't you?

MISS PRISM. It is, I regret to say, one of the Rector's
most constant duties in this parish. I have often spoken
to the poorer classes on the subject. But they don't seem
to know what thrift is.

CHASUBLE. But is there any particular infant in whom
you are interested, Mr Worthing ? Your brother was, I
believe, unmarried, was he not ?

JACK. Oh yes.

MISS PRISM [*bitterly*]. People who live entirely for
pleasure usually are.

JACK. But it is not for any child, dear Doctor. I am
very fond of children. No ! the fact is, I would like to
be christened myself, this afternoon, if you have nothing
better to do.

CHASUBLE. But surely, Mr Worthing, you have been
christened already ?

JACK. I don't remember anything about it.

CHASUBLE. But have you any grave doubts on the
subject ?

JACK. I certainly intend to have. Of course I don't
know if the thing would bother you in any way, or if you
think I am a little too old now.

CHASUBLE. Not at all. The sprinkling, and, indeed, the
immersion of adults is a perfectly canonical practice.

JACK. Immersion !

CHASUBLE. You need have no apprehensions. Sprinkling
is all that is necessary, or indeed I think advisable. Our
weather is so changeable. At what hour would you wish
the ceremony performed ?

JACK. Oh, I might trot round about five if that would
suit you.

CHASUBLE. Perfectly, perfectly ! In fact I have two
similar ceremonies to perform at that time. A case of
twins that occurred recently in one of the outlying cottages

on your own estate. Poor Jenkins the carter, a most hard-working man.

JACK. Oh! I don't see much fun in being christened along with other babies. It would be childish. Would 5 half-past five do?

CHASUBLE. Admirably! Admirably! [*Takes out watch.*] And now, dear Mr Worthing, I will not intrude any longer into a house of sorrow. I would merely beg you not to be too much bowed down by grief. What seem to us 10 bitter trials are often blessings in disguise.

MISS PRISM. This seems to me a blessing of an extremely obvious kind.

Enter CECILY *from the house.*

CECILY. Uncle Jack! Oh, I am pleased to see you back. But what horrid clothes you have got on. Do go 15 and change them.

MISS PRISM. Cecily!

CHASUBLE. My child! my child! [CECILY *goes towards* JACK ; *he kisses her brow in a melancholy manner.*]

CECILY. What is the matter, Uncle Jack? Do look 20 happy! You look as if you had toothache, and I have got such a surprise for you. Who do you think is in the dining-room? Your brother!

JACK. Who?

CECILY. Your brother Ernest. He arrived about half 25 an hour ago.

JACK. What nonsense! I haven't got a brother.

CECILY. Oh, don't say that. However badly he may have behaved to you in the past he is still your brother. You couldn't be so heartless as to disown him. I'll tell 30 him to come out. And you will shake hands with him, won't you, Uncle Jack? [*Runs back into the house.*

CHASUBLE. These are very joyful tidings.

MISS PRISM. After we had all been resigned to his loss, his sudden return seems to me peculiarly distressing.

JACK. My brother is in the dining-room ? I don't know what it all means. I think it is perfectly absurd.

Enter ALGERNON *and* CECILY *hand in hand. They come slowly up to* JACK.

JACK. Good heavens !   [*Motions* ALGERNON *away*

ALGERNON. Brother John, I have come down from town to tell you that I am very sorry for all the trouble I have 5 given you, and that I intend to lead a better life in the future. [JACK *glares at him and does not take his hand.*]

CECILY. Uncle Jack, you are not going to refuse your own brother's hand ?

JACK. Nothing will induce me to take his hand. I 10 think his coming down here disgraceful. He knows perfectly well why.

CECILY. Uncle Jack, do be nice. There is some good in every one. Ernest has just been telling me about his poor invalid friend Mr Bunbury whom he goes to visit 15 so often. And surely there must be much good in one who is kind to an invalid, and leaves the pleasures of London to sit by a bed of pain.

JACK. Oh ! he has been talking about Bunbury, has he ?

CECILY. Yes, he has told me all about poor Mr Bunbury, 20 and his terrible state of health.

JACK. Bunbury ! Well, I won't have him talk to you about Bunbury or about anything else. It is enough to drive one perfectly frantic.

ALGERNON. Of course I admit that the faults were all on 25 my side. But I must say that I think that Brother John's coldness to me is peculiarly painful. I expected a more enthusiastic welcome, especially considering it is the first time I have come here.

CECILY. Uncle Jack, if you don't shake hands with 30 Ernest I will never forgive you.

JACK. Never forgive me ?

CECILY. Never, never, never !

JACK. Well, this is the last time I shall ever do it. [*Shakes hands with* ALGERNON *and glares.*]

CHASUBLE. It's pleasant, is it not, to see so perfect a reconciliation? I think we might leave the two brothers together.

MISS PRISM. Cecily, you will come with us.

CECILY. Certainly, Miss Prism. My little task of reconciliation is over.

CHASUBLE. You have done a beautiful action to-day, dear child.

MISS PRISM. We must not be premature in our judgments.

CECILY. I feel very happy.

[*They all go off except* JACK *and* ALGERNON.]

JACK. You young scoundrel, Algy, you must get out of this place as soon as possible. I don't allow any Bunburying here.

Enter MERRIMAN.

MERRIMAN. I have put Mr Ernest's things in the room next to yours, sir. I suppose that is all right?

JACK. What?

MERRIMAN. Mr Ernest's luggage, sir. I have unpacked it and put it in the room next to your own.

JACK. His luggage?

MERRIMAN. Yes, sir. Three portmanteaus, a dressing-case, two hat-boxes, and a large luncheon-basket.

ALGERNON. I am afraid I can't stay more than a week this time.

JACK. Merriman, order the dog-cart at once. Mr Ernest has been suddenly called back to town.

MERRIMAN. Yes, sir. [*Goes back into the house.*]

ALGERNON. What a fearful liar you are, Jack? I have not been called back to town at all.

JACK. Yes, you have.

ALGERNON. I haven't heard any one call me.

JACK. Your duty as a gentleman calls you back.

ALGERNON. My duty as a gentleman has never interfered with my pleasures in the smallest degree.

JACK. I can quite understand that.

ALGERNON. Well, Cecily is a darling.

JACK. You are not to talk of Miss Cardew like that. I don't like it.

ALGERNON. Well, I don't like your clothes. You look perfectly ridiculous in them. Why on earth don't you go up and change ? It is perfectly childish to be in deep mourning for a man who is actually staying for a whole week with you in your house as a guest. I call it grotesque.

JACK. You are certainly not staying with me for a whole week as a guest or anything else. You have got to leave . . . by the four-five train.

ALGERNON. I certainly won't leave you so long as you are in mourning. It would be most unfriendly. If I were in mourning you would stay with me, I suppose. I should think it very unkind if you didn't.

JACK. Well, will you go if I change my clothes ?

ALGERNON. Yes, if you are not too long. I never saw anybody take so long to dress, and with such little result.

JACK. Well, at any rate, that is better than being always over-dressed as you are.

ALGERNON. If I am occasionally a little over-dressed, I make up for it by being always immensely over-educated.

JACK. Your vanity is ridiculous, your conduct an outrage, and your presence in my garden utterly absurd. However, you have got to catch the four-five, and I hope you will have a pleasant journey back to town. This Bunburying, as you call it, has not been a great success for you.   [*Goes into the house.*

ALGERNON. I think it has been a great success. I'm in love with Cecily, and that is everything.

Enter CECILY *at the back of the garden. She picks
up the can and begins to water the flowers.*

But I must see her before I go, and make arrangements
for another Bunbury. Ah, there she is.

CECILY. Oh, I merely came back to water the roses. I
thought you were with Uncle Jack.

5 ALGERNON. He's gone to order the dog-cart for me.

CECILY. Oh, is he going to take you for a nice drive?

ALGERNON. He's going to send me away.

CECILY. Then have we got to part?

ALGERNON. I afraid so. It's a very painful parting.

10 CECILY. It is always painful to part from people whom
one has known for a very brief space of time. The absence
of old friends one can endure with equanimity. But even
a momentary separation from any one to whom one has
just been introduced is almost unbearable.

15 ALGERNON. Thank you.

Enter MERRIMAN.

MERRIMAN. The dog-cart is at the door, sir. [ALGERNON
looks appealingly at CECILY.]

CECILY. It can wait, Merriman . . . for . . . five
minutes.

20 MERRIMAN. Yes, Miss. [*Exit* MERRIMAN.

ALGERNON. I hope, Cecily, I shall not offend you if I
state quite frankly and openly that you seem to me to
be in every way the visible personification of absolute
perfection.

25 CECILY. I think your frankness does you great credit,
Ernest. If you will allow me, I will copy your remarks
into my diary. [*Goes over to table and begins writing in
diary.*]

ALGERNON. Do you really keep a diary? I'd give any-
30 thing to look at it. May I?

CECILY. Oh no. [*Puts her hand over it.*] You see, it is

simply a very young girl's record of her own thoughts and impressions, and consequently meant for publication. When it appears in volume form I hope you will order a copy. But pray, Ernest, don't stop. I delight in taking down from dictation. I have reached "absolute 5 perfection". You can go on. I am quite ready for more.

ALGERNON [*somewhat taken aback*]. Ahem ! Ahem !

CECILY. Oh, don't cough, Ernest. When one is dictat- ing one should speak fluently and not cough. Besides, 10 I don't know how to spell a cough. [*Writes as* ALGERNON *speaks.*]

ALGERNON [*speaking very rapidly*]. Cecily, ever since I first looked upon your wonderful and incomparable beauty, I have dared to love you wildly, passionately, 15 devotedly, hopelessly.

CECILY. I don't think that you should tell me that you love me wildly, passionately, devotedly, hopelessly. Hopelessly doesn't seem to make much sense, does it ?

ALGERNON. Cecily.   20

Enter MERRIMAN.

MERRIMAN. The dog-cart is waiting, sir.

ALGERNON. Tell it to come round next week, at the same hour.

MERRIMAN [*looks at* CECILY, *who makes no sign*]. Yes. sir.   [MERRIMAN *retires.* 25

CECILY. Uncle Jack would be very much annoyed if he knew you were staying on till next week, at the same hour.

ALGERNON. Oh, I don't care about Jack. I don't care for anybody in the whole world but you. I love you, 30 Cecily. You will marry me, won't you ?

CECILY. You silly boy ! Of course. Why, we have been engaged for the last three months.

ALGERNON. For the last three months ?

CECILY. Yes, it will be exactly three months on Thursday.

ALGERNON. But how did we become engaged?

CECILY. Well, ever since dear Uncle Jack first confessed to us that he had a younger brother who was very wicked and bad, you of course have formed the chief topic of conversation between myself and Miss Prism. And of course a man who is much talked about is always very attractive. One feels there must be something in him, after all. I daresay it was foolish of me, but I fell in love with you, Ernest.

ALGERNON. Darling. And when was the engagement actually settled?

CECILY. On the 14th of February last. Worn out by your entire ignorance of my existence, I determined to end the matter one way or the other, and after a long struggle with myself I accepted you under this dear old tree here. The next day I bought this little ring in your name, and this is the little bangle with the true lover's knot I promised you always to wear.

ALGERNON. Did I give you this? It's very pretty, isn't it?

CECILY. Yes, you've wonderfully good taste, Ernest. It's the excuse I've always given for your leading such a bad life. And this is the box in which I keep all your dear letters. [*Kneels at table, opens box, and produces letters tied up with blue ribbon.*]

ALGERNON. My letters! But, my own sweet Cecily, I have never written you any letters.

CECILY. You need hardly remind me of that, Ernest. I remember only too well that I was forced to write your letters for you. I wrote always three times a week, and sometimes oftener.

ALGERNON. Oh, do let me read them, Cecily?

CECILY. Oh, I couldn't possibly. They would make you far too conceited. [*Replaces box.*] The three you wrote me after I had broken off the engagement are so beautiful, and so badly spelled, that even now I can hardly read them without crying a little.

ALGERNON. But was our engagement ever broken off?

CECILY. Of course it was. On the 22nd of last March. You can see the entry if you like. [*Shows diary.*] " To-day I broke off my engagement with Ernest. I feel it is better to do so. The weather still continues charming ".

ALGERNON. But why on earth did you break it off? What had I done? I had done nothing at all. Cecily, I am very much hurt indeed to hear you broke it off. Particularly when the weather was so charming.

CECILY. It would hardly have been a really serious engagement if it hadn't been broken off at least once. But I forgave you before the week was out.

ALGERNON [*crossing to her, and kneeling*]. What a perfect angel you are, Cecily.

CECILY. You dear romantic boy. [*He kisses her, she puts her fingers through his hair*] I hope your hair curls naturally, does it?

ALGERNON. Yes, darling, with a little help from others.

CECILY. I am so glad.

ALGERNON. You 'll never break off our engagement again, Cecily?

CECILY. I don't think I could break it off now that I have actually met you. Besides, of course, there is the question of your name.

ALGERNON. Yes, of course. [*Nervously.*]

CECILY. You must not laugh at me, darling, but it had always been a girlish dream of mine to love some one whose name was Ernest. [ALGERNON *rises*, CECILY *also*.] There is something in that name that seems to inspire absolute confidence. I pity any poor married woman whose husband is not called Ernest.

ALGERNON. But, my dear child, do you mean to say you could not love me if I had some other name?

CECILY. But what name?

ALGERNON. Oh, any name you like—Algernon—for instance . . .

CECILY. But I don't like the name of Algernon.

5 ALGERNON. Well, my own dear, sweet, loving little darling, I really can't see why you should object to the name of Algernon. It is not at all a bad name. In fact, it is rather an aristocratic name. Half of the chaps who get into the Bankruptcy Court are called Algernon. But 10 seriously, Cecily . . . [*Moving to her*] . . . if my name was Algy, couldn't you love me?

CECILY [*rising*]. I might respect you, Ernest, I might admire your character, but I fear that I should not be able to give you my undivided attention.

15 ALGERNON. Ahem! Cecily! [*Picking up hat.*] Your Rector here is, I suppose, thoroughly experienced in the practice of all the rites and ceremonials of the Church?

CECILY. Oh, yes. Dr Chasuble is a most learned man. 20 He has never written a single book, so you can imagine how much he knows.

ALGERNON. I must see him at once on a most important christening—I mean on most important business.

CECILY. Oh!

25 ALGERNON. I shan't be away more than half an hour.

CECILY. Considering that we have been engaged since February the 14th, and that I only met you to-day for the first time, I think it is rather hard that you should leave me for so long a period as half an hour. Couldn't 30 you make it twenty minutes?

ALGERNON. I'll be back in no time.

[*Kisses her and rushes down the garden.*

CECILY. What an impetuous boy he is. I like his hair so much. I must enter his proposal in my diary.

Enter MERRIMAN.

MERRIMAN. A Miss Fairfax has just called to see Mr Worthing. On very important business, Miss Fairfax states.

CECILY. Isn't Mr Worthing in his library?

MERRIMAN. Mr Worthing went over in the direction of   5
the Rectory some time ago.

CECILY. Pray ask the lady to come out here; Mr Worthing is sure to be back soon. And you can bring tea.

MERRIMAN. Yes, Miss.   [*Goes out.*

CECILY. Miss Fairfax! I suppose one of the many   10
good elderly women who are associated with Uncle Jack in some of his philanthropic work in London. I don't quite like women who are interested in philanthropic work. I think it is so forward of them.

Enter MERRIMAN.

MERRIMAN. Miss Fairfax.   15

Enter GWENDOLEN.   *Exit* MERRIMAN.

CECILY [*advancing to meet her*]. Pray let me introduce myself to you. My name is Cecily Cardew.

GWENDOLEN. Cecily Cardew? [*Moving to her and shaking hands.*] What a very sweet name! Something tells me that we are going to be great friends. I like you   20
already more than I can say. My first impressions of people are never wrong.

CECILY. How nice of you to like me so much after we have known each other such a comparatively short time. Pray sit down.   25

GWENDOLEN [*still standing up*]. I may call you Cecily, may I not?

CECILY. With pleasure!

GWENDOLEN. And you will always call me Gwendolen, won't you?   30

CECILY. If you wish.

GWENDOLEN. Then that is all quite settled, is it not ?

CECILY. I hope so. [*A pause. They both sit down together.*]

5   GWENDOLEN. Perhaps this might be a favourable opportunity for my mentioning who I am. My father is Lord Bracknell. You have never heard of papa, I suppose ?

CECILY. I don't think so.

GWENDOLEN. Outside the family circle, papa, I am glad
10 to say, is entirely unknown. I think that is quite as it should be. The home seems to me to be the proper sphere for the man. And certainly once a man begins to neglect his domestic duties he becomes painfully effeminate, does he not ? And I don't like that. It makes men so
15 very attractive. Cecily, mamma, whose views on education are remarkably strict, has brought me up to be extremely short-sighted ; it is part of her system ; so do you mind my looking at you through my glasses ?

CECILY. Oh ! not at all, Gwendolen. I am very fond
20 of being looked at.

GWENDOLEN [*after examining* CECILY *carefully through a lorgnette*]. You are here on a short visit, I suppose.

CECILY. Oh no ! I live here.

GWENDOLEN [*severely*]. Really ? Your mother, no doubt,
25 or some female relative of advanced years, resides here also ?

CECILY. Oh no ! I have no mother, nor, in fact, any relations.

GWENDOLEN. Indeed ?

30   CECILY. My dear guardian, with the assistance of Miss Prism, has the arduous task of looking after me.

GWENDOLEN. Your guardian ?

CECILY. Yes, I am Mr Worthing's ward.

GWENDOLEN. Oh ! It is strange he never mentioned to
35 me that he had a ward. How secretive of him ! He grows more interesting hourly. I am not sure, however,

that the news inspires me with feelings of unmixed delight. [*Rising and going to her.*] I am very fond of you, Cecily ; I have liked you ever since I met you ! But I am bound to state that now that I know that you are Mr Worthing's ward, I cannot help expressing a wish you were—well, 5 just a little older than you seem to be—and not quite so very alluring in appearance. In fact, if I may speak candidly——

CECILY. Pray do !—I think that whenever one has anything unpleasant to say, one should always be quite 10 candid.

GWENDOLEN. Well, to speak with perfect candour, Cecily, I wish that you were fully forty-two, and more than usually plain for your age. Ernest has a strong upright nature. He is the very soul of truth and honour. Dis- 15 loyalty would be as impossible to him as deception. But even men of the noblest possible moral character are extremely susceptible to the influence of the physical charms of others. Modern, no less than Ancient History, supplies us with many most painful examples of what I 20 refer to. If it were not so, indeed, History would be quite unreadable.

CECILY. I beg your pardon, Gwendolen, did you say Ernest ?

GWENDOLEN. Yes. 25

CECILY. Oh, but it is not Mr Ernest Worthing who is my guardian. It is his brother—his elder brother.

GWENDOLEN [*sitting down again*]. Ernest never mentioned to me that he had a brother.

CECILY. I am sorry to say they have not been on good 30 terms for a long time.

GWENDOLEN. Ah ! that accounts for it. And now that I think of it I have never heard any man mention his brother. The subject seems distasteful to most men. Cecily, you have lifted a load from my mind. I was 35 growing almost anxious. It would have been terrible if

19 S

any cloud had come across a friendship like ours, would
it not ? Of course you are quite, quite sure that it is not
Mr Ernest Worthing who is your guardian ?

CECILY. Quite sure. [*A pause.*] In fact, I am going to
be his.

GWENDOLEN [*inquiringly*]. I beg your pardon ?

CECILY [*rather shy and confidingly*]. Dearest Gwendolen,
there is no reason why I should make a secret of it to you.
Our little county newspaper is sure to chronicle the fact
next week. Mr Ernest Worthing and I are engaged to be
married.

GWENDOLEN [*quite politely, rising*]. My darling Cecily, I
think there must be some slight error. Mr Ernest Worthing
is engaged to me. The announcement will appear in the
Morning Post on Saturday at the latest.

CECILY [*very politely, rising*]. I am afraid you must be
under some misconception. Ernest proposed to me
exactly ten minutes ago. [*Shows diary.*]

GWENDOLEN [*examines diary through her lorgnette carefully*]. It is certainly very curious, for he asked me to be
his wife yesterday afternoon at 5.30. If you would care
to verify the incident, pray do so. [*Produces diary of her
own.*] I never travel without my diary. One should
always have something sensational to read in the train.
I am so sorry, dear Cecily, if it is any disappointment to
you, but I am afraid I have the prior claim.

CECILY. It would distress me more than I can tell you,
dear Gwendolen, if it caused you any mental or physical
anguish, but I feel bound to point out that since Ernest
proposed to you he clearly has changed his mind.

GWENDOLEN [*meditatively*]. If the poor fellow has been
entrapped into any foolish promise I shall consider it my
duty to rescue him at once, and with a firm hand.

CECILY [*thoughtfully and sadly*]. Whatever unfortunate
entanglement my dear boy may have got into, I will never
reproach him with it after we are married.

GWENDOLEN. Do you allude to me, Miss Cardew, as an entanglement? You are presumptuous. On an occasion of this kind it becomes more than a moral duty to speak one's mind. It becomes a pleasure.

CECILY. Do you suggest, Miss Fairfax, that I entrapped   5
Ernest into an engagement? How dare you? This is no time for wearing the shallow mask of manners. When I see a spade I call it a spade.

GWENDOLEN [*satirically*]. I am glad to say that I have never seen a spade. It is obvious that our social spheres   10
have been widely different.

Enter MERRIMAN, *followed by the footman. He carries a salver, table cloth, and plate stand.* CECILY *is about to retort. The presence of the servants exercises a restraining influence, under which both girls chafe.*

MERRIMAN. Shall I lay tea here as usual, Miss?

CECILY [*sternly, in a calm voice*]. Yes, as usual. [MERRIMAN *begins to clear table and lay cloth. A long pause.* CECILY *and* GWENDOLEN *glare at each other.*]   15

GWENDOLEN. Are there many interesting walks in the vicinity, Miss Cardew?

CECILY. Oh! yes! a great many. From the top of one of the hills quite close one can see five counties.

GWENDOLEN. Five counties! I don't think I should   20
like that; I hate crowds.

CECILY [*sweetly*]. I suppose that is why you live in town? [GWENDOLEN *bites her lip, and beats her foot nervously with her parasol.*]

GWENDOLEN [*looking round*]. Quite a well-kept garden   25
this is, Miss Cardew.

CECILY. So glad you like it, Miss Fairfax.

GWENDOLEN. I had no idea there were any flowers in the country.

CECILY. Oh, flowers are as common here, Miss Fairfax,   30
as people are in London.

GWENDOLEN. Personally I cannot understand how any-body manages to exist in the country, if anybody who is anybody does. ·The country always bores me to death.

CECILY. Ah! This is what the newspapers call agri-
5 cultural depression, is it not! I believe the aristocracy are suffering very much from it just at present. It is almost an epidemic amongst them, I have been told. May I offer you some tea, Miss Fairfax?

GWENDOLEN [*with elaborate politeness*]. Thank you.
10 [*Aside*] Detestable girl! But I require tea!

CECILY [*sweetly*]. Sugar?

GWENDOLEN [*superciliously*]. No, thank you. Sugar is not fashionable any more. [CECILY *looks angrily at her, takes up the tongs and puts four lumps of sugar into the*
15 *cup.*]

CECILY [*severely*]. Cake or bread and butter?

GWENDOLEN [*in a bored manner*]. Bread and butter, please. Cake is rarely seen at the best houses nowadays.

CECILY [*cuts a very large slice of cake and puts it on the*
20 *tray*]. Hand that to Miss Fairfax.

[MERRIMAN *does so, and goes out with footman.*
GWENDOLEN *drinks the tea and makes a grimace.
Puts down cup at once, reaches out her hand to
the bread and butter, looks at it, and finds it is
cake. Rises in indignation.*]

GWENDOLEN. You have filled my tea with lumps of sugar, and though I asked most distinctly for bread and butter, you have given me cake. I am known for the gentleness of my disposition, and the extraordinary sweet-
25 ness of my nature, but I warn you, Miss Cardew, you may go too far.

CECILY [*rising*]. To save my poor, innocent, trusting boy from the machinations of any other girl there are no lengths to which I would not go.

30 GWENDOLEN. From the moment I saw you I distrusted you. I felt that you were false and deceitful. I am never

deceived in such matters.　My first impressions of people are invariably right.

CECILY. It seems to me, Miss Fairfax, that I am trespassing on your valuable time.　No doubt you have many other calls of a similar character to make in the neighbourhood.

Enter JACK.

GWENDOLEN [*catching sight of him*]. Ernest !　My own Ernest !

JACK. Gwendolen !　Darling !　[*Offers to kiss her.*]

GWENDOLEN [*drawing back*]. A moment !　May I ask if you are engaged to be married to this young lady ? [*Points to* CECILY.]

JACK [*laughing*]. To dear little Cecily !　Of course not ! What could have put such an idea into your pretty little head ?

GWENDOLEN. Thank you.　　You may !　[*Offers her cheek.*]

CECILY [*very sweetly*]. I knew there must be some misunderstanding, Miss Fairfax.　The gentleman whose arm is at present round your waist is my guardian, Mr John Worthing.

GWENDOLEN. I beg your pardon ?

CECILY. This is Uncle Jack.

GWENDOLEN [*receding*]. Jack !　Oh !

Enter ALGERNON.

CECILY. Here is Ernest.

ALGERNON [*goes straight over to* CECILY *without noticing any one else*]. My own love !　[*Offers to kiss her.*]

CECILY [*drawing back*]. A moment, Ernest !　May I ask you—are you engaged to be married to this young lady ?

ALGERNON [*looking round*]. To what young lady.　Good heavens !　Gwendolen !

CECILY. Yes! to good heavens, Gwendolen, I mean to Gwendolen.

ALGERNON [*laughing*]. Of course not! What could have put such an idea into your pretty little head?

CECILY. Thank you. [*Presenting her cheek to be kissed.*] You may. [ALGERNON *kisses her.*]

GWENDOLEN. I felt there was some slight error, Miss Cardew. The gentleman who is now embracing you is my cousin, Mr Algernon Moncrieff.

CECILY [*breaking away from* ALGERNON]. Algernon Moncrieff! Oh! [*The two girls move towards each other and put their arms round each other's waists as if for protection.*]

CECILY. Are you called Algernon?

ALGERNON. I cannot deny it.

CECILY. Oh!

GWENDOLEN. Is your name really John?

JACK [*standing rather proudly*]. I could deny it if I liked. I could deny anything if I liked. But my name certainly is John. It has been John for years.

CECILY [*to* GWENDOLEN]. A gross deception has been practised on both of us.

GWENDOLEN. My poor wounded Cecily!

CECILY. My sweet wronged Gwendolen!

GWENDOLEN [*slowly and seriously*]. You will call me sister, will you not? [*They embrace.* JACK AND ALGERNON *groan and walk up and down.*]

CECILY [*rather brightly*]. There is just one question I would like to be allowed to ask my guardian.

GWENDOLEN. An admirable idea! Mr Worthing, there is just one question I would like to be permitted to put to you. Where is your brother Ernest? We are both engaged to be married to your brother Ernest, so it is a matter of some importance to us to know where your brother Ernest is at present.

JACK [*slowly and hesitatingly*]. Gwendolen—Cecily—it is

very painful for me to be forced to speak the truth. It is the first time in my life that I have ever been reduced to such a painful position, and I am really quite inexperienced in doing anything of the kind. However, I will tell you quite frankly that I have no brother Ernest. I have no brother at all. I never had a brother in my life, and I certainly have not the smallest intention of ever having one in the future.

CECILY [*surprised*]. No brother at all?

JACK [*cheerily*]. None!

GWENDOLEN [*severely*]. Had you never a brother of any kind?

JACK [*pleasantly*]. Never. Not even of any kind.

GWENDOLEN. I am afraid it is quite clear, Cecily, that neither of us is engaged to be married to any one.

CECILY. It is not a very pleasant position for a young girl suddenly to find herself in. Is it?

GWENDOLEN. Let us go into the house. They will hardly venture to come after us there.

CECILY. No, men are so cowardly, aren't they?

[*They retire into the house with scornful looks.*

JACK. This ghastly state of things is what you call Bunburying, I suppose?

ALGERNON. Yes, and a perfectly wonderful Bunbury it is. The most wonderful Bunbury I have ever had in my life.

JACK. Well, you've no right whatsoever to Bunbury here.

ALGERNON. That is absurd. One has a right to Bunbury anywhere one chooses. Every serious Bunburyist knows that.

JACK. Serious Bunburyist! Good heavens!

ALGERNON. Well, one must be serious about something, if one wants to have any amusement in life. I happen to be serious about Bunburying. What on earth you are serious about I haven't got the remotest idea. About everything, I should fancy. You have such an absolutely trivial nature.

JACK. Well, the only small satisfaction I have in the whole of this wretched business is that your friend Bunbury is quite exploded. You won't be able to run down to the country quite so often as you used to do, dear Algy. And a very good thing too.

ALGERNON. Your brother is a little off colour, isn't he, dear Jack? You won't be able to disappear to London quite so frequently as your wicked custom was. And not a bad thing either.

JACK. As for your conduct towards Miss Cardew, I must say that your taking in a sweet, simple, innocent girl like that is quite inexcusable. To say nothing of the fact that she is my ward.

ALGERNON. I can see no possible defence at all for your deceiving a brilliant, clever, thoroughly experienced young lady like Miss Fairfax. To say nothing of the fact that she is my cousin.

JACK. I wanted to be engaged to Gwendolen, that is all. I love her.

ALGERNON. Well, I simply wanted to be engaged to Cecily. I adore her.

JACK. There is certainly no chance of your marrying Miss Cardew.

ALGERNON. I don't think there is much likelihood, Jack, of you and Miss Fairfax being united.

JACK. Well, that is no business of yours.

ALGERNON. If it was my business, I wouldn't talk about it. [*Begins to eat muffins.*] It is very vulgar to talk about one's business. Only people like stockbrokers do that, and then merely at dinner parties.

JACK. How can you sit there, calmly eating muffins when we are in this horrible trouble, I can't make out. You seem to me to be perfectly heartless.

ALGERNON. Well, I can't eat muffins in an agitated

manner. The butter would probably get on my cuffs.
One should always eat muffins quite calmly.   It is the
only way to eat them.

JACK. I say it's perfectly heartless your eating muffins
at all, under the circumstances.   5

ALGERNON. When I am in trouble, eating is the only thing
that consoles me.   Indeed, when I am in really great
trouble, as any one who knows me intimately will tell you,
I refuse everything except food and drink.   At the present
moment I am eating muffins because I am unhappy. 10
Besides, I am particularly fond of muffins.   [*Rising.*]

JACK [*rising*]. Well, that is no reason why you should
eat them all in that greedy way. [*Takes muffins from*
ALGERNON.]

ALGERNON [*offering tea-cake*]. I wish you would have 15
tea-cake instead.   I don't like tea-cake.

JACK. Good heavens !   I suppose a man may eat his
own muffins in his own garden.

ALGERNON. But you have just said it was perfectly
heartless to eat muffins.   20

JACK. I said it was perfectly heartless of you, under the
circumstances.   That is a very different thing.

ALGERNON. That may be.   But the muffins are the
same.   [*He seizes the muffin-dish from* JACK.]

JACK. Algy, I wish to goodness you would go.   25

ALGERNON. You can't possibly ask me to go without
having some dinner.   It 's absurd.   I never go without
my dinner.   No one ever does, except vegetarians and
people like that.   Besides I have just made arrangements
with Dr Chasuble to be christened at a quarter to six 30
under the name of Ernest.

JACK. My dear fellow, the sooner you give up that nonsense the better.   I made arrangements this morning with
Dr Chasuble to be christened myself at 5.30, and I naturally will take the name of Ernest.   Gwendolen would wish 35
it.   We can't both be christened Ernest.   It 's absurd.

Besides, I have a perfect right to be christened if I like. There is no evidence at all that I have ever been christened by anybody. I should think it extremely probable I never was, and so does Dr Chasuble. It is entirely different in 5 your case. You have been christened already.

ALGERNON. Yes, but I have not been christened for years.

JACK. Yes, but you have been christened. That is the important thing.

ALGERNON. Quite so. So I know my constitution can 10 stand it. If you are not quite sure about your ever having been christened, I must say I think it rather dangerous your venturing on it now. It might make you very unwell. You can hardly have forgotten that some one very closely connected with you was very nearly carried 15 off this week in Paris by a severe chill.

JACK. Yes, but you said yourself that a severe chill was not hereditary.

ALGERNON. It usen't to be, I know—but I daresay it is now. Science is always making wonderful improvements 20 in things.

JACK [*picking up the muffin-dish*]. Oh, that is nonsense ; you are always talking nonsense.

ALGERNON. Jack, you are at the muffins again ! I wish you wouldn't. There are only two left. [*Takes them.*] I 25 told you I was particularly fond of muffins.

JACK. But I hate tea-cake.

ALGERNON. Why on earth then do you allow tea-cake to be served up for your guests ? What ideas you have of hospitality !

30 JACK. Algernon ! I have already told you to go. I don't want you here. Why don't you go !

ALGERNON. I haven't quite finished my tea yet ! and there is still one muffin left. [JACK *groans, and sinks into a chair.* ALGERNON *still continues eating.*]

ACT DROP.

THIRD ACT

SCENE.—*Morning-room at the Manor House.*
GWENDOLEN *and* CECILY *are at the window, looking out into the garden.*

GWENDOLEN. The fact that they did not follow us at once into the house, as any one else would have done, seems to me to show that they have some sense of shame left.

CECILY. They have been eating muffins. That looks like repentance.   5

GWENDOLEN [*after a pause*]. They don't seem to notice us at all. Couldn't you cough?

CECILY. But I haven't got a cough.

GWENDOLEN. They're looking at us. What effrontery.

CECILY. They're approaching. That's very forward of   10
them.

GWENDOLEN. Let us preserve a dignified silence.

CECILY. Certainly. It's the only thing to do now.

Enter JACK *followed by* ALGERNON. *They whistle some dreadful popular air from a British Opera.*

GWENDOLEN. This dignified silence seems to produce an unpleasant effect.   15

CECILY. A most distasteful one.

GWENDOLEN. But we will not be the first to speak.

CECILY. Certainly not.

GWENDOLEN. Mr Worthing, I have something very particular to ask you. Much depends on your reply.   20

CECILY. Gwendolen, your common sense is invaluable. Mr Moncrieff, kindly answer me the following question. Why did you pretend to be my guardian's brother?

ALGERNON. In order that I might have an opportunity of meeting you.   25

CECILY [*to* GWENDOLEN]. That certainly seems a satisfactory explanation, does it not ?

GWENDOLEN. Yes, dear, if you can believe him.

CECILY. I don't.   But that does not affect the wonderful beauty of his answer.

GWENDOLEN. True.   In matters of grave importance, style, not sincerity is the vital thing.   Mr Worthing, what explanation can you offer to me for pretending to have a brother ?   Was it in order that you might have an opportunity of coming up to town to see me as often as possible ?

JACK. Can you doubt it, Miss Fairfax ?

GWENDOLEN. I have the gravest doubts upon the subject.   But I intend to crush them.   This is not the moment for German scepticism. [*Moving to* CECILY.] Their explanations appear to be quite satisfactory, especially Mr Worthing's.   That seems to me to have the stamp of truth upon it.

CECILY. I am more than content with what Mr Moncrieff said.   His voice alone inspires one with absolute credulity.

GWENDOLEN. Then you think we should forgive them ?

CECILY. Yes.   I mean no.

GWENDOLEN. True !   I had forgotten.   There are principles at stake that one cannot surrender.   Which of us should tell them ?   The task is not a pleasant one.

CECILY. Could we not both speak at the same time ?

GWENDOLEN. An excellent idea !   I nearly always speak at the same time as other people.   Will you take the time from me ?

CECILY. Certainly.   [GWENDOLEN *beats time with uplifted finger.*]

GWENDOLEN and CECILY [*speaking together*]. Your Christian names are still an insuperable barrier.   That is all !

JACK and ALGERNON [*speaking together*]. Our Christian

names! Is that all? But we are going to be christened this afternoon.

GWENDOLEN [*to* JACK]. For my sake you are prepared to do this terrible thing?

JACK. I am.   5

CECILY [*to* ALGERNON]. To please me you are ready to face this fearful ordeal?

ALGERNON. I am!

GWENDOLEN. How absurd to talk of the equality of the sexes! Where questions of self-sacrifice are concerned, 10 men are infinitely beyond us.

JACK. We are. [*Clasps hands with* ALGERNON.]

CECILY. They have moments of physical courage of which we women know absolutely nothing.

GWENDOLEN [*to* JACK]. Darling!   15

ALGERNON [*to* CECILY]. Darling! [*They fall into each other's arms.*]

Enter MERRIMAN. *When he enters he coughs loudly, seeing the situation.*

MERRIMAN. Ahem! Ahem! Lady Bracknell!

JACK. Good heavens!

Enter LADY BRACKNELL. *The couples separate in alarm. Exit* MERRIMAN.

LADY BRACKNELL. Gwendolen! What does this mean? 20

GWENDOLEN. Merely that I am engaged to be married to Mr Worthing, mamma.

LADY BRACKNELL. Come here. Sit down. Sit down immediately. Hesitation of any kind is a sign of mental decay in the young, of physical weakness in the old. 25 [*Turns to* JACK] Apprised, sir, of my daughter's sudden flight by her trusty maid, whose confidence I purchased by means of a small coin, I followed her at once by a luggage train. Her unhappy father is, I am glad to say, under the impression that she is attending a more than usually lengthy lecture by the University Extension Scheme on the Influence of a permanent income on Thought. I do not propose to undeceive him. Indeed I have never undeceived him on any question. I would consider it wrong. But of course, you will clearly understand that all communication between yourself and my daughter must cease immediately from this moment. On this point, as indeed on all points, I am firm.

JACK. I am engaged to be married to Gwendolen, Lady Bracknell!

LADY BRACKNELL. You are nothing of the kind, sir. And now as regards Algernon ! . . . Algernon !

ALGERNON. Yes, Aunt Augusta.

LADY BRACKNELL. May I ask if it is in this house that your invalid friend Mr Bunbury resides ?

ALGERNON [*stammering*]. Oh ! No ! Bunbury doesn't live here. Bunbury is somewhere else at present. In fact, Bunbury is dead.

LADY BRACKNELL. Dead ! When did Mr Bunbury die ? His death must have been extremely sudden.

ALGERNON [*airily*]. Oh ! I killed Bunbury this afternoon. I mean poor Bunbury died this afternoon.

LADY BRACKNELL. What did he die of ?

ALGERNON. Bunbury ? Oh, he was quite exploded.

LADY BRACKNELL. Exploded ! Was he the victim of a revolutionary outrage ? I was not aware that Mr Bunbury was interested in social legislation. If so, he is well punished for his morbidity.

ALGERNON. My dear Aunt Augusta, I mean he was found out ! The doctors found out that Bunbury could not live, that is what I mean—so Bunbury died.

LADY BRACKNELL. He seems to have had great confidence in the opinion of his physicians. I am glad however, that he made up his mind at the last to some definite course of action, and acted under proper medical advice.

And now that we have finally got rid of this Mr Bunbury, may I ask, Mr Worthing, who is that young person whose hand my nephew Algernon is now holding in what seems to me a peculiarly unnecessary manner ?

JACK. That lady is Miss Cecily Cardew, my ward. 5
[LADY BRACKNELL *bows coldly to* CECILY.]

ALGERNON. I am engaged to be married to Cecily, Aunt Augusta.

LADY BRACKNELL. I beg your pardon ?

CECILY. Mr Moncrieff and I are engaged to be married, 10 Lady Bracknell.

LADY BRACKNELL [*with a shiver, crossing to the sofa and sitting down*]. I do not know whether there is anything peculiarly exciting in the air of this particular part of Hertfordshire, but the number of engagements that go 15 on seems to me considerably above the proper average that statistics have laid down for our guidance. I think some preliminary inquiry on my part would not be out of place. Mr Worthing, is Miss Cardew at all connected with any of the larger railway stations in London ? I 20 merely desire information. Until yesterday I had no idea that there were any families or persons whose origin was a Terminus. [JACK *looks perfectly furious, but restrains himself.*]

JACK [*in a clear, cold voice*]. Miss Cardew is the grand- 25 daughter of the late Mr Thomas Cardew of 149 Belgrave Square, S.W. ; Gervase Park, Dorking, Surrey ; and the Sporran, Fifeshire, N.B.

LADY BRACKNELL. That sounds not unsatisfactory. Three addresses always inspire confidence, even in trades- 30 men. But what proof have I of their authenticity ?

JACK. I have carefully preserved the Court Guides of the period. They are open to your inspection, Lady Bracknell.

LADY BRACKNELL [*grimly*]. I have known strange errors 35 in that publication.

JACK. Miss Cardew's family solicitors are Messrs Markby, Markby, and Markby.

LADY BRACKNELL. Markby, Markby, and Markby? A firm of the very highest position in their profession. Indeed I am told that one of the Mr Markby's is occasionally to be seen at dinner parties. So far I am satisfied.

JACK [*very irritably*]. How extremely kind of you, Lady Bracknell! I have also in my possession, you will be pleased to hear, certificates of Miss Cardew's birth, baptism, whooping cough, registration, vaccination, confirmation, and the measles; both the German and the English variety.

LADY BRACKNELL. Ah! A life crowded with incident, I see; though perhaps somewhat too exciting for a young girl. I am not myself in favour of premature experiences. [*Rises, looks at her watch.*] Gwendolen! the time approaches for our departure. We have not a moment to lose. As a matter of form, Mr Worthing, I had better ask you if Miss Cardew has any little fortune?

JACK. Oh! about a hundred and thirty thousand pounds in the Funds. That is all. Good bye, Lady Bracknell. So pleased to have seen you.

LADY BRACKNELL [*sitting down again*]. A moment, Mr Worthing. A hundred and thirty thousand pounds! And in the Funds! Miss Cardew seems to me a most attractive young lady, now that I look at her. Few girls of the present day have any really solid qualities, any of the qualities that last, and improve with time. We live, I regret to say, in an age of surfaces. [*To* CECILY] Come over here, dear. [CECILY *goes across.*] Pretty child! your dress is sadly simple, and your hair seems almost as Nature might have left it. But we can soon alter all that. A thoroughly experienced French maid produces a really marvellous result in a very brief space of time. I remember recommending one to young Lady Lancing, and after three months her own husband did not know her.

JACK. And after six months nobody knew her.

LADY BRACKNELL [*glares at* JACK *for a few moments. Then bends, with a practised smile, to* CECILY]. Kindly turn round, sweet child. [CECILY *turns completely round.*] No, the side view is what I want. [CECILY *presents her profile.*] Yes, quite as I expected. There are distinct social possibilities in your profile. The two weak points in our age are its want of principle and its want of profile. The chin a little higher dear. Style largely depends on the way the chin is worn. They are worn very high, just at present. Algernon!

ALGERNON. Yes, Aunt Augusta!

LADY BRACKNELL. There are distinct social possibilities in Miss Cardew's profile.

ALGERNON. Cecily is the sweetest, dearest, prettiest girl in the whole world. And I don't care twopence about social possibilities.

LADY BRACKNELL. Never speak disrespectfully of Society, Algernon. Only people who can't get into it do that. [*To* CECILY] Dear child, of course you know that Algernon has nothing but his debts to depend upon. But I do not approve of mercenary marriages. When I married Lord Bracknell I had no fortune of any kind. But I never dreamed for a moment of allowing that to stand in my way. Well, I suppose I must give my consent.

ALGERNON. Thank you, Aunt Augusta.

LADY BRACKNELL. Cecily, you may kiss me!

CECILY [*kisses her*]. Thank you, Lady Bracknell.

LADY BRACKNELL. You may also address me as Aunt Augusta for the future.

CECILY. Thank you, Aunt Augusta.

LADY BRACKNELL. The marriage, I think, had better take place quite soon.

ALGERNON. Thank you, Aunt Augusta.

CECILY. Thank you, Aunt Augusta.

19 T

LADY BRACKNELL. To speak frankly, I am not in favour of long engagements. They give people the opportunity of finding out each other's character before marriage, which I think is never advisable.

5 JACK. I beg your pardon for interrupting you, Lady Bracknell, but this engagement is quite out of the question. I am Miss Cardew's guardian, and she cannot marry without my consent until she comes of age. That consent I absolutely decline to give.

10 LADY BRACKNELL. Upon what grounds, may I ask? Algernon is an extremely, I may almost say an ostentatiously, eligible young man. He has nothing, but he looks everything. What more can one desire?

JACK. It pains me very much to have to speak frankly 15 to you, Lady Bracknell, about your nephew, but the fact is that I do not approve at all of his moral character. I suspect him of being untruthful. [ALGERNON *and* CECILY *look at him in indignant amazement.*]

LADY BRACKNELL. Untruthful! My nephew Algernon? 20 Impossible! He is an Oxonian.

JACK. I fear there can be no possible doubt about the matter. This afternoon during my temporary absence in London on an important question of romance, he obtained admission to my house by means of the false 25 pretence of being my brother. Under an assumed name he drank, I 've just been informed by my butler, an entire pint bottle of my Perrier-Jouet, Brut, '89; wine I was specially reserving for myself. Continuing his disgraceful deception, he succeeded in the course of the 30 afternoon in alienating the affections of my only ward. He subsequently stayed to tea, and devoured every single muffin. And what makes his conduct all the more heartless is, that he was perfectly well aware from the first that I have no brother, that I never had a brother, and 35 that I don't intend to have a brother, not even of any kind. I distinctly told him so myself yesterday afternoon.

LADY BRACKNELL. Ahem ! Mr Worthing, after careful consideration I have decided entirely to overlook my nephew's conduct to you.

JACK. That is very generous of you, Lady Bracknell. My own decision, however, is unalterable. I decline to 5 give my consent.

LADY BRACKNELL [*to* CECILY]. Come here, sweet child. [CECILY *goes over.*] How old are you, dear ?

CECILY. Well, I am really only eighteen, but I always admit to twenty when I go to evening parties.

LADY BRACKNELL. You are perfectly right in making some slight alteration. Indeed, no woman should ever be quite accurate about her age. It looks so calculating. . . . [*In a meditative manner*] Eighteen, but admitting to twenty at evening parties. Well, it will not be very 15 long before you are of age and free from the restraints of tutelage. So I don't think your guardian's consent is, after all, a matter of any importance.

JACK. Pray excuse me, Lady Bracknell, for interrupting you again, but it is only fair to tell you that according 20 to the terms of her grandfather's will Miss Cardew does not come legally of age till she is thirty-five.

LADY BRACKNELL. That does not seem to me to be a grave objection. Thirty-five is a very attractive age. London society is full of women of the very highest birth 25 who have, of their own free choice, remained thirty-five for years. Lady Dumbleton is an instance in point. To my own knowledge she has been thirty-five ever since she arrived at the age of forty, which was many years ago now. I see no reason why our dear Cecily should not be 30 even still more attractive at the age you mention than she is at present. There will be a large accumulation of property.

CECILY. Algy, could you wait for me till I was thirty-five ? 35

ALGERNON. Of course I could, Cecily. You know I could.

CECILY. Yes, I felt it instinctively, but I couldn't wait all that time. I hate waiting even five minutes for anybody. It always makes me rather cross. I am not punctual myself, I know, but I do like punctuality in 5 others, and waiting, even to be married, is quite out of the question.

ALGERNON. Then what is to be done, Cecily?

CECILY. I don't know, Mr Moncrieff.

LADY BRACKNELL. My dear Mr Worthing, as Miss Cardew 10 states positively that she cannot wait till she is thirty-five —a remark which I am bound to say seems to me to show a somewhat impatient nature—I would beg of you to reconsider your decision.

JACK. But my dear Lady Bracknell, the matter is 15 entirely in your own hands. The moment you consent to my marriage with Gwendolen, I will most gladly allow your nephew to form an alliance with my ward.

LADY BRACKNELL [*rising and drawing herself up*]. You must be quite aware that what you propose is out of the 20 question.

JACK. Then a passionate celibacy is all that any of us can look forward to.

LADY BRACKNELL. That is not the destiny I propose for Gwendolen. Algernon, of course, can choose for himself. 25 [*Pulls out her watch.*] Come, dear, [GWENDOLEN *rises*] we have already missed five, if not six, trains. To miss any more might expose us to comment on the platform.

Enter DR CHASUBLE.

CHASUBLE. Everything is quite ready for the christenings.

LADY BRACKNELL. The christenings, sir! Is not that 30 somewhat premature?

CHASUBLE [*looking rather puzzled, and pointing to* JACK *and* ALGERNON]. Both these gentlemen have expressed a desire for immediate baptism.

LADY BRACKNELL. At their age? The idea is grotesque

and irreligious ! Algernon, I forbid you to be baptized. I will not hear of such excesses. Lord Bracknell would be highly displeased if he learned that that was the way in which you wasted your time and money.

CHASUBLE. Am I to understand then that there are to 5 be no christenings at all this afternoon ?

JACK. I don't think that, as things are now, it would be of much practical value to either of us, Dr Chasuble.

CHASUBLE. I am grieved to hear such sentiments from you, Mr Worthing. They savour of the heretical views of 10 the Anabaptists, views that I have completely refuted in four of my unpublished sermons. However, as your present mood seems to be one peculiarly secular, I will return to the church at once. Indeed, I have just been informed by the pew-opener that for the last hour and a 15 half Miss Prism has been waiting for me in the vestry.

LADY BRACKNELL [*starting*]. Miss Prism ! Did I hear you mention a Miss Prism ?

CHASUBLE. Yes, Lady Bracknell. I am on my way to join her. 20

LADY BRACKNELL. Pray allow me to detain you for a moment. This matter may prove to be one of vital importance to Lord Bracknell and myself. Is this Miss Prism a female of repellent aspect, remotely connected with education ? 25

CHASUBLE [*somewhat indignantly*]. She is the most cultivated of ladies, and the very picture of respectability.

LADY BRACKNELL. It is obviously the same person. May I ask what position she holds in your household ?

CHASUBLE [*severely*]. I am a celibate, madam. 30

JACK [*interposing*]. Miss Prism, Lady Bracknell, has been for the last three years Miss Cardew's esteemed governess and valued companion.

LADY BRACKNELL. In spite of what I hear of her, I must see her at once. Let her be sent for. 35

CHASUBLE [*looking off*]. She approaches ; she is nigh.

Enter MISS PRISM *hurriedly.*

MISS PRISM. I was told you expected me in the vestry,
dear Canon. I have been waiting for you there for an
hour and three-quarters. [*Catches sight of* LADY BRACK-
NELL, *who has fixed her with a stony glare.* MISS PRISM
5 *grows pale and quails. She looks anxiously round as if
desirous to escape.*]

LADY BRACKNELL [*in a severe, judicial voice*]. Prism !
[MISS PRISM *bows her head in shame.*] Come here, Prism !
[MISS PRISM *approaches in a humble manner.*] Prism !
10 Where is that baby ? [*General consternation. The* CANON
starts back in horror, ALGERNON *and* JACK *pretend to be
anxious to shield* CECILY *and* GWENDOLEN *from hearing the
details of a terrible public scandal.*] Twenty-eight years
ago, Prism, you left Lord Bracknell's house, Number 104,
15 Upper Grosvenor Street, in charge of a perambulator that
contained a baby of the male sex. You never returned.
A few weeks later, through the elaborate investigations of
the Metropolitan police, the perambulator was discovered
at midnight standing by itself in a remote corner of Bays-
20 water. It contained the manuscript of a three-volume
novel of more than usually revolting sentimentality.
[MISS PRISM *starts in involuntary indignation.*] But the
baby was not there. [*Every one looks at* MISS PRISM.]
Prism ! Where is that baby ? [*A pause.*]

25 MISS PRISM. Lady Bracknell, I admit with shame that
I do not know. I only wish I did. The plain facts
of the case are these. On the morning of the day you
mention, a day that is for ever branded on my memory,
I prepared as usual to take the baby out in its perambu-
30 lator. I had also with me a somewhat old, but capacious
hand-bag in which I had intended to place the manuscript of a work of fiction that I had written during my
few unoccupied hours. In a moment of mental abstrac-
tion, for which I never can forgive myself, I deposited

the manuscript in the basinette, and placed the baby in the hand-bag.

JACK [*who has been listening attentively*]. But where did you deposit the hand-bag?

MISS PRISM. Do not ask me, Mr Worthing.

JACK. Miss Prism, this is a matter of no small importance to me. I insist on knowing where you deposited the hand-bag that contained that infant.

MISS PRISM. I left it in the cloak-room of one of the larger railway stations in London.

JACK. What railway station?

MISS PRISM [*quite crushed*]. Victoria. The Brighton line. [*Sinks into a chair.*]

JACK. I must retire to my room for a moment. Gwendolen, wait here for me.

GWENDOLEN. If you are not too long, I will wait here for you all my life.   [*Exit* JACK *in great excitement.*

CHASUBLE. What do you think this means, Lady Bracknell?

LADY BRACKNELL. I dare not even suspect, Dr Chasuble. I need hardly tell you that in families of high position strange coincidences are not supposed to occur. They are hardly considered the thing.

       [*Noises heard overhead as if some one was throwing trunks about. Every one looks up.*

CECILY. Uncle Jack seems strangely agitated.

CHASUBLE. Your guardian has a very emotional nature.

LADY BRACKNELL. This noise is extremely unpleasant. It sounds as if he was having an argument. I dislike arguments of any kind. They are always vulgar, and often convincing.

CHASUBLE [*looking up*]. It has stopped now. [*The noise is redoubled.*]

LADY BRACKNELL. I wish he would arrive at some conclusion.

GWENDOLEN. This suspense is terrible. I hope it will last.

Enter JACK *with a hand-bag of black leather in his hand.*

JACK [*rushing over to* MISS PRISM]. Is this the hand-bag, Miss Prism ? Examine it carefully before you speak. The happiness of more than one life depends on your answer.

5　MISS PRISM [*calmly*]. It seems to be mine. Yes, here is the injury it received through the upsetting of a Gower Street omnibus in younger and happier days. Here is the stain on the lining caused by the explosion of a temperance beverage, an incident that occurred at Leamington. And
10 here, on the lock, are my initials. I had forgotten that in an extravagant mood I had had them placed there. The bag is undoubtedly mine. I am delighted to have it so unexpectedly restored to me. It has been a great inconvenience being without it all these years.

15　JACK [*in a pathetic voice*]. Miss Prism, more is restored to you than this hand-bag. I was the baby you placed in it.

MISS PRISM [*amazed*]. You ?

JACK [*embracing her*]. Yes . . . mother !

20　MISS PRISM [*recoiling in indignant astonishment*]. Mr Worthing, I am unmarried !

JACK. Unmarried ! I do not deny that is a serious blow. But after all, who has the right to cast a stone against one who has suffered ? Cannot repentance wipe
25 out an act of folly ? Why should there be one law for men, and another for women ? Mother, I forgive you. [*Tries to embrace her again.*]

MISS PRISM [*still more indignant*]. Mr Worthing, there is some error. [*Pointing to* LADY BRACKNELL.] There is the
30 lady who can tell you who you really are.

JACK [*after a pause*]. Lady Bracknell, I hate to seem inquisitive, but would you kindly inform me who I am ?

LADY BRACKNELL. I am afraid that the news I have to give you will not altogether please you. You are the son of my poor sister, Mrs Moncrieff, and consequently Algernon's elder brother.

JACK. Algy's elder brother! Then I have a brother after all. I knew I had a brother! I always said I had a brother! Cecily,—how could you have ever doubted that I had a brother? [*Seizes hold of* ALGERNON.] Dr Chasuble, my unfortunate brother. Miss Prism, my unfortunate brother. Gwendolen, my unfortunate brother. Algy, you young scoundrel, you will have to treat me with more respect in the future. You have never behaved to me like a brother in all your life.

ALGERNON. Well, not till to-day, old boy, I admit. I did my best, however, though I was out of practice.

[*Shakes hands.*

GWENDOLEN [*to* JACK]. My own! But what own are you? What is your Christian name, now that you have become some one else?

JACK. Good heavens! . . . I had quite forgotten that point. Your decision on the subject of my name is irrevocable, I suppose?

GWENDOLEN. I never change, except in my affections.

CECILY. What a noble nature you have, Gwendolen!

JACK. Then the question had better be cleared up at once. Aunt Augusta, a moment. At the time when Miss Prism left me in the hand-bag, had I been christened already?

LADY BRACKNELL. Every luxury that money could buy, including christening, had been lavished on you by your fond and doting parents.

JACK. Then I was christened! That is settled. Now, what name was I given? Let me know the worst.

LADY BRACKNELL. Being the eldest son you were naturally christened after your father.

JACK [*irritably*]. Yes, but what was my father's Christian name?

LADY BRACKNELL [*meditatively*]. I cannot at the present

moment recall what the General's Christian name was. But I have no doubt he had one. He was eccentric, I admit. But only in later years. And that was the result of the Indian climate, and marriage, and indigestion, and other things of that kind.

JACK. Algy! Can't you recollect what our father's Christian name was?

ALGERNON. My dear boy, we were never even on speaking terms. He died before I was a year old.

JACK. His name would appear in the Army Lists of the period, I suppose, Aunt Augusta?

LADY BRACKNELL. The General was essentially a man of peace, except in his domestic life. But I have no doubt his name would appear in any military directory.

JACK. The Army Lists of the last forty years are here. These delightful records should have been my constant study. [*Rushes to bookcase and tears the books out.*] M. Generals . . . Mallam, Maxbohm, Magley, what ghastly names they have—Markby, Migsby, Mobbs, Moncrieff! Lieutenant 1840, Captain, Lieutenant-Colonel, Colonel, General 1869, Christian names, Ernest John. [*Puts book very quietly down and speaks quite calmly.*] I always told you, Gwendolen, my name was Ernest, didn't I? Well, it is Ernest after all. I mean it naturally is Ernest.

LADY BRACKNELL. Yes, I remember now that the General was called Ernest. I knew I had some particular reason for disliking the name.

GWENDOLEN. Ernest! My own Ernest! I felt from the first that you could have no other name!

JACK. Gwendolen, it is a terrible thing for a man to find out suddenly that all his life he has been speaking nothing but the truth. Can you forgive me?

GWENDOLEN. I can. For I feel that you are sure to change.

JACK. My own one!

CHASUBLE [*to* MISS PRISM]. Lætitia! [*Embraces her.*]

MISS PRISM [*enthusiastically*]. Frederick! At last!

ALGERNON. Cecily! [*Embraces her.*] At last!

JACK. Gwendolen! [*Embraces her.*] At last!

LADY BRACKNELL. My nephew, you seem to be displaying signs of triviality.   5

JACK. On the contrary, Aunt Augusta, I 've now realised for the first time in my life the vital Importance of Being Earnest.

TABLEAU.

CURTAIN.

X
NOTES

NOTES

THE KNIGHT OF THE BURNING PESTLE

INDUCTION

It was a common practice for gallants of the day to have stools actually on the stage. Dekker refers to this in *The Gull's Horn-book*.

31 4 goodman boy. Note throughout the use of " boy ". Companies of boy actors were common and of course all women's parts were played by boys till after the Restoration, when in 1662 actresses came over from France and were at first very unpopular.

31 9 The London Merchant. There was a play of this name by Ford, which was never printed.—*Dyce*.

31 19 play the Jacks : Mockers.

33 16 reparel : an old form of *apparel*.

33 23 fear : transitive ; *i.e.* frighten.

33 30-34 " By Heavens, methinks ", etc. A parody of Hotspur's speech (*Henry IV.*, Part I., Act I., iii.).

34 3 before : redundant—from the next line. This is probably a printer's error.

34 25 shawms : a shawm is an instrument similar to a hautboy ; a kind of oboe.

34 35 o'er the water : the waits of Southwark were on the other side of the Thames from the theatre.

35 10 taxes : in the same sense as " to tax one with it " ; *i.e.* accusations.

ACT I

SCENE I

35 24 staples : markets.

SCENE II

38 11 lets : hindrances. For use as a verb, see Hamlet's " By heaven I'll make a ghost of him that lets me " (I. iv. 85).

39 9 Moncaster : Richard Mulcaster, the famous headmaster of Merchant Taylors School (1561-86).

293

SCENE II

78 2 **cap :** arrest.—*Dyce*.
78 5 **beholding :** beholden, under an obligation.
80 3 **won :** " dwell " ; archaic.
80 4 **ycleped :** called. Dyce has Barbarosso, but Barbaroso is more usually accepted.
80 9 **gent :** noble and courteous.
80 10 **copper basin :** part of the barber surgeon's stock-in-trade Cervantes' barber wore his on his head.
80 18 **bord :** circumference—the bowl again.
80 19 **bullets,** or balls of soap.
81 18-19 **Ninevie :** The puppet show of Nineveh, which seems to have been tremendously popular.

SCENE III

81 27 **presently :** immediately.

SCENE IV

82 26 **tooth :** a common practice with barbers, who, it must be remembered, were also surgeons and tooth-drawers.
83 9 **fond :** foolish.
83 9 **wight :** man.
84 14 **sable :** dark, gloomy.
84 23 **vild :** vile. The quartos have " wild ", but *vild* is a regular old form of " vile ".
85 8 **curled locks . . . tied :** a fashion of the day.
85 21 **eke :** also.

SCENE V

87 26 **conductor :** carrier.
88 30 **ingrant :** ignorant, or, more probably, " ingrate ", ungrateful.
90 3 **lavolta :** a sprightly dance for two.
90 31 **Fading :** named from the burden of an Irish song.
91 8 **points :** used to fasten hose or breeches to doublet. Feste puns on this in *Twelfth Night*, I. v. 24.

ACT IV

SCENE I

92 5 **flirt-gill :** loose woman.
92 9 **Arches :** the prison of the Court of Arches.
92 10 **sing peccavi :** acknowledge his guilt. (Latin : *peccavi*—I have sinned.)

92 16 **Sophy of Persia :** An allusion to a play *The Travailes of the Three English Brothers* (1607).—*Dyce.*

92 19 **Red Bull :** a playhouse of the time. Collier suggests it was originally an inn-yard—the forerunner of the theatre.

93 3 **prentice to a grocer in London ?**—No. He was a knight in *Morte D'Arthur.* He was King Arthur's fool and was knighted by him.

93 4 **Four Prentices :** a play by Heywood.

Scene II

94 11 **nipitato :** strong ale.

95 14 **butter :** the ointment used for anointing the fallen horse's back.

95 25 **properer :** handsomer.

Scene III

97 17 **hoits :** indulges in riotous mirth.—*Wheeler.*

98 14 **purchased :** incurred by his deeds.

Scene IV

99 15 **say :** a subject for experiments.

100 31 **cypress, yew :** inseparable accompaniments of death and the grave. *Cf.* " And in sad cypress let me be laid " and " My shroud of white stuck all with yew " from Feste's song " Come away, Death ", in *Twelfth Night.*

102 6 **fear me not :** fear not for me.

Scene V

103 5 **denier :** copper coin worth one-twelfth of a sou.

104 32 **with all his scarfs,** etc. : costume of a May Lord, who with his Lady has always been an important character in May Day festivities.

106 4 **hobby-horse :** always a feature of May Day celebrations with morris dancing.

106 10 **mewed :** shut up. A hawking term. The hawks were mewed in darkness until taken out for the chase. *Cf.* mews, which though now stables (or usually garages !) were once where the King's hawks were kept.

106 13 **rascal :** young deer, lean and out of season.

106 13 **pricket :** a two-year-old buck.

106 17-18 **with bells . . . scarfs and garters :** The dress of a morris dancer—coloured garters, scarves and shoulder-knots, and bells on the legs which rang in the jigs.

107 2 **thrumming of our caps :** sowing threads on ; *i.e.* useless work.

107 4 **tabor:** drum and tabor provided the music for the morris dancing.

ACT V

SCENE I

107 10 **rosemary:** for remembrance—used at funerals and weddings. *Cf.* Ophelia, *Hamlet*, IV. v. 174.

109 8 **St Faith's church under Paul's:** mentioned by Dekker in *The Shoemaker's Holiday*. See also Stow: "At the west end . . . under the choir of Paul's also was a parish church of St Faith, commonly called St Faith under Paul's".

SCENE II

Some of the procedure and many of the remarks in this scene, *e.g.* "Sergeant, call a muster", "As you were again", "Open your files", "Proceed, Sergeant" (Carry on, Sergeant!) are extraordinarily "modern".

110 22 **Ancient:** Ensign; used for the colours and the colour-bearer.

112 14 **furious fields:** Mile End, whither they have now in imagination marched.

112 28 **whose care,** *i.e.* food, the result of the care their wives had taken to see they were provided for.

113 8 **galley-foist:** the old name for the Lord Mayor's barge.

SCENE III

113 10 **stoop:** a measure or vessel of wine. "A stoup of wine" is a commonly recurrent phrase of the period.

113 19, 20 **"Sing we",** etc. A madrigal composed by Henry VIII.

113 23 **Mimon:** C. B. Wheeler suggests "the world".

114 8, 9 **"Thou art welcome",** etc. Burlesquing the speech of Andreas' ghost in *The Spanish Tragedy*.

117 29 **lingel:** cobbler's thread or thong.

120 3 **pottle:** two quarts.

THE CRITIC

PROLOGUE

The Prologue gives an excellent epitome of the Drama
of the preceding hundred years

143 6 **Villiers criticised what Dryden writ.** George Villiers, Duke of Buckingham, wrote *The Rehearsal* (1671) burlesquing heroic tragedy, of which Dryden was one of the chief exponents at the time. In the play he is represented as Bayes. The two plays are the classic examples of burlesque, *The Critic* having retained the greater popularity partly owing to its more general application.

143 7 The Tragic Queen: Melpomene, the Muse of Tragedy.

143 11 Comic Sister: Thalia, the Muse of Comedy.

ACT I

Scene 1

145 1 Brutus to Lord North. Lord North's actions at the time of the American War subjected him to much newspaper criticism, one of *The Letters of Junius* being addressed to him.

145 2 To the First L dash D, etc., First Lord of the Admiralty, John Montague, Earl of Sandwich, also much criticised.

145 4 St Kitt's: St Christopher's Island in the West Indies, where the poet Byron's grandfather was English Vice-Admiral at this time.

145 4 Coxheath Intelligence: an encampment of militia formed at Coxheath near Maidstone in anticipation of a French invasion.

145 5 Sir Charles Hardy: appointed Commander of the Channel Fleet as successor to Keppel (1779). All these references, which Dangle, whose sole interest is "the theatre", naturally dismisses with a contemptuous "Pshaw", provide interesting topical allusions.

145 8 Morning Chronicle: noted for its theatrical news.

145 12 Spanish Armada: a recrudescence of interest in the defeat of the Armada at this period, due to the fear of a French invasion, gave Sheridan the clue for the title of Puff's play.

146 8 Roman signatures: a common practice in correspondence to the newspapers.

146 20 Maecenas: the famous patron of Roman authors.

147 11 Dorinda: a character in *The Beaux' Stratagem*, by Farquhar (1707); Polly, in *The Beggar's Opera* by Gay (1728)

147 25 Westminster associations: of volunteer militia.

147 25 trailing . . . Ground: near Bunhill fields, the drill ground of the H.A.C. This reminds one strangely of Ralph's exploit in *The Knight of the Burning Pestle*, V. ii.

147 31 "the mirror of Nature", and "the abstract, and brief chronicles of the time": Both quotations from *Hamlet*. *The Critic* was originally performed as an after-piece to *Hamlet*.

149 13 genteel comedy: a hit at the sentimental comedy, at which Sheridan had aimed several shafts—though, indeed, the Julia-Falkland passages of *The Rivals* incline to this sentimental type.

149 14 taken from the French. The French influence on both comedy and tragedy has been noted in the Introduction, pp. 126-7, and 205-6.

149 21 I am quite . . . : All this, of course, is aimed at the critics of *The School for Scandal.*

149 34 Vanbrugh . . . : A reference to his own adaptation of Vanbrugh's *Relapse* into *A Trip to Scarborough*?

150 6 comedy, on a very new plan : another hit at the sentimental comedy.

150 23 Sir Fretful Plagiary : a satirical portrait of Richard Cumberland, the dramatist, of whom the pretended indifference to adverse criticism, while actually being acutely susceptible to it, was a well-known and obvious characteristic which he frequently betrays in his letters and memoirs.

153 7 he might take out some of the best things . . . comedy. In this connection a story is told that Cumberland went with his children to a performance of *The School for Scandal* and when they laughed heartily he rebuked them with these words, " What are you laughing at, my dear little folks ? You should not laugh, my angels, there is nothing to laugh at ! ", adding, *sotto voce,* " Keep still, you little dunces ". On hearing this, Sheridan is said to have remarked : " It was ungrateful of Cumberland to have been displeased with his children for laughing at my comedy, for when I went to see his tragedy I laughed from beginning to end ". It is only fair to add that in his *Memoirs* Cumberland denies this story.

153 28 Sincerely then . . . From here to the end of the scene, with his repeated " angling " for criticism and his behaviour when he gets what he has asked for (even though it *is* hastily invented by Sneer), is perfectly typical of Cumberland's character.

Professor Nettleton quotes here from Thomas Davis's chapter on Cumberland in *The Life of David Garrick,* referring to criticisms of Cumberland's *The Choleric Man* : " The criticisms thrown out in the newspapers against this play, seem to have affected the author very much. In his Dedication to Detraction, he enters into a long defence of Terence, and his manner of writing comedy, and endeavours to convince his anonymous opponent of malice and ignorance. . . . Mr Cumberland tugs too much at the critic's arrow in his side, and yet affects to despise the hand from whence it came ". (II. 272-73.)

SCENE II

161 27 winter managers : the season at Covent Garden and Drury Lane theatres was during the winter months—September to May.

164 6 Marshalsea : debtors' prison in Southwark, abolished in 1849.

164 11 pressed : forcible recruiting for the navy was carried out by the " Press Gangs ".

165 20 Mr Dodd : created the part of Dangle. Professor

Nettleton quotes Boaden as follows : " Dodd, with more confined powers (than Palmer) was one of the most perfect actors that I have ever seen. He was the fopling of the *drama* rather than the age. . . . He was, to be sure, the prince of pink heels, and the soul of empty eminence ". (*Memoirs of the Life of John Philip Kemble*, I. 55.)

165 22 **Mr Palmer :** originally played Sneer, and was also an excellent Joseph Surface in *The School for Scandal*.

165 25 **Mr King :** the original Puff, who had played Sir Peter Teazle.

165 28 **De Loutherbourg :** a famous designer of scenery and scenic effects, the chief designer at Drury Lane and responsible for the first production of *The Critic*.

167 28 **scan. mag. :** scandalum magnatum—slander of " high personages of the realm ".

168 30 **Morning Chronicle :** see note to I. i. 8 above.

169 8 **style of Junius.** The famous letters of Junius appeared in *The Public Advertiser*. They were full of invective against the King and Government and their author remains unidentified.

169 9 **The Thames navigation.** The dredging and cleaning of the Thames and its harbours, as the names " Misomud " and " Anti-shoal " imply, was at this time a subject of controversy.

169 12 **Paul Jones :** John Paul Jones (1747-92), an " American privateer " who had been for some years a menace to British shipping.

169 13 **Indiamen :** ships of the East India Company.

169 13 **Byron :** Vice-Admiral John Byron. See note I. i. 4 above.

169 17 **Public Advertiser :** noted for its devotion to topics of public interest.

169 18 **to shoot Charles Fox in the Morning Post :** noted for scurrilous personal attacks under the editorship of Henry Bate, imprisoned in 1780 for a libel on the Duke of Richmond.

ACT II

Scene i

169 21 **what Shakespeare says of actors :** Hamlet's remarks to Polonius about the players contain these words which Dangle has already quoted.

171 19 **Mr Hopkins :** he had appeared as prompter in a farce by Garrick, produced at Drury Lane in 1767.

Scene ii

172 4 **(Clock strikes)** *et seq.* See Introduction, p. 125 for this question of description in opening scenes of the type of play *The Critic* burlesques.

172 21 **Sir Christopher Hatton :** Lord Chancellor (1587). Won a reputation as a dancer.

173 23 **When virgin Majesty :** a reference to Queen Elizabeth's review of troops at Tilbury Fort in 1588.

173 30 **The State some danger apprehends :** a perfect anticlimax.

178 17 **Oh, never mind,** etc. This, and almost every remark Sneer makes, affords an excellent example of the aptness of his name : there is nearly always a scarcely concealed barb and a delightful possibility of two interpretations in his speeches.

179 10 **(Cannon twice).** See note at foot of p. 179. Here, I think, is an excellent example of a possible interpolation from an acting copy of the play. There is no proof that the edition of 1781 had Sheridan's personal supervision. In this case a rather rich piece of burlesque would be missed by the omission of the two superfluous morning guns.

179 23 **minuet in Ariadne :** from an opera by Handel. In the ale-house scene of *She Stoops to Conquer* one of Tony Lumpkin's cronies says " his bear dances only to the very genteelest of tunes— *Water Parted* or the minuet in Ariadne ".

179 24 **Now has the whispering breath,** etc. An excellent example of a burlesque of the descriptive setting discussed in the Introduction, p. 124-5.

182 31 **borrowed from the French.** For the French influence on the type of Heroic Tragedy, see Introduction, p. 126.

183 16 **parry carte :** the " parry in quart " is the parry to the " thrust in quart ".

183 18 **flankonade :** the thrust in the side.

ACT III

Scene 1

190 6 **I am not for making slavish distinctions,** etc. Puff's defence of his style might in some degree be put forward by Congreve and Sheridan, whose main object was wit at almost any price—and from any mouth. The same feature is noteworthy in Wilde's dialogue.

190 9 **Now pray mark this scene.** It has been suggested that this burlesque of the absurd recognition scenes of contemporary dramas may be a specific parody of a situation in Home's tragedy *Douglas*.

192 11 **Gad! Now you put me in mind on't.** There is something almost Falstaffian in Puff's escape from the accusation of rank plagiarism from *Othello*, III. iii. 90.

197 1 **For all eter—.** A reminiscence of Hotspur's dying speech in *Henry IV*, Part I :

> . . . and food for— *(Dies)*
>   *Prince.* For worms, brave Percy.

198 13 **white satin . . . white linen :** a very right and proper distinction ! The confidante was a legacy from the French drama.

200 — **Handel's Water Music :** a suite of twenty-one movements, " first performed on the Thames, Aug. 22, 1715, when George I and the Royal Family sailed from Limehouse to Whitehall. Handel followed the Royal barge with his orchestra, and performed this suite to the delight of the king, who asked the name of its composer ". (*Cyclopedia of Music and Musicians*, III. 566.)

200 — **Judas Maccabaeus :** another composition by Handel.

THE IMPORTANCE OF BEING EARNEST

ACT I

The first act is neatly constructed. It is always necessary to put the audience in possession of certain essential knowledge. Here we are introduced to nearly all the main characters and learn something of Cecily and Miss Prism of the second act. We are let into the secret of Bunburying (see Introduction, p. 211), and have more than a hint of the importance to Jack of being Ernest.

226 4 **French drama :** The beginnings of the break-away from the French influence of Sardou and Labiche came with Robertson.

226 30 **Gwendolen :** In his early plays Shaw had directed shrewd blows at the conventional type of Victorian heroine—the ingenuous maiden who shrinkingly and blushingly accepted the wooing of the dominating male. Shaw's heroines are much stronger minded, more vital creatures, and Gwendolen lives in the same street.

228 2 **Mary Farquhar :** cleverly engineered and obviously a line which gets a laugh after Algy's remarks to Jack earlier in the Act.

237 23 **Is that clever ?** This question and its answer might well be applied to much of the dialogue.

239 18 **Empire :** then a small music hall popular with " men about town ".

241 18 **I do my best :** this is in the best tradition of comedy butlers ; it is the sort of remark that Jeeves would make.

ACT II

Both Cecily and Gwendolen keep diaries—a practice much in vogue with young ladies of the period.

248 28 **womanthrope :** Miss Prism has stolen this from Mrs Malaprop. She means, of course, " woman-hater " and should have said misogynist.

272 19 **science :** this hit at the scientists of Wilde's day might slip very easily into a modern play.

276 28 **social legislation :** social problems were arousing increasing interest, which is reflected in the drama of the period.

ACT III

The modern stage usually demands a " curtain " at the end of each act, and in order to make this effective dramatists are inevitably occasionally guilty of staginess. Well-handled, an effective curtain helps to preserve realism. The final curtain here is the best of the three. The other acts are rather inclined to fizzle out.

XI
APPENDIX

APPENDIX

This is not an exhaustive list, but it aims at providing a reference to the more important plays of the authors mentioned in the Introduction and Interchapters. The dates after the titles of the plays refer, wherever possible, to the date of production or approximate composition.

DATE	AUTHOR	PLAY
1505–1556	Nicholas Udall	Ralph Roister Doister, 1553–54
? –1608 (*fl.* 1546–60)	John Still ? } W. Stevenson ? }	Gammer Gurton's Needle, printed 1575
1536–1608 1532–1584	Thomas Sackville } Thomas Norton }	Gorboduc, 1562
1554 ?–1606	John Lyly	Campaspe, 1579–80
		Sapho and Phao, 1581
		Galatea, 1582(?)
		Endymion, 1585
		Love's Metamorphosis, 1584–8(?)
		Midas, 1589
		Mother Bombie, 1590
		The Woman in the Moon, 1591–93
1558 ?–1597 ?	George Peele	The Arraignement of Paris, printed 1584
		Edward I, printed 1593
		The Battle of Alcazar, printed 1594
		The Old Wive's Tale, printed 1595
		David and Bethsabe, printed 1599
1558–1592	Robert Greene	Friar Bacon and Friar Bungay, 1589–91
		James IV, 1590–91
1558 ?–1594	Thomas Kyd	The Spanish Tragedy, 1588–
1564–1593	Christopher Marlowe	Tamburlaine the Great, 1587–88
		Doctor Faustus, 1588(?)

DATE	AUTHOR	PLAY
1564–1593	Christopher Marlowe	The Jew of Malta, 1592
		Edward II, 1592
1573 ?–1637	Ben Jonson	Every Man in His Humour, 1598
		Every Man out of His Humour, 1599
		Volpone, or the Fox, 1605–6
		Epicoene, or the Silent Woman, 1609
		The Alchemist, 1610
1579–1625	John Fletcher } Francis Beaumont }	The Faithful Sheperdess, (before 1610)
		The Knight of the Burning Pestle, 1609(?)
		Philaster, 1610
		The Maid's Tragedy, 1611
		A King and No King, 1611
		Bonduca, (not later than 1614)
		Thierry and Theodoret, 1617
		The Wild Goose Chase, 1621
1570–1641 ?	Thomas Dekker	The Shoemakers' Holiday, printed 1600
		Old Fortunatus, printed 1600
		The Honest Whore, Part I, printed 1604 ; Part II, printed 1630
1580 ?–1625 ?	John Webster	The White Devil, 1611(?), printed 1612
		The Duchess of Malfi, 1614(?), printed 1623
1583–1640	Philip Massinger	The Virgin Martyr, printed 1622
		A New Way to Pay Old Debts, (before 1626)
		The Maid of Honour, 1622–31
1631–1700	John Dryden	The Wild Gallant, 1663
		Marriage à la Mode, 1672
		All for Love, 1678
1635 ?–1691 ?	George Etherege	The Comical Revenge, or Love in a Tub, 1664
		She would if she could, 1668
		The Man of the Mode, or Sir Fopling Flutter, 1676

DATE	AUTHOR	PLAY
1640?–1715	William Wycherly	The Country Wife, 1672
		The Plain Dealer, 1674
1670–1729	William Congreve	The Double Dealer, 1693
		Love for Love, 1695
		The Way of the World, 1700
1728–1774	Oliver Goldsmith	The Good-natured Man, 1767
		She Stoops to Conquer, 1772
1751–1816	Richard Brinsley Sheridan	The Rivals, 1775
		St Patrick's Day, 1775
		The Duenna, 1775
		The School for Scandal, 1777
		The Critic, 1779
1829–1871	T. W. Robertson	David Garrick, 1864
		Society, 1865
		Ours, 1866
		Caste, 1867
1851–1929	Henry Arthur Jones	(More than fifty plays)
		The Silver King, 1882
		Saints and Sinners, 1884
		Michael and his Lost Angel, 1896
1855–1934	A. W. Pinero	The Profligate, 1889
		The Second Mrs Tanqueray, 1893
		Trelawney of the Wells, 1898
		Iris, 1901
		His House in Order, 1906
1856–	George Bernard Shaw	(More than forty plays)
		Arms and the Man, 1894
		Candida, 1895
		You Never Can Tell, 1898
		Pygmalion, 1913
		Back to Methuselah, 1921
		St Joan, 1923
1858–1900	Oscar Wilde	Lady Windermere's Fan, 1892
		A Woman of No Importance, 1893
		The Importance of Being Earnest, 1895